Encyclopedia of
VEGETARIAN
CUISINE

Editorial Director: Kate Mascaro
Editor: Helen Adedotun
Translated from the French by Julia Chalkley (pp. 13-143 and 152-203)
and Carmella Abramowitz Moreau (pp. 9, 146-51, and 207-407)
Design: Alice Leroy
Copyediting: Penelope Isaac
Typesetting: Gravemaker+Scott
Proofreading: Nicole Foster
Indexing: JMS Books
Color Separation: IGS, Angoulême, France
Printed in China by Toppan Leefung

Originally published in French as *Encyclopédie de la cuisine végétarienne*
© Flammarion, S.A., Paris, 2015

English-language edition
© Flammarion, S.A., Paris, 2016

editions.flammarion.com

16 17 18 3 2 1

ISBN: 978-2-08-020276-5

Legal Deposit: 10/2016

Estérelle Payany

Photography by Nathalie Carnet

Foreword by Régis Marcon

Encyclopedia of
VEGETARIAN
CUISINE

Flammarion

How to use this book

Techniques (pp. 11–143)
All the basic techniques, with specialist step-by-step explanations

Step-by-step photos

Level of difficulty,
from 1 to 3 stars

Easily visible
chapter headings

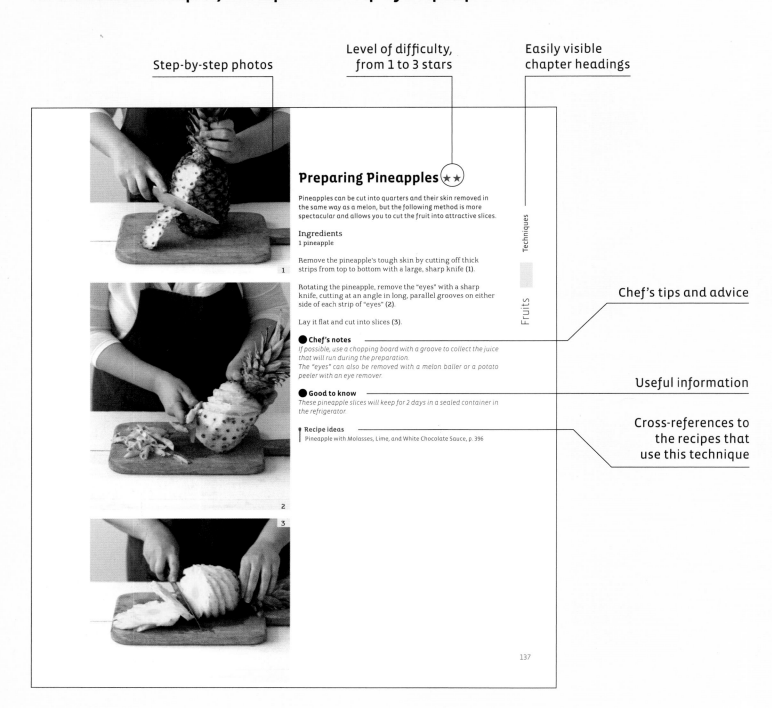

Preparing Pineapples ★★

Pineapples can be cut into quarters and their skin removed in the same way as a melon, but the following method is more spectacular and allows you to cut the fruit into attractive slices.

Ingredients
1 pineapple

Remove the pineapple's tough skin by cutting off thick strips from top to bottom with a large, sharp knife (1).

Rotating the pineapple, remove the "eyes" with a sharp knife, cutting at an angle in long, parallel grooves on either side of each strip of "eyes" (2).

Lay it flat and cut into slices (3).

● **Chef's notes**
If possible, use a chopping board with a groove to collect the juice that will run during the preparation.
The "eyes" can also be removed with a melon baller or a potato peeler with an eye remover.

● **Good to know**
These pineapple slices will keep for 2 days in a sealed container in the refrigerator.

▌ **Recipe ideas**
Pineapple with Molasses, Lime, and White Chocolate Sauce, p. 396

Techniques

Fruits

Chef's tips and advice

Useful information

Cross-references to
the recipes that
use this technique

137

Recipes (pp. 205–407)
Ninety basic recipes, with ten additional recipes created and tested by Michelin star chefs

Easily visible
chapter headings

Level of difficulty,
from 1 to 3 stars

Gluten-free recipe

Vegan recipe

Indonesian Bean Salad ★★

Serves 4
Preparation time: 20 minutes
Cooking time: 20 minutes

For the spicy coconut paste (*sambal*)
Peel the garlic. Squeeze the lime. Remove the stem and seeds of the chili pepper. Cut the coconut flesh into pieces. Peel the galangal. Chop the palm sugar roughly.

In the bowl of the food processor or blender, chop the garlic, chili pepper, and palm sugar. Add the galangal and kaffir lime leaves and process until the ingredients form a paste. Next, add the coconut, using the pulse function rather than processing continuously, until the paste reaches the texture of bread crumbs. Season with salt and pepper.

For the salad
Trim the snake beans and cook them in salted boiling water for 5 minutes, then refresh in ice water. Cut them into slices about ⅛–¼ inch (3–5 mm) long. Finely slice the cucumber. Wash the soy sprouts and dry them carefully. Rinse and dry the Thai basil and pick off the leaves. Combine all the ingredients with the Thai basil.

Heat a small skillet over high heat and cook the coconut paste for 1 to 2 minutes. Pour it over the salad, mix through, and place in the refrigerator to chill. Serve well chilled.

● **Chef's notes**
Coconut sambal is traditionally prepared with red curry paste rather than the fresh chili pepper indicated here. Curry paste usually contains dried shrimps, so check the list of ingredients if you wish to use it

● **Good to know**
This refreshing salad, typical of the center of the island of Java, is known locally as trancam. It may also include shredded cabbage or banana. It's the sambal seasoning—a spicy coconut paste—that gives it its distinctive taste.

Techniques
Preparing Chilies, p. 23
Peeling Fresh Ginger, p. 29
Blanching, p. 41
Opening a Coconut, p. 129

Ingredients
Spicy coconut paste (*sambal*)
1 clove garlic
1 lime
1 small fresh red chili pepper
3 ½ oz. (100 g) fresh coconut
⅔ oz. (20 g) piece galangal
⅔ oz. (20 g) palm sugar
2 kaffir lime leaves
Fine salt

Salad
8 oz. (250 g) fresh snake beans,
or fresh green beans
1 small cucumber (about 5 oz./150 g)
4 handfuls mung bean sprouts
1 bunch Thai basil
1 lime

Equipment
Food processor or blender

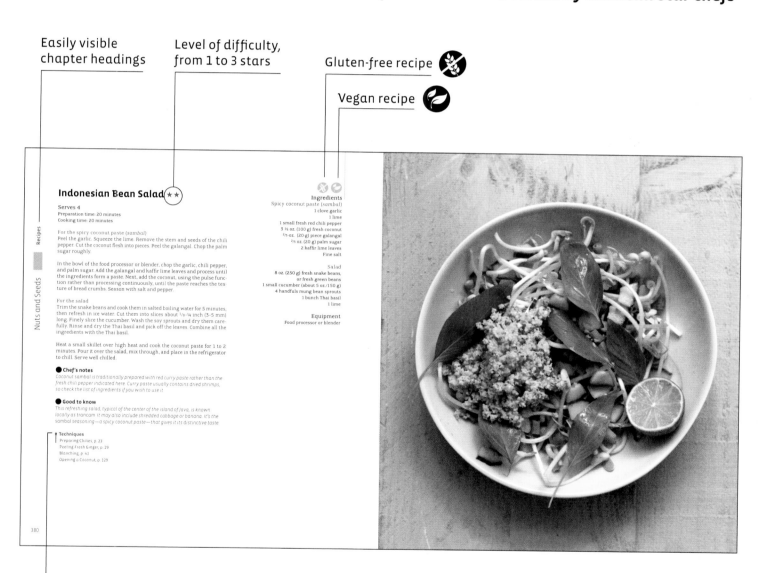

Cross-references
to the techniques
used in this recipe

Contents

Recipes

Michelin star chefs introduce each category and share the secrets of one of their creations.

Foreword

By Régis Marcon
Three Michelin star chef

In this *Encyclopedia of Vegetarian Cuisine*, you will find the very best that nature has to offer the home chef. An astounding variety of vegetables, grains, pulses, and fruits is presented, through a myriad of instructive photographs, so let's take full advantage of the bounty so generously provided by the earth and enjoy the wealth of its diversity by preparing dishes that are good to eat, good for our spirit, good for the environment, and good for our health.

Now, get that apron on! This book is here to guide you, step by step. Once you have ensured you have all the right equipment, take the time to read through the recipes before you begin: the chef's notes and tips will help you to get it just right.

Cook with the seasons, and embark on a voyage of discovery into this world of plants where there is still much to explore. You will soon realize that it is easy to cook delicious and healthy dishes using just vegetables, mushrooms, pulses, grains, dairy products, nuts, and fruit.

I'm delighted to be able to invite you into this lush, green universe, where pleasure, good health, and sustainability can be combined, and a whole new culinary adventure awaits you.

Happy Cooking!

Techniques

Preparation

Cutting

Cooking

Vegetables

Preparing Baby Artichokes ★ ★

Baby artichokes are so tender they can be eaten raw once their chokes are removed.

Ingredients
Baby artichokes
Lemon

Cut off the stalks of the artichokes, leaving 2 in. (5 cm) remaining (**1**).

First, simply pull the small lower petals from the stalk. Hold the artichoke in your hand and cut off all the leaves around the base with a small sharp knife, working it backward and forward (**2**).

When all the large leaves have been removed, cut off the leaves surrounding the choke to reveal the heart (**3**).

Rub the heart with the cut surface of half a lemon to prevent discoloration (**4**). Squeeze the juice of the other lemon half and add it to a large bowl of water.

Peel the stalk with a small knife (**5**) or vegetable peeler. Place in the bowl of water with lemon juice as you prepare each artichoke and set aside until needed (**6**). If the heart still has any of the choke attached, simply lift it out with a spoon.

● Chef's notes
Artichoke juice tends to stain the skin: rub your hands immediately with half a lemon or wear disposable gloves.
To prepare large globe artichokes, use a similar technique: pull off the main part of the stalk, which is fibrous, then remove the large leaves and trim away the smaller leaves with a small knife, working it backward and forward. Next, cook the artichoke—it is easier to remove the choke afterward.

● Good to know
Once they have been prepared, baby artichokes can be eaten raw, braised with spring vegetables such as peas or fava beans, or simply cooked in a blanc (see technique p. 43).

❘ Recipe ideas
Asparagus and Lima Bean Paella, p. 241
Mediterranean Vegetable Tartlets, p. 375

1

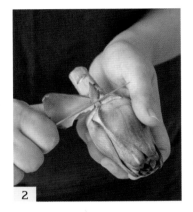

2

3

4

5

6

1

Preparing Swiss Chard ★

Swiss chard commonly has white stalks but they can also be pink, yellow, or red. They are all prepared in the same way.

Ingredients
Swiss chard

Cut off the base from the bunch of Swiss chard to separate the ribs (1). Wash and dry the ribs.

Cut the green leaves away from the ribs, cutting close to the edge (2).

Lay the leaves on top of each other, roll them up, and slice them thinly (3).

Chop the white ribs finely, removing any fibrous parts (see technique for rhubarb, p. 138) (4).

● **Chef's notes**

Swiss chard leaves are prepared in the same way as spinach; the ribs need a longer time to cook. When braising both, first sweat the ribs in a little stock for 10 minutes, then add the sliced leaves. Continue to cook for an additional 10 minutes.

▎ **Recipe ideas**
▎ Swiss Chard and Goat Cheese Focaccia, p. 257

2

3

4

Preparing Fennel ★

The awkward shape of this vegetable is easy to manage using the method that follows.

Ingredients
Fennel bulbs

Remove the feathery fronds from the fennel (1). Reserve them for flavoring your broths, soups, and bouquets garnis. They can also be dried.

Cut off the base of the fennel (2). If the outside layers of the bulb are tough or discolored, remove them (3). Reserve them for juicing or for use in a soup that will be blended. The outer leaves of spring fennel and baby fennel are not fibrous, so there will be no need to remove them.

Cut off the stalks as close as possible to the heart (4). Sauté them or use them in soups, stocks, etc.

Cut the heart in two from top to bottom, then slice finely (5) or use a mandolin to give you evenly shaped slices.

Recipe ideas
Fennel Tortilla, p. 364

Preparing Squash ★

Butternut, red kuri, and spaghetti squash are prepared in different ways.

Ingredients
Red kuri, or other squash

Cut the kuri squash in half on a chopping board (1). If you are using a butternut squash, cut across where it begins to swell, to give a round section and an oblong section. Cut the round section in half, as for the kuri squash.

Remove the seeds from the kuri squash with a spoon (2). Do the same for all types of squash. Remove any remaining fibers by rinsing the squash, then drying it. Cut the kuri squash in half again (3), then into half-moon shapes. For butternut squash, cut the oblong section in two, then in four; cut the round section into quarters.

The thin skin of kuri squash can be left on, as long as it has been scrubbed well first. Peel all other types of squash, such as butternut squash, with a vegetable peeler (4), as their skin is much thicker. Cut the squash into chunks according to the recipe (5).

To prepare spaghetti squash, cut the squash in half as in step 1. Remove the seeds as in step 2. Preheat the oven to 350°F (180°C/Gas Mark 4). Brush the squash with oil and season lightly with salt, then place it cut side down on a large baking sheet and bake for 35 to 45 minutes. Leave to cool, then remove the pulp using a fork: it will separate out naturally into spaghetti-like strands (6).

● Chef's notes
Half-moon slices of squash are delicious brushed with oil and spices and simply roasted in the oven (see technique p. 46).

● Good to know
The flesh of spaghetti squash goes well with all types of pasta sauce. It can also be used in gratins, tarts, etc.

❗ Recipe ideas
Creamed Pumpkin Soup and Sage Tempura, p. 211
Bulgur and Squash Kibbe, p. 268
Three Sisters Soup with Squash, Corn, and Beans, p. 294

Techniques

Vegetables

1

Preparing Corn ★

Corn grilled on a barbecue is a real treat. The kernels are also delicious when removed from the ear and cooked.

Ingredients
Corn ears

Pull the green leaves away from the ears and remove the silky fibers surrounding the corn with your hands (1).

Break off the base of the ears in one movement (2) and discard; rinse and dry the ears. Remove the corn kernels from the cobs by slicing down the length with a large knife (3). Gather up the kernels into a large bowl.

Bring a large pan of salted water to a boil. Add the kernels and cook for 20 minutes. Break up the cobs (4) and either add them to the pan with the kernels or reserve them to flavor a soup or stock.

● **Chef's notes**
You can blanch the kernels for 1 minute in boiling water, then drain and freeze to be used throughout the year.

● **Good to know**
Corn kernels can be cooked in the same way as a risotto: brown, then simmer slowly in a stock. They will become soft with a creamy texture.

❙ **Recipe ideas**
Three Sisters Soup with Squash, Corn, and Beans, p. 294

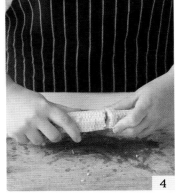

1

2

3

Preparing Cauliflower "Steaks" ★

Cauliflower is most often separated into florets before steaming. A less common yet tasty alternative is to cut it into thick slices to be served in the form of a "steak."

Cooking time: 20 minutes

Ingredients
Cauliflower
Olive oil (for cooking)

Remove and discard the outer green leaves of the cauliflower. Wash and dry it. Cut it in half from top to bottom (1).

Cut a slice approximately ¾ in. (2 cm) thick from the widest part of each half (2).

Preheat the oven to 375°F (190°C/Gas Mark 5). Heat a splash of olive oil in a skillet and lightly brown the slices of cauliflower, turning them over gently with a spatula. Season with salt and pepper, then finish cooking in the oven for 15 minutes. Serve with pesto or a sauce of your choice (3).

● Chef's notes
The remaining pieces of cauliflower can be separated into florets and steamed (see technique p. 41) or used to make cauliflower "couscous" (see technique p. 20).

● Good to know
Cauliflower has a delicate flavor when fresh: be sure to use it promptly after purchasing it.

❢ Recipe ideas
Roasted Cauliflower, Red Tahini, and Preserved Lemon, p. 371

Preparing Cauliflower "Couscous" ★

This delicious vegetable "couscous" can replace traditional wheat couscous, giving a different texture to your salads.

Ingredients
Florets of raw cauliflower

Cut the florets into small pieces, or use the remaining pieces after preparing cauliflower "steaks" (see technique p. 19) **(1)**.

Put the pieces in a blender or food processor **(2)**. Process briefly using the pulse option to obtain a coarse "couscous."

This "couscous" can be eaten raw **(3)**, mixed in a salad. It can also be precooked by marinating in lemon juice or salt for 2 hours, or steamed for 2 minutes in cheesecloth.

● Chef's notes
Process small quantities of cauliflower at a time to obtain the correct texture.

❙ Recipe ideas
As a replacement for wheat couscous:
Berber-Style Mint and Vegetable Couscous, p. 262
Falafel and Tabbouleh, p. 304

1

2

3

1

2

3

Preparing Parsnips ★

Certain large root vegetables have a fibrous core that is slow to cook and can give them an unpleasant taste. This is true of parsnips, which need to be prepared using the method that follows once they get to a certain size.

Ingredients
Parsnips, 2-3 in. (6-8 cm) or more in diameter at their
  thickest end

Peel the parsnips with a vegetable peeler or scraper. Rinse and dry them, and cut them in half lengthwise (1).

Cut each half in two lengthwise again (2) to give four pieces in total.

Remove the central core from each piece; it will appear paler than the surrounding flesh and have visible fibers (3). Reserve them for use in a soup. Cut up the parsnips according to your recipe (cubes, slices, etc.).

● Chef's notes
This technique can also be used for large carrots at the end of winter.

❘ Recipe ideas
Miso- and Maple-Glazed Roasted Root Vegetables, p. 226

Preparing Bell Peppers ★

It is easy to peel a raw bell pepper if it is first cut up correctly.

Ingredients
Bell peppers

Remove the stalk from the bell pepper and cut off the top (1). Pull out the ribs and the seeds (2). Cut along the natural lines marked on the bell pepper (3). Peel each piece with a vegetable peeler (4).

Cut up the bell peppers according to your recipe (cubes, slices, etc.).

● Good to know
At the start, all bell peppers are green! Depending on their variety, they turn yellow, red, or purple as they ripen, and vary in sweetness and strength.

❢ Recipe ideas
Shakshuka, p. 359

1

2

3

Preparing Chilies ★

Red or green, medium hot or extra-strong—there's a chili for every taste.

Ingredients
Fresh chilies

It is essential that you wear disposable gloves when preparing chilies.

Cut off the stalks (1). Split the chilies lengthwise down one side (2) and open up. Gently scrape out all the seeds with a small knife (3).

Finely chop the chilies according to your recipe (4).

● Chef's notes
The capsaicin contained in chilies, which gives them their hotness, can make your nose, mouth, and eyes sting painfully. Washing your hands will not always remove it, hence the need to wear gloves. Throw gloves away immediately after use and avoid touching your face after preparing chilies.

Recipe ideas
Biryani, p. 245
Pad Thai, p. 246
Amaranth Patties and Avocado Cream, p. 277
Three Sisters Soup with Squash, Corn, and Beans, p. 294
Spicy Potato *Dosas*, p. 297
Urad Dhal with Mango and Pomegranate Raita, p. 303
Two-Bean Chili Sin Carne, p. 307
Gado-Gado with Tempeh, p. 323
Shakshuka, p. 359
Paneer and Spinach Curry, p. 360
Hot Pepper and Walnut Dip with Pita Chips, p. 379
Indonesian Bean Salad, p. 380

4

1

Cleaning Leeks ★

With its tightly packed leaves, soil often gets trapped in this vegetable.

Ingredients
Leeks

Cut off the root end of the leeks and remove the thick, outer leaves by splitting them lengthwise (1).

Shorten the leeks by cutting off the dark green section at the top (2) and slit the remaining leaves lengthwise through the middle to about halfway down the white section.

Turn the leeks on their side and make a second, parallel slit (3). Rinse the leeks under running water, spreading the leaves apart to allow any trapped soil to be flushed out.

● Chef's notes
Reserve the tough, outer leaves for use in a bouquet garni. The leek tops can be used in soups or broths.

2

3

● Good to know
When blanching leeks (see technique p. 41) or steaming them (see technique p. 41), tie them into a bundle so they hold their shape and are easier to handle.

❢ Recipe ideas
Wild Rice–Stuffed Jack Be Little Squash, p. 237
One-Eyed Bouillabaisse, p. 363

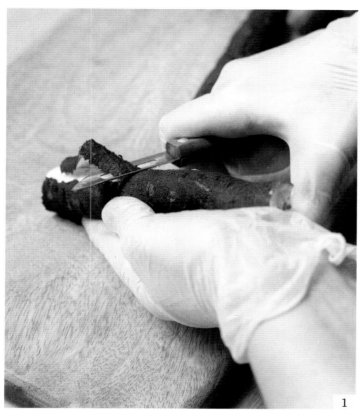

Preparing Salsifies ★

The white salsify is a root vegetable that needs careful preparation, as does the black salsify (scorzonera).

Ingredients
Salsifies
Juice of 1 lemon

Put on disposable gloves and rinse the salsifies under running water. Fill a large bowl with cold water and add the lemon juice.

Cut off the extremities and peel with a vegetable peeler (1).

Cut up the salsifies according to your recipe (2). Rinse, adding them to the bowl of acidulated water as you rinse them, to prevent discoloration (3).

Cook according to your recipe: in general, it is recommended that salsifies be cooked in a *blanc* (see technique p. 43).

Recipe ideas
Miso- and Maple-Glazed Roasted Root Vegetables, p. 226

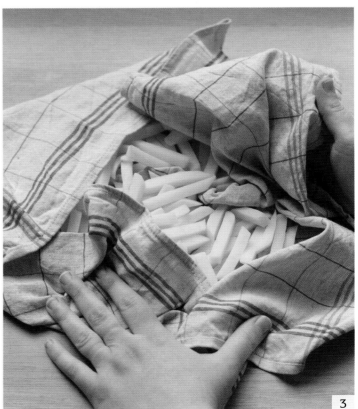

4

5

6

Making French Fries ★★

The secret for getting crisp, golden fries with soft centers is to deep-fry them twice.

Preparation time: 20 minutes
Cooking time: 15 minutes

Ingredients
2 ¼ lb. (1 kg) floury potatoes (e.g. Russet or King Edward)
1 quart (1 liter) frying oil (e.g. olive oil or peanut oil)
Fine salt and fleur de sel

Peel the potatoes, immersing them immediately in cold water to prevent discoloration. Cut them into sticks the size of your index finger using a knife or fry cutter (1). Rinse them in several changes of hot water until the water is clear (2). Spread them out on a clean cloth or dish towel and dry thoroughly until they no longer appear moist or shiny (3).

Heat the oil in the fryer to 300°F-320°F (150°C-160°C), using a thermometer to check the temperature. Once the oil has reached the desired temperature (little bubbles should form around the potato sticks when they are immersed in the oil), add half of the potato fries to the frying basket and immerse (4). Cook half of the fries at a time.

Cook the fries for 6 to 8 minutes, depending on their thickness: they should just color lightly (5). Drain them and increase the temperature to 360°F-370°F (180°C-190°C). Immerse the fries for a second time in the oil for 5 to 6 minutes, until they are crisp and golden.

Drain thoroughly (6). Season generously with salt and add a little fleur de sel when serving.

● **Chef's notes**
Use three times the volume of oil to potatoes. Do not overfill the frying basket: all the fries must be coated with the oil to cook correctly. It is best to fry them in several batches rather than all at once.

● **Good to know**
Filter the cold frying oil after use in order to use it once or twice more.
You can make fries from sweet potatoes, or from celeriac, which requires less rinsing as it contains less starch but which still should be thoroughly dried before frying.

Making Potato Puree ★

To be eaten just as it is, or for preparing potato croquettes, dauphine potatoes, or *aligot* (mashed potato with melted cheese, a specialty from Aubrac).

Preparation time: 15 minutes
Cooking time: 20 to 25 minutes

Ingredients
2 ¼ lb. (1 kg) floury potatoes (e.g. Russet or King Edward)
1 ¼ cups (300 ml) milk
4 tablespoons (50 g) butter, cold and diced
1 tablespoon kosher salt
Fine salt, freshly ground pepper, and nutmeg

Peel the potatoes, cut them into chunks, and rinse them in plenty of water. Put them in a large pan, cover with cold water, and add the kosher salt. Bring to a boil and cook for 20 to 25 minutes, until the tip of a knife pierces them easily.

Drain immediately to prevent them becoming waterlogged. Pass them through a potato ricer or vegetable mill (1) into the pan they were cooked in.

Dry the puree a little over a low heat (2), stirring continually with a wooden spatula.

Meanwhile, bring the milk to a boil in a small pan, add it to the potato in a thin stream, with the heat turned off (3). Stir, then add the cold diced butter; add the pepper and the nutmeg. Stir vigorously to allow the butter to melt and form an emulsion with the puree. Taste to check the seasoning, adding more if needed (4). Serve hot.

● **Chef's notes**
Use a bain-marie when reheating potato puree.

● **Good to know**
Never use a food processor to make potato puree: it processes it too quickly, giving it an unpleasant, glue-like texture.

❙ **Recipe ideas**
❙ Dulse Croquettes with Asparagus Salad, p. 343

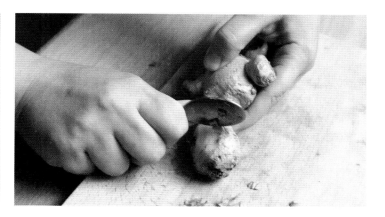

Peeling Fresh Ginger ★

The most aromatic essential oils found in fresh ginger lie just beneath the skin. Follow this method to peel it very thinly.

Ingredients
Fresh ginger

Remove the fine skin covering the ginger using the edge of a teaspoon **(see photo above)**. A teaspoon allows you to peel the ginger's irregular surface easily.

● **Good to know**
You can use the same technique for peeling fresh galangal and turmeric root.

Recipe ideas
Chickpea Curry with Cauliflower, Sweet Potatoes, and Coconut Milk, p. 219
Biryani, p. 245
Soba Noodles with Broccoli and Watercress, p. 281
Sautéed Spinach and Chanterelle Mushrooms with Tofu, p. 320
Buddha's Delight: *Lo Han Chai*, p. 327
Paneer and Spinach Curry, p. 360
Indonesian Bean Salad, p. 380
Pears Poached in White Wine, p. 397
Rhubarb, Red Currant, and Ginger Parfait , p. 407

Preparing Garlic ★

Ingredients
Garlic cloves

Removing the green shoot from the center of the cloves
This step is essential for making garlic digestible.
Peel the garlic cloves. Cut them in half lengthwise **(1)** and remove the green shoot using the tip of a small knife **(2)**. Chop finely according to your recipe.

Bruising garlic
Use this technique when you want the flavor of garlic to penetrate a stock or a dish without chopping and frying it. The whole clove can be removed once it has imparted its flavor. Pressing down on the flat surface of a large knife, lightly crush the whole clove with its skin on: it can then be removed easily **(3)**. Add the clove directly to the dish being prepared.

● **Good to know**
New season's garlic does not contain green shoots.

Recipe ideas
Miso- and Maple-Glazed Roasted Root Vegetables, p. 226
Ful Medames, p. 300

Making a Bouquet Garni ★

Indispensable for flavoring broths and slow-cooked dishes.

Ingredients
1 leek
1 bay leaf
2-3 sprigs thyme
Stalks of fresh herbs, e.g. parsley, cilantro, chervil

Slit open a leek and remove an outside leaf (1). Use either the white or the green part to wrap around the fresh herbs and bay leaf (2).

Wind a piece of string around the bundle of herbs (3) and tie it securely to hold everything in place (4). Trim off any stalks protruding from the bouquet garni (5).

● Chef's notes
The composition of bouquets garnis varies according to the recipe, the season, and the market! Thyme, bay leaf, parsley, and leek form the classic base, but do not hesitate to include other aromatic herbs such as fresh sage, rosemary, oregano, etc.

Preparing Vegetable Broth ★

An indispensable base ingredient, vegetable broth can be made in large quantities to be stored in the refrigerator or freezer.

Preparation time: 20 minutes
Cooking time: 30 minutes

Ingredients
1 onion
2 large carrots
1 leek
2 sticks celery, leaves intact, or replace with 3 ½ oz. (100 g) celeriac
1 tablespoon olive oil
8 cups (2 liters) water
4 cloves garlic
1 small piece kombu
1 small piece ginger, peeled
3 sprigs thyme
2 bay leaves
Approximately 12 parsley stalks, leaves intact
2 teaspoons fine salt

Peel and chop all the vegetables (1). Bruise the garlic (see technique p. 29).

Heat the oil in a deep pan and soften the vegetables in it. Pour over the water (2). Add the garlic, kombu, ginger (3), thyme, bay leaves, parsley, and salt. Bring to a boil and simmer for 30 minutes (4).

Strain (5), leave to cool, then store in the refrigerator in a sealed container.

⬤ **Good to know**
You can store the broth for up to 5 days in the refrigerator. You can also freeze it—either in large quantities or in an ice-cube tray to be used in small quantities as and when you require—for up to 5 months.

Recipe ideas
Creamed Pumpkin Soup and Sage Tempura, p. 211
Avgolemono Soup with Zucchini, p. 234
Spring Vegetable Risotto, p. 238
Swiss Chard and Goat Cheese Focaccia, p. 257
Cauliflower Mac and Cheese, p. 265
Barley and Mushroom Risotto, p. 282
Three Sisters Soup with Squash, Corn, and Beans, p. 294
Southern Black-Eyed Peas with Greens and Cornbread, p. 298
Two-Bean Chili Sin Carne, p. 307
Iranian Herby Yogurt Soup, p. 354

Blending Soup ★

How to achieve the perfect texture.

Ingredients
Vegetables cooked in a broth

Strain the cooked vegetables, reserving the cooking liquid, and put the strained vegetables in the jar of a blender. Pour over enough of their cooking liquid to cover.

Process until you have a smooth texture. Add any other ingredients mentioned in your soup recipe (cream or milk, for example), and process again, then gradually add enough broth to give the texture you require. Taste and correct the seasoning as necessary.

● Chef's notes
By adding the broth gradually, after the other ingredients, you can control the overall consistency of the soup. If, nevertheless, it is too liquid for your taste you can thicken it by adding a little mashed potato (fresh, frozen, or dehydrated flakes), cooked zucchini, or rice. You could also dilute potato flour with a little cold water and add it in a thin stream to the hot soup, then bring everything to a boil and cook for 3 minutes over a low heat.

❗ Recipe ideas
Creamed Pumpkin Soup and Sage Tempura, p. 211

Using a Juicer ★

The centrifugal force of a juicer allows juice to be gently extracted from fruit and vegetables, preserving all their nutrients. It is indispensable for making green juices and extracting the maximum nutritive value from vegetables.

Ingredients
Vegetables: carrots, cucumbers, beets, fennel, celery, etc.
Fruits: apples, pears, etc.
Herbs or ginger

Rinse the fruit and vegetables. If they are organic, do not peel them. Cut them up so they fit through the funnel of the juicer: it may be large enough for some fruit to remain whole. Position a container to collect the juice and another to collect the dry pulp. Put the fruit in the funnel and turn the juicer on (1).

Some varieties of vegetable (beets, cucumber) do not yield all their juice the first time round. Their pulp can therefore be put through the juicer a second time to extract more (2).

● Chef's notes
Avoid using fruits that have a soft texture such as mangoes, bananas, apricots, peaches: it is better to use them in smoothies because they do not give their best result when juiced. (These fruits are used commercially to produce "nectar," meaning their pulp is mixed with water and sugar.)

● Good to know
Juicing vegetables allows you to make the most of their less appetizing parts and avoid waste: broccoli and cabbage stalks, limp salad leaves, stalks from aromatic herbs, pea pods, etc. Their juices make a good base for risottos or other grain dishes.

1

Preparing Kale Chips ★

This method for preparing the curly-leaved cabbage has made it popular the world over.

Preparation time: 10 minutes
Cooking time: 10 minutes

Ingredients
6 large leaves kale
2 tablespoons olive oil
1 teaspoon spice of your choice: curry, sweet paprika, smoked paprika, garam masala, etc.
Fleur de sel

Preheat the oven to 340°F (170°C/Gas Mark 3).

Remove the ribs from the center of the kale leaves (1); you can use them as part of a green juice made in a centrifugal juicer (see technique p. 32) or a broth. Tear the leaves into large pieces and lay them on a baking sheet.

Mix the olive oil and spices in a small bowl.

Spread the oil over the leaves and gently massage it into them using your fingers (2): this helps to tenderize the leaves. Make sure that the kale leaves do not overlap on the baking sheet so they dry out evenly and become crisp; bake them in batches if necessary.

Add a generous sprinkling of fleur de sel and cook in the oven for 10 minutes (3). Leave to cool before serving.

● **Good to know**
You can also dry out the leaves for 12 hours at 100°F (40°C) in a dehydrator.
The chips will keep for 3 days in a well-sealed container.

❗ **Recipe ideas**
Portobello Burgers and Kale Chips, p. 347

2

3

1

2

Making Celery Salt ★

A delicious homemade seasoning using the often neglected part of celeriac or celery.

Preparation time: 15 minutes
Cooking time: 30 minutes

Ingredients
Stalks and leaves of a celeriac or leaves from a bunch of celery
Fine salt

3

Preheat the oven to 210°F (100°C/Gas Mark ¼). Cut off the stalks and leaves from the celeriac (1). Remove the leaves from the stalks and discard the stalks (2). If you are using a bunch of celery, cut off the leaves.

Spread the leaves in a single layer on a baking sheet (3). They should not overlap. Bake for 30 minutes, stirring them twice so they dry out uniformly: they should not brown.

Crumble the dried leaves between your fingers, discarding any tough parts (4). You can then reduce the leaves to a powder in a food processor. Measure their volume, add the same volume of salt, and mix together.

4

Celery salt keeps for 3 months in a sealed container away from the light. It is an ideal seasoning for salads, burgers, or vegetarian hot dogs, as well as tomato-based mixtures (juice, soup, etc.).

● Chef's notes
You can also make celery gomasio (see technique p. 119) in the same way by adding half salt and half sesame seeds to the crumbled celery leaves.

5

1

2

3

Preparing Pickled Vegetables ★

Vegetables preserved in vinegar and sugar can be kept for a long time, thanks to the lacto-fermentation that takes place, or they can be eaten after 3 days, as in this recipe.

For one 1-quart (1-liter) jar

Ingredients
3 carrots (approximately 7 oz./200 g)
1 large radish (approximately 7 oz./200 g): Red or Green Meat radishes, black radishes, white radishes, etc.
A few slices of red onion
½ cup (3 ½ oz./100 g) granulated sugar
Scant ½ cup (100 ml) rice vinegar
1 level teaspoon fine salt
1 ¼ cups (300 ml) water
1 star anise
10 coriander seeds
5 peppercorns
Chili pepper (optional)

Peel and slice the vegetables finely on a mandolin (see technique p. 40) (1). You can also slice them into julienne by hand. Place them in a large bowl.

Place all the remaining ingredients in a pan, stir, and bring to a boil.

Pour the boiling liquid over the prepared vegetables (2) and leave to cool.

Sterilize the jar and its lid (see technique p. 143) and fill it with the vegetables and their marinade (3).

Place in the refrigerator for at least 3 days before sampling. Consume within 2 months.

● Chef's notes
Add a teaspoon of black tea leaves to your marinade for even crunchier vegetables.
Sharp, vinegary, and spicy, these tasty pickled vegetables can be used to enhance sandwiches and salads.

● Good to know
Beware of the slightest hint of a bad odor, traces of mold, or a bulge in the jar's lid: do not consume the pickles. These are signs that there has been a problem with the sterilization or temperature of the jar's contents, preventing the development of the good bacteria necessary for their conservation.

Peeling Asparagus ★

Whether white or green, these delicate vegetables require careful handling!

Ingredients
White or green asparagus

Cut off any damaged parts of the asparagus stalks (1). Peel them with a vegetable peeler, starting just below the tip toward the stalk (2).

Remove any small, protruding "buds" attached to the tips using the tip of a small knife. Reserve the stalks, peelings, and trimmings for flavoring a broth.

Rinse and dry the asparagus. Tie them together in a bundle if you wish to blanch them (see technique p. 41).

Recipe ideas
Spring Vegetable Risotto, p. 238
Asparagus and Lima Bean Paella, p. 241
Japanese-Style Soy Balls with Wakame-Cucumber Salad, p. 344

1

2

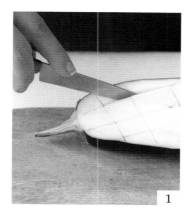

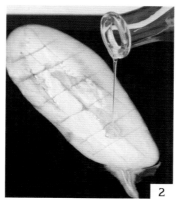

Making Eggplant (Aubergine) "Caviar" ★

This is a recipe found throughout the Mediterranean and the Middle East that can be enhanced in various ways.

Preparation time: 15 minutes
Cooking time: 30 to 40 minutes

Ingredients
1 eggplant
4 tablespoons (60 ml) olive oil
Thyme or dried oregano
Fine salt and freshly ground pepper
According to your taste, add either: 2-3 tablespoons tahini;
    2-3 tablespoons fromage blanc, or strained or Greek yogurt;
    or 2 tablespoons black olive puree.

Preheat the oven to 350°F (180°C/Gas Mark 4).

Wash and dry the eggplant. Cut in half lengthwise and mark the flesh into squares without cutting down to the skin (1).

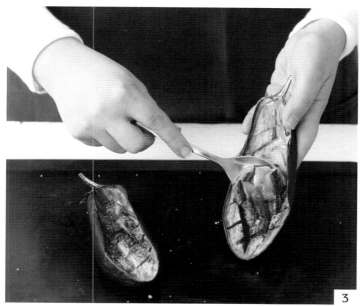

Baste the flesh with a tablespoon of the olive oil (2), reserving the remainder; season lightly with salt and sprinkle with the thyme or oregano.

Bake for 30 to 40 minutes until the eggplant flesh is tender and its surface has lightly browned.

Leave to cool, then scoop out the flesh with a spoon (3). Process the flesh in a food processor with the tahini, yogurt, or black olive puree.

Add the remaining olive oil in a thin stream through the funnel with the motor running, until you have a smooth, creamy texture. Taste, and adjust the seasoning if necessary.

● **Chef's notes**
Eggplant "caviar" will keep for 3 days in the refrigerator in a sealed container.

● **Good to know**
This is a great replacement for mayonnaise in a sandwich, topping for canapés, or accompaniment for grains and crudités, and is, along with hummus, one of the most popular vegetarian foods. Make sure you always have it to hand when in season.

Preparing Fresh Herbs ★

This is how to extend the life of parsley, mint, chervil, dill, and many other herbs.

Ingredients
Bunch of fresh herbs

Wash the herbs in a large bowl of cold water. Lift them out carefully, leaving any soil behind in the bottom of the bowl. Dry them in a salad spinner.

For immediate use: remove the leaves from the stalks **(1)**, using scissors where necessary. Chop the herbs finely. Keep parsley, chervil, and dill stalks for flavoring broths and soups and for using in bouquets garnis.

To extend their shelf life: once you have washed and dried the herbs, spread them out in a single layer on slightly damp paper towel, then roll them up in it **(2)**. Store in the refrigerator, moistening the paper regularly.

For a readily available stock of herbs or to use up the remains of a bunch: put your choice of fresh herbs in a food processor and pour 1 or 2 tablespoons of olive oil through the funnel with the motor running **(3)**. Spoon the resulting mixture into an ice-cube tray **(4)**, pressing down lightly, and place in the freezer. These herb ice cubes will keep for 3 or 4 months. No need to defrost them before using them: add them directly to your dish as they melt quickly.

❙ Recipe ideas
Freekeh-Stuffed Eggplant, p. 254
Berber-Style Mint and Vegetable Couscous, p. 262
Falafel and Tabbouleh, p. 304
Iranian Herby Yogurt Soup, p. 354
Coconut and Verbena Tapioca with Raspberry Coulis, p. 404

Dicing Onions ★

Dicing an onion—chopping it into small, evenly sized cubes—is a culinary technique that's needed regularly.

Ingredients
Onions of your choice: white, red, yellow, etc.

Cut off the top of the onion (1). Never remove the base—it will help to hold the onion together when you are dicing it.

Peel the onion (2). Cut it in two through the base (3).

Slice each half through the center horizontally, taking care not to cut all the way to the base (4). Holding the onion firmly at its base, which should remain intact, make three or four downward cuts (5).

Finally, slice crossways to obtain small dice (*brunoise*) (6).

● Chef's notes
Following this method using a sharp knife greatly reduces the risk of tears!

Techniques

Vegetables

Using a Mandolin ★★

The light and effective Japanese mandolin is indispensable for slicing vegetables thinly.

Hold the mandolin at an appropriate angle for the shape of slice you wish to obtain. Use with caution when you slice small vegetables such as radishes or carrots: the mandolin is extremely sharp, so stop slicing before you get to the end of the vegetable, to keep your fingers safe! **(1)**. Leftover pieces can be used up in soups or broths.

To regulate the thickness of the slices, use the screw positioned on the back, at the center of the mandolin **(2)**.

You can also make julienne of varying thicknesses with a mandolin: change the blade carefully using the screw on the side **(3)**.

To slice vegetables lengthwise and make julienne, use the pusher supplied with the mandolin; push it firmly into the vegetable you are slicing **(4)**.

● Chef's notes
To make a really crunchy salad, immerse the vegetable slices in a bowl of ice water as you slice. Drain, dry, and dress them just before serving to preserve their texture.

● Good to know
Be particularly careful and attentive when using a mandolin, as it is very easy to cut yourself.
Special gloves are available for stress-free slicing—a good precaution for the more inattentive or clumsy cook.

❱ Recipe ideas
Citrus Beet and Sprouted Buckwheat Salad, p. 278
Vegetable *Maki* with Miso Soup, p. 336
Japanese-Style Soy Balls with Wakame-Cucumber Salad, p. 344
Fennel Tortilla, p. 364
Mediterranean Vegetable Tartlets, p. 375

1

2

3

4

Blanching ★

Blanching green vegetables entails boiling them in a large quantity of salted water for a few minutes until they are al dente.

Ingredients
Green vegetables: green beans, peas, fava beans, etc.
Kosher salt: 1 tablespoon per 4 cups (1 liter) water

Bring a large pan of water to a boil with the kosher salt. Immerse the vegetables in the boiling water and cook over a high heat, just until they are al dente (1).

Remove the vegetables using a strainer and refresh them by immersing them immediately in a bowl of cold water with ice cubes (2). Let the vegetables cool in the water, then drain them. Use according to your recipe–in sautés, for example, or reheated with a little butter–seasoning them to taste.

● Chef's notes
Blanched vegetables absorb very little salt while cooking, so ensure they are seasoned correctly afterward.
Other, non-green vegetables can also be blanched in salted water but it has less impact on their color.
Root vegetables should be added to cold salted water before it is brought to a boil.

● Good to know
Blanching preserves the color and texture of green vegetables better than steaming.
Cooking over a high heat helps preserve the color of green vegetables.

❙ Recipe ideas
Pea, Spinach, and Sprouted Seed Muffins, p. 224
Spring Vegetable Risotto, p. 238
Soba Noodles with Broccoli and Watercress, p. 281
Gado-Gado with Tempeh, p. 323

Steaming ★

A simple technique for cooking vegetables at a low temperature. It is easy to overcook them, so pay close attention to their cooking time.

Ingredients
Vegetables of your choice, cleaned, prepared, chopped, etc.

Bring a large pan of water to a boil: the longer the cooking time required for the vegetables, the more water you will need. Put the vegetables in a steam basket and place it over the boiling water (1). It should not come into direct contact with the water. Cover (2) and leave to cook, topping up the water at intervals to ensure there is always plenty of steam. Check whether the vegetables are cooked using the tip of a knife. They should be al dente (tender but not soft).

● Chef's notes
If you wish to lightly flavor the vegetables, place some fresh herbs at the bottom of the steam basket, not in the cooking water.

● Good to know
Steamers, bamboo steamers, couscous pots, etc., all work in the same way and have a receptacle pierced with holes to allow the circulation of steam, a second one for boiling water, and a lid to maintain the temperature.

❙ Recipe ideas
Colcannon, p. 216
Banana and Coconut Milk Cake, p. 249
Berber-Style Mint and Vegetable Couscous, p. 262
Cauliflower Mac and Cheese, p. 265
Bulgur and Squash Kibbe, p. 268
Soba Noodles with Broccoli and Watercress, p. 281
Herby Spring Rolls with Sesame Sauce, p. 315

Guidelines for Cooking Vegetables

VEGETABLE	METHOD OF COOKING IN WATER	COOKING TIME IN WATER	COOKING TIME IN STEAM
Artichoke	From cold, in a *blanc* (see technique p. 43)	40 minutes, covered	30 minutes (cooking in a *blanc* is preferable, see technique p. 43)
Asparagus, green	Tied in a bunch	15–25 minutes, depending on diameter	8–15 minutes, depending on diameter
Asparagus, white	Boiling water, tied in a bunch	20–25 minutes (until they no longer float in the pan)	20–25 minutes, depending on diameter
Beets (Beetroot)	Unpeeled	1 ½–2 hours, depending on size (a pressure cooker reduces the time by ²/₃)	2–2 ½ hours
Belgian endive (Chicory)	Whole	20 minutes	10 minutes
Broccoli	Boiling water, in florets	4–5 minutes, uncovered	10–15 minutes, in florets
Brussels sprouts	Boiling water	10 minutes, uncovered	12–18 minutes
Carrots	Boiling water, in rounds	6–10 minutes, uncovered	20 minutes, in rounds
Cauliflower	Boiling water, in florets	10 minutes, uncovered	15–20 minutes, in florets
Celeriac	From cold, in cubes	15–20 minutes, uncovered	15–20 minutes, diced
Eggplant (Aubergine)	Not recommended	/	20–30 minutes, diced
Fennel	Not recommended	/	10 minutes, diced
Green beans	Boiling water	4–5 minutes, uncovered	12–15 minutes
Leeks	Boiling water, whole	10–15 minutes, uncovered	25 minutes, in rounds
Peas	Boiling water, shelled	3 minutes, then refreshed	10 minutes
Potatoes	From cold	20–25 minutes, depending on size	20 minutes, diced
Pumpkin/Red kuri squash	Diced	20–25 minutes	20 minutes
Romanesco cauliflower	In florets	7–8 minutes, then refreshed in ice water	8–10 minutes, in florets
Spinach	Boiling water, stalks removed	1 minute	3 minutes
Sweet potatoes	From cold, diced	15–20 minutes, depending on size	25 minutes, diced
Turnips	From cold, diced	10–15 minutes, covered	10–15 minutes, in quarters
Zucchini (Courgette)	Not recommended	/	8–10 minutes, in rounds or batons

Cooking in a *Blanc* ★

This technique of cooking in water to which flour, lemon juice, and salt has been added prevents the oxidation of certain vegetables.

Ingredients
1 tablespoon all-purpose flour
Juice of 2 lemons
½ teaspoon kosher salt
6 cups (1.5 liters) water

Pour the water into a large pan. Mix the flour to a paste with a spoonful of water, then add to the pan with the lemon juice and salt and stir (1).

Bring to a boil, then add the vegetables to the pan and cook until al dente (2).

● Chef's notes
This cooking method is used for salsifies, tuberous-rooted chervil, and artichokes.
Once they are cooked, you can keep these vegetables in the refrigerator for 24 hours or freeze them for 2 months.

Baking in a Salt Crust ★★

Inspired by one of French chef Alain Passard's signature recipes, this cooking method intensifies the flavor of root vegetables. It can be used for beets, celeriac, and even pineapple!

Preparation time: 5 minutes
Cooking time: 3 hours 15 minutes

Ingredients
1 celeriac, weighing approximately 1 ¼ lb. (600 g)
3 ½ lb. (1.5 kg) gray unrefined sea salt if available, or kosher salt
Olive oil for serving

Preheat the oven to 340°F (170°C/Gas Mark 3). Pour 2 ¼ lb. (1 kg) salt onto a baking sheet to a thickness of ¾ in. (2 cm) (1).

Wash and dry the celeriac and place it on the salt in the center of the baking sheet. Pack the remaining salt onto and around the celeriac (2), pressing firmly with your hands to form a dome (3) and covering it completely. The humidity in the salt will help it to adhere. Bake for 3 hours 15 minutes.

Remove from the oven and leave to cool for 30 minutes. Crack the top of the dome by gently tapping it to create an opening (4). Lift out the celeriac flesh with a spoon (5) and serve with a splash of olive oil.

● Chef's notes
To adapt the cooking time to the weight of your celeriac, allow 30 minutes per 3 ½ oz. (100 g).
This spectacular way of cooking celeriac can also be achieved in a large, cast-iron casserole filled with kosher salt; the crust can then be cracked at the table. For a celebratory meal, serve with a few shavings of truffle and a splash of olive oil.
If you do not have gray unrefined sea salt or kosher salt to hand, use table salt mixed with an egg white—the crust will form more easily.

Peeling Bell Peppers ★

Although bell peppers can be peeled raw using a vegetable peeler (see technique p. 22), the traditional method that has always been used in Mediterranean countries entails grilling them, either in the oven or on a barbecue, to cook them and allow their skin, which can be difficult to digest, to be easily removed.

Preparation time: 15 minutes
Cooking time: 30 minutes

Ingredients
Bell peppers

Preheat the broiler in your oven. Wash and dry the bell peppers and place them whole on a baking sheet (1). Cook them under the broiler for approximately 15 minutes, turn them over and cook for an additional 15 minutes. Their skin should blister and blacken (2).

Remove from the oven, and put the warm peppers in a large bowl. Cover with a plate so the peppers release their juices as they cool down (3): the steam created will enable the skins to be removed easily. Leave to cool for approximately 30 minutes.

Gently remove the blackened skins using a sharp knife (4). Do not rinse the peppers so they retain all of their flavor.

Remove the stalk and seeds (5). Wipe off any remaining seeds and cut into strips to be used as a garnish, in sauces, etc.

To make a salad of the prepared bell peppers, season with olive oil, lemon juice, finely chopped garlic, and salt and pepper. Set them aside to marinate for at least 8 hours before serving.

Recipe ideas

Solaris, p. 209
Hot Pepper and Walnut Dip with Pita Chips, p. 379

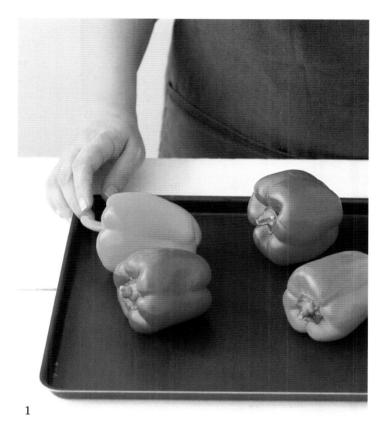

1

2

3

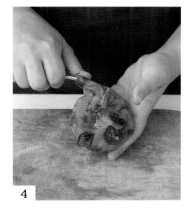

4

5

Roasting Vegetables ★

This cooking method, which allows dishes to be prepared in advance, preserves the texture of vegetables and intensifies their flavor.

Preparation time: 20 minutes
Cooking time: 45 minutes

Ingredients

3 ½ lb. (1.5 kg) vegetables: either winter root vegetables (parsnips, carrots, beets, turnips, Jerusalem artichokes, celariac) or a summer mix (bell peppers, zucchini, eggplants), with or without sliced onion, according to your taste
2–4 cloves garlic, according to taste
3 tablespoons olive oil
2 teaspoons dried thyme or oregano
1 bay leaf
1 teaspoon fleur de sel
Spices: curry, *piment d'Espelette*, paprika, etc. (optional)

1

Preheat the oven to 425°F (220°C/Gas Mark 7). Peel and chop the vegetables into evenly sized pieces. Bruise the garlic (see technique p. 29). Crumble the bay leaf between your fingers and mix it with the olive oil and thyme in a small bowl. Add the spices, if using.

Spread the vegetables and garlic in a single layer in a large baking dish. Pour over the herb and oil mixture, season with salt, and mix everything together with your hands until well coated (1).

Roast for approximately 45 minutes, depending on the texture of the vegetables, giving them a stir two or three times so that the vegetables brown lightly on all sides. Serve hot or warm (2).

● Chef's notes

You can prepare the vegetables in advance and mix them with the flavored oil in a large freezer bag or sealed container. They will keep for 24 to 48 hours in the refrigerator, before roasting. When cold, these roasted vegetables will keep in a sealed container in the refrigerator for 48 hours.

● Good to know

Roasting vegetables concentrates their natural sugars by removing their water content. Intensify the caramelization process by adding a little maple syrup or rice syrup to your marinade.

❘ Recipe ideas
Miso- and Maple-Glazed Roasted Root Vegetables, p. 226
Nut and Vegetable Millet Torte, p. 285

2

1

2

Cooking Asparagus ★

In addition to blanching or steaming, green asparagus can also be roasted, for a more original texture and taste.

Preparation time: 10 minutes
Cooking time: 7 to 9 minutes

Ingredients
1 bunch prepared asparagus (see technique p. 36)
2 tablespoons (25 g) butter
Scant ½ cup (100 ml) water (or vegetable broth, see technique p. 31)
A good pinch fine salt

Melt the butter in a skillet. Add the asparagus and color on all sides, shaking the skillet gently so they remain whole (1).

When they have lightly browned, add the water (or broth) and salt (2).

Cover the skillet and cook for 7 to 9 minutes, depending on their thickness. Check whether they are cooked using the tip of a knife (3): they should glisten and feel tender.

● Chef's notes
Asparagus cooked in this way is the perfect accompaniment to all egg dishes (boiled, baked, etc.).

❙ Recipe ideas
Spring Vegetable Risotto, p. 238
Asparagus and Lima Bean Paella, p. 241

Preparation

Cooking

Rice

Making Creole Rice ★

This is the simplest way to cook rice, in a large quantity of water. However, the rice loses some of its flavor and nutrients.

Ingredients
1 ¼ cups (9 oz./250 g) long grain rice
8 cups (2 liters) water
1 ½ teaspoons fine salt

Pour the rice into a fine-mesh sieve. Rinse it thoroughly under running cold water (1). Put the water into a large pan, add the salt, and bring to a boil. Add the rice in a steady stream (2) and stir immediately with a wooden spoon. Bring back to a boil, then simmer uncovered. The cooking time will depend on the type of rice (see the table below). Taste the rice to check if it is cooked, drain, and serve hot or cold.

● Chef's notes
This cooking method is particularly suited to parboiled long grain rice, or long grain rice (Thai, basmati) that is to be eaten cold in a salad or reheated as fried rice.

● Good to know
Cooked rice keeps for 2 days in a sealed container in the refrigerator and 1 month in the freezer. Chill immediately after it has cooled following cooking, if not using immediately.

❢ Recipe ideas
Avgolemono Soup with Zucchini, p. 234
Fried Rice with Shiitake, Bok Choy, and Cashew Nuts, p. 242

Cooking Rice by Absorption
(Slow-Cooked, Risotto, in a Rice Cooker, etc.)

TYPE OF RICE	VOLUME OF LIQUID (for 1 volume of rice)	COOKING TIME (approx.)
White rice (basmati, Thai)	2	16–18 minutes
Red rice	2.2	30 minutes
Brown rice	2.2	45–60 minutes*
Wild rice	3	30–40 minutes*
Sushi rice	1.15–1.25	10–13 minutes
Brown sushi rice	2	40 minutes
Risotto rice (arborio, etc.)	3	15–20 minutes

* The time can be reduced by soaking for 30 minutes before cooking.

1

2

Making Slow-Cooked (Pilaf) Rice ★

This method of cooking rice—which is also known as Indian pilaf or pilau rice—involves the absorption of water or broth. Consequently, it is more fragrant and has a perfect texture.

Ingredients
Scant 1 cup (7 oz./200 g) long grain rice (basmati, Thai)
1 tablespoon (15 g) olive oil or clarified butter
2 ½ cups (600 ml) boiling water
½ teaspoon fine salt
Optional: spices (star anise, cloves, cardamom) or a bouquet garni

Rinse the rice in a fine-mesh sieve. Heat the oil or butter in a heavy-bottom pan or cast-iron casserole. Add the rice (1), stir with a wooden spoon, and cook for 1 to 2 minutes until colored (2).

Pour over the boiling water and add your chosen spices (3), or the bouquet garni, and the salt. Bring to a boil, cover, and lower the heat.

Let the rice cook over a low heat for the time required for the type of rice. Five minutes before the end of the cooking time, remove the pan from the heat, and let stand for 5 minutes, covered, to finish cooking.

Take off the lid, remove any spices that need removing or the bouquet garni, and separate the grains with a fork before serving (4).

● Chef's notes
This method of cooking is particularly suitable for long grain rice (basmati, Thai). If you use brown rice, remember to increase the quantity of water accordingly; see table p. 50.
Pilaf rice can also be cooked in a casserole in the oven. Begin preparing the recipe in the same way, cover the casserole, then put it in the oven at 400°F (200°C/Gas Mark 6) for 20 minutes. Remove from the oven and let stand for 10 to 15 minutes, covered. For brown rice, allow 50 minutes in the oven.

● Good to know
Traditional pilaf rice also contains onions fried in butter and broth is used for the cooking liquid. It is usually cooked in butter.

❙ Recipe ideas
Thai-Style Sautéed Organic Red Camargue Rice, with Spring Vegetables and Tofu, p. 233.

1

2

3

4

Making Risotto ★★

Risotto is actually quite simple to make, as long as care is taken not to overcook it.

Ingredients
3 cups (750 ml) vegetable broth (see technique p. 31)
1 onion
1 carrot
1 stick celery
3 tablespoons olive oil
1 ¼ cups (9 oz./250 g) risotto rice (e.g. *arborio*, *carnaroli*, *vialone nano*)
Generous ½ cup (150 ml) dry white wine
6 tablespoons (75 g) cold butter
2 oz. (60 g) freshly grated vegetarian Parmesan-style hard cheese, plus extra to serve
Fine salt and freshly ground pepper

Heat the broth in a covered pan to prevent evaporation. Peel and dice the onion and carrot; wash and dry the celery, then dice into small cubes.

Heat the olive oil in a heavy-bottom pan. Add the diced vegetables **(1)**, soften for 2 minutes, then add the rice. Cook for 1 to 2 minutes until the grains are coated in oil and translucent **(2)**.

Pour in the wine **(3)**. Stir thoroughly until it has been completely absorbed. Add a ladleful of broth **(4)** and let the rice cook until it is nearly all absorbed. Stir, then add another ladleful.

Repeat the process, adding a ladleful of the broth at a time and stirring continuously, until the rice is tender. Make sure there is always a little broth in the pan when you add the next ladleful; you should not wait for it to be absorbed completely **(5)**.

Cut the butter into small cubes. Turn off the heat and mix it in **(6)**, then add the grated cheese **(7)**.

Stir vigorously so that the starch in the rice forms an emulsion with the butter and cheese **(8)**, to create the risotto's creamy texture.

Season to taste with salt and pepper. Serve in preheated soup plates.

● Chef's notes

To work out the quantity of broth necessary for your quantity of rice, multiply the volume of rice by three (see table p. 50). The emulsion created between the starch released by the rice into the broth and the butter and cheese, traditionally Parmesan, is called mantecatura: *it's what gives risotto its wonderfully creamy texture. Stir thoroughly and vigorously to obtain an airy texture.*

● Good to know

Tradition dictates that the broth is added one ladleful at a time, stirring continuously. However, you can achieve excellent results by adding two thirds of the broth and leaving it to cook for approximately 12 minutes, only stirring from time to time. Add the remainder of the broth a ladleful at a time.

❚ Recipe ideas
Spring Vegetable Risotto, p. 238
Barley and Mushroom Risotto, p. 282

Using Rice-Paper Wrappers ★

Rice-paper wrappers are thin sheets made from finely ground rice, used for making spring rolls. They are folded or rolled in a similar way to filo pastry, but need moistening before they become pliable.

Ingredients
Cold water
Rice-paper wrappers
Filling ingredients according to the recipe

Equipment
Clean dish towels

Place a clean dish towel on your work surface. Fill a large bowl with cold water.

Dip a rice sheet quickly into the water (1).

Lay it on the dish towel. Place the filling on top, leaving ½ in. (1 cm) clear at the base and ½ in. (1 cm) on each side (2).

Fold over the sides (3), then the base (4) of the sheet to enclose the filling. Roll it up (5) and press down firmly to seal it.

● **Good to know**
Some people prefer to dampen the rice-paper wrappers by placing them between two wet dish towels for approximately 1 minute. Experiment with both techniques to find which one works best for you.

Recipe ideas
Herby Spring Rolls with Sesame Sauce, p. 315

1

2

Making Sushi Rice ★★

The essential base for *maki* and sushi.

Ingredients

2 ¾ cups (1 lb. 2 oz./500 g) round grain sushi rice
3 cups (750 ml) cold water

Seasoning
¼ cup (60 ml) rice vinegar
3 ½ tablespoons (1 ½ oz./40 g) granulated sugar
2 teaspoons fine salt

Place the rice in a fine-mesh sieve and rinse under running water until it runs clear (1). Leave the rice to dry at room temperature for a minimum of 1 hour (2).

3

Put the water in a heavy-bottom pan or cast-iron casserole and add the rice (3). Cover and bring to a boil. Lower the heat and simmer for about 10 to 13 minutes, until all the water has been absorbed. Remove from the heat and let stand for 10 to 15 minutes, covered.

Meanwhile, prepare the seasoning. Mix the vinegar, sugar, and salt in a small pan. Place over a low heat until the sugar and salt have dissolved (4).

4

Put the hot rice in a large bowl, with a flat bottom if possible. The traditional receptacle is made of wood but you can use one made of glass or plastic; metal bowls, however, should never be used. Pour the vinegar mixture over the rice to cover the whole surface (5), then mix with a wooden spatula, turning the rice over gently to avoid crushing the grains (6).

Leave to cool at room temperature before use. Do not place in the refrigerator.

● Chef's notes

If you are using brown sushi rice, allow 1 volume of rice to 2 volumes of water. Prepare in the same way, allowing 40 minutes cooking time (see table p. 50).
You can also use a rice cooker, and then season the rice as described above.
Depending on the sushi rice, you need 15–25% more water than rice (see table p. 50). The rice should not be too soggy, so that it sticks together and the sushi or maki can hold their shape.

▮ Recipe ideas
Vegetable *Maki* with Miso Soup, p. 336

5

6

Making *Maki* ★★

It requires a little precision to make this classic Japanese dish successfully—as well as dexterity.

Ingredients
Sheets of nori
Sushi rice
Filling of your choice

Equipment
Maki mats (*makisu*)

Wash and dry an area of your kitchen work surface; place a bowl of cold water and a hand towel within easy reach. Place the *maki* mat on the work surface so the strings are aligned vertically.

Lay a sheet of nori on the *maki* mat, shiny side downward and touching the mat (1).

Lightly moisten your hands and take a small amount of the sushi rice (enough to form a small ball). Spread the rice evenly over the nori sheet, leaving a gap of approximately ¾ in. (2 cm) at the top and ½ in. (1 cm) on each side.

Arrange the filling ingredients in a strip along the bottom half of the rice (2). Enclose the filling in the nori sheet by taking hold of the bottom edge of the *maki* mat with two hands (3) and rolling it firmly away from you (4). Remove the rolled *maki* from the mat (5).

Cut the *maki* in half, then cut each half into two or three pieces using a well-sharpened knife (6). Serve immediately.

● **Chef's notes**
If the maki *is not to be served immediately, wrap it in plastic wrap to prevent it drying out. Consume within 2 hours, before the nori turns soft.*

● **Good to know**
To make an inverted maki, *first cover the* maki *mat with a layer of plastic wrap, then spread the rice over it thickly. Lay a sheet of nori on top and lastly the filling ingredients. Roll and cut up as described above.*

▾ **Recipe ideas**
Vegetable *Maki* with Miso Soup, p. 336

1

2

3

4

5

6

Making Rice Milk ★

A classic nondairy drink that can easily be prepared at home.
It is most suitable for use in sweet recipes.

Ingredients
4 cups (1 liter) water, preferably filtered
Generous ½ cup (3 ½ oz./100 g) Thai rice
1 pinch fine salt
Flavorings: 1-2 teaspoons syrup sweetener (malted rice, agave,
    or maple), or ½ vanilla bean or 1 teaspoon vanilla extract

Equipment
Blender

Bring 2 cups (500 ml) of the water to a boil and add the
rice. Cook it for 5 minutes only, then drain and let it cool
completely.

If you are using a vanilla bean, scrape out the seeds.

Pour the rice into a blender with the remaining water and
salt **(1)**. Process thoroughly. Add the syrup sweetener of your
choice, or the vanilla seeds or extract.

Strain through a cheesecloth or nut milk bag **(2)**. Squeeze it
firmly to extract the maximum amount of rice milk **(3)**.

Pour into a clean bottle and keep in the refrigerator. Shake
the bottle to homogenize the milk before use.

● Chef's notes
Use the milk within 3 days.
If you prefer a thicker consistency, do not strain the milk.
*This homemade milk differs from commercial rice milks because
it does not contain malted rice. It thickens naturally when
cooked.*

❦ Recipe ideas
Chia Pudding with a Green Smoothie, p. 383

3

1

2

Cooking Rice in a Rice Cooker ★

This is a useful piece of equipment if you cook rice on a regular basis in large quantities. It also has the added advantage of keeping the rice warm.

Ingredients
1 volume of rice
2-3 volumes water, depending on the type of rice (see table p. 51)
Fine salt to taste

Rinse the rice. Place it in the rice cooker, ensuring it does not exceed the limit indicated. Cover with cold water, ensuring it does not exceed the limit indicated (1).

Season lightly with salt. Close the lid and turn on the cooker. The machine will stop automatically when all the water has been absorbed.

Put the machine on the "keep warm" setting if the rice is not going to be served immediately. Otherwise open it, being careful of the steam that will escape (2). Serve.

● Chef's notes
Suitable for long grain rice (basmati, Thai), sushi rice, parboiled rice, and wild rice, this cooker can also be used to cook a variety of cereals.

Recipe ideas
Wild Rice-Stuffed Jack Be Little Squash, p. 237
Fried Rice with Shiitake, Bok Choy, and Cashew Nuts, p. 242

Preparation

Cooking

Wheat and Other Grains

Making Yeast-Raised Dough ★ ★

Whether you are preparing dough for bread, pizza, or focaccia, the technique is the same, only the quantity of liquid varies. The following recipe is for making focaccia and is particularly moist and pliable.

Serves 6 to 8
(for a 16 × 14-in./40 × 35-cm baking sheet)
Preparation time: 25 minutes
Resting time: 10 minutes
Rising time: 4 hours 30 minutes
Cooking time: 15 to 20 minutes

Ingredients
¾ oz. (20 g) fresh yeast or 1 tablespoon (⅓ oz./10 g) dried yeast
1 ¼ cups (300 ml) warm water (approximately 85°F/30°C)
¾ oz. (20 g) granulated sugar, honey, or agave syrup
4 ½ cups (1 ¼ lb./560 g) flour (all-purpose, spelt)
2 teaspoons (10 g) fine salt
Scant ½ cup (100 ml) white wine
3 tablespoons (50 ml) olive oil plus extra for the baking sheet

For baking
2 tablespoons (30 ml) water
1 ½ tablespoons (25 ml) olive oil
Fleur de sel

Crumble the fresh yeast. Add the water with the sugar, honey, or agave syrup. Mix together and let rest for 10 minutes: the mixture should begin foaming on the surface.

Mix the flour with the salt in a large bowl. Form a well in the center and pour the yeast mixture into it (1), then the wine and oil (2).

Knead the dough for 10 minutes: it should be moist and pliable (3). The dough can also be kneaded in a food processor using the dough blade or in a stand mixer fitted with a dough hook.

Cover with a clean damp cloth that has been well wrung out (4) and leave to rise for 2 to 3 hours at room temperature, until it doubles in size.

Generously oil the baking sheet and place the risen dough on it. It should be very pliable (5).

Spread it out with your hands (6), then with the tips of your fingers until the surface of the baking sheet is covered. Press down firmly to prevent the dough from shrinking back; small depressions should form (7).

Cover with a damp cloth again and leave to rise for 1 hour 30 minutes.

Preheat the oven to 450°F (230°C/Gas Mark 8). Mix the water with the olive oil for baking in a bowl. Brush the surface of the dough with the mixture, making sure all the small depressions are filled (8). This will keep the focaccia soft while baking.

Bake for 15 to 20 minutes.

● Chef's notes
For a pizza dough, use the following proportions:
4 cups (17 ¾ oz./500 g) flour
⅓ oz. (10 g) fresh yeast, or 1 ½ teaspoons (⅙ oz./5 g) dried yeast
1 teaspoon salt
1 teaspoon sugar
1 cup (250 ml) warm water
2 tablespoons olive oil

Let rise for 2 hours before rolling out thinly and baking for 10 minutes at 450°F (230°C/Gas Mark 8).

❘ Recipe ideas
Swiss Chard and Goat Cheese Focaccia, p. 257

Making Pastry Dough with Oil ★

To make a change from pastry dough made with butter, this vegan tart dough is enriched with cereal flakes to give it a more rustic, crunchy texture.

For one 9-10-in. (22-24-cm) tart pan
Preparation time: 10 minutes
Cooking time: 40 minutes

Ingredients

1 cup plus 2 tablespoons (5 oz./150 g) white whole-wheat flour
1 ¾ oz. (50 g) oats, buckwheat, or millet flakes
2 tablespoons seeds (sesame, poppy, chia, etc.)
¼ teaspoon fine salt
3 tablespoons (40 ml) olive oil
6 tablespoons (90 ml) water

Mix the flour with the cereal flakes, seeds, and salt. Add the oil and roughly mix it in using your fingertips (1).

Add the water (2); pour it in gradually, as you may need a little less, or a little more, depending on the absorption rate of your flour. Bring everything together quickly to form a ball (3).

Preheat the oven to 350°F (180°C/Gas Mark 4).

Sprinkle your work surface lightly with flour. Roll out the dough to the desired thickness and line the tart pan. Bake blind (see technique p. 76) for 10 minutes; allow to cool a little, then add your filling and bake for an additional 25 to 30 minutes.

● Chef's notes

Vary the oil depending on your tart's filling: walnut oil is good for a mushroom tart, sesame oil goes well with a carrot filling, etc.

● Good to know

You can also use a food processor fitted with the knife blade to make this pastry dough. Use the pulse setting to add the oil and water.
The dough will keep for 3 days covered in plastic wrap in the refrigerator, or for 2 months in the freezer.

1

2

3

Making Shortcrust Pastry Dough ★ ★

Rich in butter and very crisp, this pastry is more fragile to work with but makes a delicious base for all kinds of fillings, particularly fruit.

For one 9-10-in. (22-24-cm) tart pan
Preparation time: 10 minutes
Resting time: 1 hour
Cooking time: 15 minutes

Ingredients
1 ½ cups (6 ⅓ oz./180 g) all-purpose flour, plus extra for rolling
¼ teaspoon fine salt
7 tablespoons (4 oz./110 g) cold butter, cut into cubes, plus extra
  for the pan
3 tablespoons (45 ml) ice water
1 teaspoon cider vinegar, lemon juice, or white vinegar

Mix the flour and salt together in a large bowl. Form a well in the center and add the butter. Rub the butter into the flour with your fingertips, until you obtain a texture resembling coarse bread crumbs (1). Mix the water and vinegar together, then add to the dough mixture (2). Knead lightly until you have a ball of dough (3). Cover with plastic wrap, flatten with the palm of your hand, and place in the refrigerator for 1 hour.

Remove the dough from the plastic wrap and roll it out between two sheets of parchment paper (see technique p. 66). Line your tart pan and bake blind for 15 minutes (see technique p. 76) before using.

● Chef's notes
If the weather is very warm, cut up the butter in advance and put it in the freezer on a sheet of parchment paper for 30 minutes before making the pastry.
It is not necessary to rub the butter into the flour completely: you should still be able to see pea-sized lumps.

● Good to know
You can also use a food processor fitted with the knife blade to make this pastry dough. Mix the dry ingredients together, then add the butter in stages, using the pulse setting. Next, add the liquid ingredients through the funnel. Stop the machine as soon as the dough forms a ball.
The dough will keep for 3 days in the refrigerator, covered in plastic wrap, or for 2 months in the freezer.

❚ **Recipe ideas**
❚ Chicago Navy Bean Pie, p. 308

1

2

3

Rolling Out Pastry Dough ★★

Less fragile pastry doughs, such as those made with oil, are easy to roll out on a floured work surface. For doughs rich in butter with a more crumbly texture, the following technique is preferable. It also has the advantage of being completely hygienic as the dough is not in direct contact with the work surface and the rolling pin.

Ingredients
1 quantity chilled pastry dough of your choice, in plastic wrap

Equipment
Parchment paper
Rolling pin

Cut two pieces of parchment paper approximately 16 in. (40 cm) long. Remove the plastic wrap from the chilled dough (1). Place the dough in the center of one of the sheets of parchment paper.

Lay the second piece of parchment paper on top of the dough and roll it out with the rolling pin (2).

Gently remove the top sheet of parchment paper (3).

● Chef's notes
Using parchment paper when rolling out dough has many advantages. The dough can be handled more easily, it remains cooler resulting in less shrinkage as it bakes, and its texture isn't altered by the use of extra flour for rolling.
You can also use a silicone mat instead of parchment paper for rolling out pastry.

❙ Recipe ideas
Chicago Navy Bean Pie, p. 308
Mediterranean Vegetable Tartlets, p. 375
Nut and Maple Syrup Tart, p. 384
Onion, Apple, and Whiskey Pie, p. 393

Lining a Tart Pan ★

This is a simple technique that is quick to master.

Refrigeration time: 30 minutes

Ingredients
1 quantity pastry dough of your choice, rolled out on parchment
   paper (see technique p. 66)
Butter, for greasing the tart pan

Equipment
Tart pan
Rolling pin

Butter the tart pan. Take the rolled-out dough on its sheet
of parchment paper and lay it over the pan as centrally as
possible, with the paper side facing upward (1).

Gently remove the paper, sliding the dough down onto the
base of the pan and overlapping the sides (2). Press the
base and sides of the dough firmly into the pan to line it
uniformly.

Cut off the excess dough: use a knife or simply roll your
rolling pin across the pan to level it off (3).

Place the lined pan in the refrigerator for 30 minutes for
the dough to rest, to prevent shrinkage as the dough bakes.
Remove from the refrigerator and bake blind (see technique
p. 76).

● Chef's notes
*To line a square or rectangular pan, roll out the pastry into a strip
rather than a round.*

❙ Recipe ideas
Chicago Navy Bean Pie, p. 308
Nut and Maple Syrup Tart, p. 384

1

2

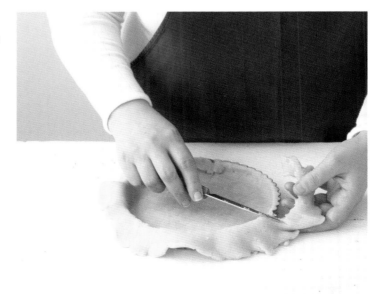

3

Preparing Seitan ★★

Perfected by Chinese Buddhist monks, seitan then became widespread throughout Asia; it was adopted and given pride of place in macrobiotic cuisine. Its name, which comes from Japanese, means "made from proteins." Seitan is traditionally prepared from wheat that has been repeatedly washed to remove its starch, leaving only the gluten—hence its alternative name "wheat gluten." This gluten is used as the base for a meat substitute with a texture comparable to white meats, and it will take on the flavor of the spices and broth that it is cooked in. It can be purchased from stores, but homemade seitan will be much tastier and is quick to prepare from dehydrated gluten, available from organic food stores.

Makes 1 lb. 5 oz.-1 ½ lb. (600-700 g) seitan
Preparation time: 30 minutes
Resting time: 8 hours
Cooking time: 30 to 45 minutes

Ingredients
Dough
7 oz. (200 g) wheat gluten powder
¾ oz. (20 g) potato flour, arrowroot starch, or cornstarch
¼ cup (¾ oz./20 g) ground almonds
⅓ oz. (10 g) brewer's yeast tablets
1 teaspoon spices of your choice: curry, sweet paprika, smoked paprika, etc.

Broth for preparing the dough
1 ½ cups (350 ml) vegetable broth (see technique p. 31)
2 tablespoons (30 ml) soy sauce
1 tablespoon olive oil or sesame oil, depending on the final use of the seitan

Broth for cooking the seitan
8 cups (2 liters) vegetable broth (see technique p. 31)
3 ½ tablespoons (50 ml) soy sauce
1 small piece kombu
2 cloves garlic, finely chopped

Equipment
Stand mixer

Put the gluten powder, starch of your choice, ground almonds, brewer's yeast, and spices of your choice into the bowl of a stand mixer and stir to mix together (1).

Mix all the ingredients for the first broth together and add them to the dry ingredients (2). Stir quickly to mix until the liquid has been completely absorbed (3).

Knead the mixture for 7 to 10 minutes either by hand or in the stand mixer fitted with a dough hook (strongly recommended) (4), until the dough is smooth and shiny and comes away completely from the sides of the bowl.

Place the seitan on a floured work surface and cut it to the size you require (depending on your recipe or what you wish to make with it) using a pair of scissors (5); the mixture will be sticky.

Put the 8 cups (2 liters) of the second broth, soy sauce, kombu, and garlic in a large pan and bring to a boil. Immerse the seitan pieces in the broth and poach on a very low heat for approximately 30 to 45 minutes, according to the size of your pieces. Allow to cool in the broth, then remove with a skimmer (6). Put the pieces in a container with sufficient broth to cover; once completely cold, seal and place in the refrigerator. Chill for a minimum of 8 hours before using.

● Chef's notes
Homemade seitan keeps for 3 days in broth. It can also be frozen, well drained and laid flat on a sheet of parchment paper, for up to 2 months.
Gluten has no flavor of its own: you can give it different flavors by varying the spices, adding herbs and other seasonings (mustard, smoked spices, etc.), or using a mushroom broth, depending on the recipe you are following.
Gluten swells considerably while it is cooking: be sure to use a large pan.

● Good to know
Seitan can also be cooked in the oven: its texture will be drier but firmer with a more defined shape. Divide the dough in two and roll into sausage shapes. Cover with aluminum foil and bake for 1 hour 30 minutes at 300°F (150°C/Gas Mark 2). Allow to cool before cutting into slices.

❙ Recipe ideas
Seitan Kebabs with *Dengaku* Sauce, p. 266

Shaping Chinese Dumplings ★★

The technique for folding these dumplings is the same, whether you are using thin store-bought disks or thicker homemade dough.

Ingredients
Disks of dumpling dough
Filling of your choice

Place a disk of dough on your work surface. Moisten the edges with water using a pastry brush (1).

Place 1 ½–2 teaspoons of filling in the center of the disk (2); the dumpling should not be overfilled or it will burst while cooking. However, bear in mind that some fillings shrink in volume during cooking, and you could end up with half-filled dumplings. Fold the disk into a half-moon shape (3).

Seal the edges by pinching them firmly between your fingers (4), then pleat them all the way round to ensure they are completely closed (5). Press the base of the dumpling lightly to ensure that the stuffing is evenly spread (6).

Repeat the process with the remaining disks of dough, placing each one on a tray lightly sprinkled with flour as soon as it is prepared.

Either steam the dumplings, or cook them in a skillet as follows: heat 3 tablespoons sunflower oil in a skillet over medium-high heat. Working in batches, place the dumplings in the skillet, making sure they do not touch, and fry for 2 to 3 minutes, until lightly golden. Pour in 3 tablespoons (50 ml) water, immediately cover with a lid, and cook for 5 minutes, until all the water has been absorbed. Continue with the remaining dumplings.

⬤ Good to know
Store-bought dough disks freeze well. Defrost them 12 hours in advance in the refrigerator, then use them just like fresh ones. Filled dumplings can also be frozen before cooking. They keep for 2 to 3 months, depending on the filling. They are best steamed from frozen, allowing an additional 5 minutes' cooking time.

❙ Recipe ideas
Chinese Tofu and Black Mushroom Dumplings, p. 316

Preparing Polenta ★

Whether white or yellow, this cornmeal is a traditional ingredient in Italian cooking. It can also be found in the cuisine of other Western European countries, under various names.

Serves 6 to 8
Preparation time: 5 minutes
Cooking time: 3 to 4 minutes

Ingredients
5 cups (1.25 liters) water, vegetable or mushroom broth, or a
   mixture of half water, half milk (cow, soya, etc.)
1 teaspoon fine salt
1 ¼ cups (9 oz./250 g) precooked polenta flour
Butter and/or freshly grated vegetarian Parmesan-style hard
   cheese, for serving (depending on the recipe)

Bring your chosen liquid to a boil with the salt in a large, deep pan. Add the polenta flour in a steady stream (1) and cook for 3 to 4 minutes, stirring continuously, until the polenta is smooth (2).

Polenta has a tendency to "erupt" when cooking and spatter; always use a large, deep pan.

Depending on the recipe, butter, cheese, herbs, or spices are added to the polenta once it is cooked.

● Chef's notes
If you wish to make a firm polenta for slicing (see technique p. 72), do not use milk when preparing it, as the mixture will be too soft to handle.

● Good to know
If using cornmeal that has not been precooked, allow approximately 45 minutes' cooking time, stirring frequently to prevent the mixture sticking to the bottom of the pan.

❢ Recipe ideas
Mushroom and Apricot Polenta, p. 339

71

Making Polenta Slices ★

Polenta can also be served in slices—easy to prepare in advance.

Preparation time: 10 minutes
Resting time: 3 hours
Cooking time: 5 minutes

Ingredients
Hot, cooked polenta (see technique p. 71)
Olive oil, for frying

Select a baking sheet with sides or a gratin dish–preferably nonstick, otherwise oil it lightly. Pour in the hot polenta (1).

Spread out the polenta evenly using a large spatula (2). Leave to firm up for a minimum of 3 hours at room temperature or place in the refrigerator until required.

Turn out the polenta onto a chopping board covered with parchment paper, then slice it up as desired (3). You can use a cookie cutter or even a glass to cut out rounds.

Heat a splash of olive oil in a skillet. When it is really hot, add the slices and brown lightly for 5 minutes on each side (4).

● **Chef's notes**
Polenta can be kept for 3 days in the refrigerator before slicing and frying it.
These slices can also be brushed with oil and lightly browned under a broiler.

● **Good to know**
Chickpea flour cooked in water and semolina can both be prepared in the same way as the cornmeal: spread them out on a baking sheet when cooked, let cool, then cut up and either broil or fry.

❚ **Recipe ideas**
Gnocchi *alla Romana*, p. 261

Sprouting Cereal Grains

2–3 level tablespoons of grain are enough to produce a generous quantity of sprouts, without overfilling your sprouting jar, which can be a source of bacteria.

If the weather is hot, rinse the grains more often—up to three times a day.

Mucilaginous grains (so called because they develop a viscous gel when they come into contact with water) such as buckwheat and amaranth need to be rinsed particularly thoroughly.

The skins of certain grains split when sprouting: it is preferable to remove them to prevent the risk of bacteria developing. Soak them for 2 to 3 minutes in a large bowl of water, then remove the skins that float to the surface.

Never eat grains that smell at all rotten or moldy. Check them carefully to ensure they do not contain any traces of mold.

TYPE OF GRAIN	SOAKING TIME	SPROUTING TIME	CONSUMPTION
Quinoa	4 hours (rinse before soaking)	3–4 days. Rinse generously twice a day.	As soon as the sprouts appear, and until sprouts are ¾–1 in. (2–3 cm) long. Put in the refrigerator and consume within 2 days.
Amaranth	6 hours (rinse before soaking)	2–3 days. Rinse generously twice a day.	As soon as the sprouts appear. Put in the refrigerator and consume within 2 days.
Whole-grain millet	Overnight	2–4 days. Rinse twice a day.	The millet sprout is tiny and wraps itself around the grain. Put in the refrigerator and consume within 2 days.
Oats/Wheat/Spelt/ Einkorn wheat/ Barley	Overnight	3–5 days. Rinse twice a day.	At every stage of sprouting, as soon as the sprouts appear. Can be eaten raw, steamed, or dried. Green shoots can be cut and their juice extracted in a juicer.
Brown rice	24 hours	3–6 days	Raw or steamed. Put in the refrigerator and consume within 2 days.

Wheat and Other Grains

73

Sprouting Buckwheat ★

Buckwheat, slightly mucilaginous, softens considerably once it has sprouted and develops a milder flavor. It can be eaten whole in a salad or sandwich, or ground to make a raw, gluten-free "porridge" packed with nutrients.

Soaking time: 12 hours

Ingredients
2-3 tablespoons buckwheat grains
Water

Equipment
Sprouting jar (or large jelly jar covered with a piece of muslin or cheesecloth, held in place by an elastic band)

Soak the buckwheat in plenty of water for 12 hours. Rinse very thoroughly, then put the buckwheat in a sprouting jar (or large jelly jar) and leave to sprout in a warm room (approximately 68°F/20°C) in natural light, avoiding direct sunlight on the jar (1).

Rinse thoroughly twice a day (2), ideally in the morning and evening, and drain well by shaking the jar over the sink (3).

Once the sprouts have grown to the desired length (this can vary from the first emerging shoots to sprouts ¾-1 in./2-3 cm long), rinse and drain them thoroughly.

Keep in the refrigerator and eat within 2 days.

● Chef's notes
Be sure not to use toasted buckwheat, also known as kasha: it will not sprout.

❚ Recipe ideas
Citrus Beet and Sprouted Buckwheat Salad, p. 278

Cooking Quinoa ★

In order to preserve all of its flavor, it is best to cook quinoa using the absorption method, as is the case for amaranth, too.

Preparation time: 5 minutes
Cooking time: 12 minutes
Resting time: 5 minutes

Ingredients
1 ¼ cups (200 g) quinoa
1 ¾ cups (420 ml) water
½ teaspoon fine salt

Rinse the quinoa thoroughly in a fine-mesh sieve to remove the saponin surrounding the grains (**1**).

Bring the water to a boil with the salt in a pan that has a lid. Pour the quinoa into the boiling water (**2**). Bring back to a boil, cover, and cook for 12 minutes over a medium heat.

Remove the pan from the heat and leave to rest, covered, for 5 minutes, to let the grains swell fully and finish absorbing the liquid (**3**).

● Chef's notes
Red and black quinoa are both a little firmer than the white variety when cooked. Cook them a little longer if you prefer them soft.
You can also replace the water with broth and add a bouquet garni or spices of your choice.

● Good to know
Allow 1 volume of quinoa to 1.7 volumes of water to obtain an ideal texture.
Amaranth can be prepared in the same way as quinoa: allow 1 volume of water to 1 volume of amaranth and cook for 25 minutes. Leave to rest for 5 minutes before serving. Amaranth is slightly viscous, like tapioca.

❙ Recipe ideas
Quinoa Soup, p. 274
Amaranth Patties and Avocado Cream, p. 277
Portobello Burgers and Kale Chips, p. 347

Wheat and Other Grains

Toasting Buckwheat ★

Lightly toasting cereal grains before cooking using the absorption method gives them an interesting, slightly nutty flavor. This technique is also recommended for millet.

Preparation time: 5 minutes
Cooking time: 7 minutes
Resting time: 15 to 20 minutes

Ingredients
1 cup plus 3 tablespoons (7 oz./200 g) buckwheat
Generous 1 ½ cups (400 ml) hot water
½ teaspoon fine salt

Lightly toast the buckwheat grains in a heavy-bottom pan over medium heat; they should give off an aroma of hazelnuts and turn golden. Add the hot water and salt, bring to a boil, and cook for 7 minutes, covered, over a medium heat. Remove the pan from the heat and let rest to allow the grains to swell for 15 to 20 minutes, still covered: they will absorb any remaining water and finish cooking without sticking to the bottom of the pan. Fluff the grains with a fork before serving.

● Chef's notes
Buckwheat tends to be viscous and turns sticky if boiled in lots of water. By following this method, the grains will remain well separated.
You can replace the water with broth and add a bouquet garni or spices of your choice.

● Good to know
It is essential to note that for 1 volume of buckwheat you will always need 1.5 volumes of water.
Hulled millet is best cooked using the same technique. For 1 volume of millet you will need 2 volumes of water. Cook for 5 minutes, followed by 10 minutes resting time, covered, once it is removed from the heat.

Baking Blind ★

For a perfectly cooked tart, without a soggy crust.

Cooking time: 10 to 30 minutes

Ingredients
1 unbaked tart shell made with your choice of pastry, chilled

Equipment
Parchment paper
Pie weights

Preheat the oven to 350°F (180°C/Gas Mark 4). Cut out a disk of parchment paper larger in diameter than your tart pan: this will make it easier to remove the hot pie weights after baking. Take the tart shell in its tart pan out of the refrigerator. Lay the disk of paper over the shell and cover it with the pie weights. Place in the oven: to prebake the shell, cook for 10 to 15 minutes; to bake it completely, cook for 30 minutes, then remove the paper with the weights, place back in the oven and continue cooking for an additional 5 minutes, to allow the shell to turn golden brown.

● Chef's notes
When prebaking blind, place your tart shell near the bottom of the oven, for a perfectly cooked and crispy base, even after a moist filling is added.

● Good to know
Pie weights ensure an even distribution of heat and help the pastry to cook uniformly. However, if you don't have any to hand, you can use dried beans or even rice in the same way, reserving them just for this purpose.

❙ Recipe ideas
Chicago Navy Bean Pie, p. 308
Nut and Maple Syrup Tart, p. 384

1

2

3

Breading ★

A simple technique for making food, such as croquettes, deliciously crunchy.

Ingredients
All-purpose flour
Egg whites
Bread crumbs
Oil for frying

Put the flour in a shallow dish, the egg whites in a second one, and the bread crumbs in a third (1). Lightly beat one or more egg whites (depending on the quantities to be breaded) with a fork to make them liquid without turning them frothy.

Dip and coat the food to be breaded in each of the three dishes in turn: first the flour, then the egg white, and lastly the bread crumbs (2).

Heat the oil in a skillet and fry the breaded pieces until golden (3), then leave to drain on paper towel.

Keep warm in an oven preheated to 210°F (100°C/Gas Mark ¼) if they are not to be served immediately.

● **Chef's notes**
The item to be breaded must have a completely dry surface—that is why it is first rolled in flour—so that it turns nice and crispy when fried.
If you are breading moist food such as tofu, ensure that it is pressed and dried thoroughly (see technique p. 88), before preparing it in this way.

● **Good to know**
Preparations with a high water content and therefore a less rigid texture, such as those made from vegetable or potato purees, can be shaped then chilled for at least an hour in the refrigerator, or even in the freezer. It is easier to bread chilled or frozen items; they will just take a bit longer to cook.

❙ **Recipe ideas**
Glamorgan Sausages, p. 267
Dulse Croquettes with Asparagus Salad, p. 343

Pulses

Sprouting Pulses ★

Sprouting significantly increases the nutritive value of pulses, both in terms of vitamins and minerals, and transforms their starch content, making them easier to digest.

Ingredients
2-3 tablespoons pulses
Water

Equipment
Sprouting jar (or large jelly jar covered with a piece of muslin or cheesecloth, held in place by an elastic band)
Fine-mesh sieve

Soak the pulses (1) according to the table below. After soaking, put them in your sprouting jar or jelly jar.

Rinse thoroughly in the morning and evening, either in your sprouting jar or in a fine-mesh sieve (2). When rinsing, ensure that any skins (from alfalfa, lentils, etc.) are removed; the best way to do this is to place the sprouts in a large bowl of cold water for 2 to 3 minutes, then remove the skins that float to the surface.

The pulses should be kept in a moist atmosphere but should not be allowed to get saturated with water. Place them in natural light, but not direct sunlight.

When the pulses have sprouted to the required length, put them in a sealed container in the refrigerator; they will keep for 2 to 3 days.

● Chef's notes
Mung beans and alfalfa are eaten raw. Adzuki beans, lentils, and chickpeas require cooking; sprouting reduces their cooking time to approximately 15 to 20 minutes. They can then be eaten in the usual way. Sprouting also makes them easier to digest and maximizes their nutritive value.

❙ Recipe ideas
Pea, Spinach, and Sprouted Seed Muffins, p. 224
Gado-Gado with Tempeh, p. 323
Indonesian Bean Salad, p. 380

Guidelines for Sprouting Pulses

TYPE OF PULSE	SOAKING TIME	SPROUTING TIME
Alfalfa	4–8 hours	3–7 days
Adzuki	14–18 hours	3–5 days
Chickpeas	14–18 hours	2–3 days
Lentils	8–12 hours	2–5 days
Mung beans	8–12 hours	3–4 days

Making Hummus ★

Both a dish in itself and a base ingredient, this puree of chickpeas with tahini is very versatile. It can be used for canapés, as a dip, as a sandwich spread, and even for breakfast with extra chickpeas, olive oil, and yogurt.

Ingredients
3 scant cups (14 oz./400 g) cooked chickpeas, drained and cooled
2 cloves garlic
3 tablespoons (1 oz./30 g) tahini (sesame seed paste)
1 teaspoon fine salt
Juice of 1 lemon
1–3 tablespoons (20–40 ml) water or cooking liquid from the chickpeas, depending on the texture required
2–3 tablespoons (30–40 ml) olive oil

Peel the garlic and remove the green shoot (see technique p. 29).

Put the chickpeas, garlic, tahini, and salt in a blender (1). Process roughly, then add the lemon juice and some of the water (or cooking liquid) and blend again, until you obtain a smooth, creamy texture. Add more water or liquid if necessary.

Place the hummus in a bowl and dress generously with the olive oil (2) to serve.

● **Chef's notes**
You can use canned chickpeas: drain—reserving some of their liquid to adjust the texture of the hummus—rinse them well, and drain again thoroughly.

● **Good to know**
Hummus can be kept for 5 days in a sealed container in the refrigerator. It can be enhanced by adding beet or squash puree, or pine nuts. You can also garnish it with spices such as za'atar.

Soaking Glass Noodles ★

These fine, transparent noodles are an indispensable ingredient in Asian cooking. They are made from the starch contained in mung beans, although they are often incorrectly labeled as edamame or green soybean noodles, a different product with a more robust texture.

Ingredients
3 ½ oz. (100 g) glass noodles
4 cups (1 liter) boiling water

Put the noodles in a bowl and pour the boiling water over them. Leave to swell for 15 minutes. Drain, rinse, and then cut them up with a pair of scissors.

Use these noodles in spring rolls or simply stir-fried with vegetables.

● **Good to know**
The noodles keep for 3 days in a sealed container in the refrigerator.

❦ **Recipe ideas**
Herby Spring Rolls with Sesame Sauce, p. 315

Cooking Pulses ★

Here are a few simple guidelines to ensure success every time when cooking dried beans, chickpeas, lentils, etc.

Ingredients
Water (preferably filtered)
Pulses of your choice
½ teaspoon lemon juice or cider vinegar
1 piece kombu
1 bouquet garni (optional)
Fine salt

If necessary, soak the pulses in a large quantity of cold water with the lemon juice or cider vinegar (1), for the time indicated in the table on p. 83.

Rinse the soaked pulses well (2), then place in a pan with cold water to cover. Add the kombu (3), and the bouquet garni, if using. Bring to a boil, then lower the heat, cover the pan, and simmer for the time shown in the table on p. 83.

Check regularly to ensure there is enough water in the pan to prevent the contents sticking (4).

Take off the heat, remove the kombu and bouquet garni, season with salt and serve, or use according to your recipe.

● Good to know
The weight of uncooked pulses increases three- or fourfold during cooking.
Bicarbonate of soda (baking soda) is often recommended to help cook pulses: unfortunately, it also destroys the vitamin B content. It is preferable to add kombu, which aids the cooking process and makes the pulses all the tastier.

Recipe ideas
Minestrone, p. 215
Chickpea Curry with Cauliflower, Sweet Potatoes, and Coconut Milk, p. 219
Asparagus and Lima Bean Paella, p. 241
Three Sisters Soup with Squash, Corn, and Beans, p. 294
Southern Black-Eyed Peas with Greens and Cornbread, p. 298
Ful Medames, p. 300
Two-Bean Chili Sin Carne, p. 307
Chicago Navy Bean Pie, p. 308

Guidelines for Cooking Pulses

The cooking time can vary depending on:
• The hardness of your water (calcium content).
Use filtered water if you live in an area where the calcium content is high.

• The freshness of your pulses.
The longer they have been in your pantry, the longer they will take to cook.

• The altitude, which will extend the cooking time.
The boiling point of water drops by about 1.8°F (1°C) for every 961 feet (293 meters) of altitude—a difference that might seem minimal but that can really affect your cooking on a daily basis.

If you do not have time for soaking:
• Immerse the pulses in a pan of boiling water for 5 minutes, remove from the heat, and let cool for 1 hour in the water.

• Rinse and cook them as indicated in the technique on p. 82: they will cook more quickly but will have retained some of their phytic acid, making them less easy to digest.

You can store your cooked pulses:
• For up to 5 days in a sealed container in the refrigerator.

• For up to 6 months in the freezer.

TYPE OF PULSE	SOAKING TIME	COOKING TIME IN BOILING WATER	COOKING TIME IN A PRESSURE COOKER
Adzuki beans	Overnight	1 hour	20 minutes
Black-eyed peas (beans)	Overnight	1 ½–2 hours	30–40 minutes
Chickpeas	Overnight	1 ½–2 hours	30–40 minutes
Flageolet beans	4 hours	1 ½ hours	30 minutes
Green lentils	Optional	30–45 minutes	10–15 minutes
Green or yellow dried peas	Overnight	2–3 hours	40–60 minutes
Lima (butter) beans	8 hours	1–1 ½ hours	20–30 minutes
Mung beans	Overnight	30–45 minutes	10–15 minutes
Red kidney beans	Overnight	1 ½–2 hours	30–40 minutes
Red lentils	Unnecessary	20–30 minutes	Not recommended
Split peas	Optional	1 hour	20 minutes
Navy (haricot) beans	Overnight	1 ½–2 hours	30–40 minutes
Yellow soybeans	Overnight	1 hour	20 minutes

Preparation

Cooking and Rehydration

Soybeans

Making Soy Milk ★ ★ ★

It may be the most commonly found nondairy milk product in stores, but that's no reason not to try your hand at making your own—you will be astonished by the flavor.

Makes approximately 7 cups (1.7 liters)

Ingredients
1 ½ cups (9 oz./250 g) yellow soybeans, hulled
8 cups (2 liters) cold water, plus extra for soaking

Equipment
Blender
Fine-mesh sieve
Thermometer

Thoroughly rinse the soybeans. Put them in a large bowl, cover generously with cold water **(1)** and soak for 12 hours. Rinse them, change the water, and soak for an additional 12 hours. Rinse again and then process in a blender with 2 cups (500 ml) of the cold water **(2)**.

Pour the mixture into a deep pan, as it will foam and rise as it cooks. Add the remaining 6 cups (1.5 liters) of water and stir. The mixture should not fill more than two thirds of the pan. Bring to a boil (watch it carefully), immediately lower the heat, and cook for 30 minutes at 160°F (70°C) **(3)**, stirring frequently.

Strain the hot mixture through a sieve **(4)**. Press down firmly on the solid residue to extract as much liquid as possible **(5)**. Pour into a clean bottle, let cool, then place in the refrigerator.

Use within 3 days, and shake the bottle each time to homogenize the milk.

● Chef's notes
You can also add the seeds from half a vanilla bean to the freshly strained soy milk while it is still hot.
Soy milk is sticky, so wash your equipment immediately after use.

● Good to know
It is essential to cook soybeans for a long time in order to deactivate the trypsin inhibitors found in them that can interfere with the metabolism of proteins in the body.
The soybean solids that remain once the milk has been extracted are called okara. They keep for 2 days in a sealed container in the refrigerator. You can use them in vegetable patties, cookies, or just sprinkled over vegetables to increase their protein content.

❙ Recipe ideas
Milk Flan with Apricot and Caramelized Nuts, p. 248
Vanilla Flans with Peach Coulis, p. 348
Chia Pudding with a Green Smoothie, p. 383
Dried Apricot Flan, p. 400

Making Tofu ★★★

It is well worth trying to make homemade tofu, to discover the taste when it is ultra-fresh. However, tofu's flavor is inextricably linked to the quality of the soy milk used, so the results and the texture can be variable.

Makes 4 ¼-5 ¼ oz. (120-150 g) tofu

Ingredients
2-4 g *nigari* (approximately ¼ teaspoon)
2 tablespoons (30 ml) water
4 cups (1 liter) soy milk

Equipment
Cheesecloth
A mold pierced with holes

Mix the *nigari* in the water until dissolved. Heat the soy milk to 150°F-155°F (65°C-68°C). Pour the dissolved *nigari* into the soy milk (1). Stir once in a figure of eight. Wait for 10 minutes to allow the curds to form.

Pour the curds into a mold with holes for making curd cheese or a traditional wooden Japanese mold (as pictured), lined with cheesecloth, and place the mold on a plate or tray (2).

Leave to drain for a while (3), fold the cheesecloth over the tofu, lift it out of the mold, and squeeze it over a bowl. (Keep the drained whey to use in pancakes, clafoutis, sauces, and dressings: it is rich in nutrients.) Put the tofu back in the mold, place a weight on top to press it, and let it drain some more, for approximately 15 minutes (4).

Take the tofu out of the mold and keep in cool water for a maximum of 2 days.

● Chef's notes

Nigari (magnesium chloride) is the traditional coagulant used in Japan. It can be purchased in organic food stores. It can give tofu a bitter taste and sometimes a granular texture.

The firmness of tofu depends on the draining time. Adjust this to obtain the texture you want.

You may find it simpler to use vinegar or lemon juice to separate your soy milk. The tofu will have a more acidic taste, which is not a problem for savory dishes. Choose the mildest vinegar possible, such as white balsamic. The texture of the tofu will be much softer and more fragile, comparable to silken tofu.

❗ Recipe ideas

Sautéed Red Cabbage with Smoked Tofu and Chestnuts, p. 319
Sautéed Spinach and Chanterelle Mushrooms with Tofu, p. 320
Chow Mein with Tofu, p. 324

1 2

Pressing Tofu ★

This is an essential technique to ensure your tofu is really firm and won't crumble during cooking.

Ingredients
1 block of firm tofu (see technique p. 87)

Cut the block of tofu into slices approximately ¾ in. (2 cm) thick. Place them on a chopping board **(1)** or on a smooth surface covered with paper towel.

Lay a sheet of paper towel over the tofu slices, place another chopping board on top, and place a weight on it (cans of food, cartons of milk, a casserole dish, or similar) **(2)**. Leave for 30 minutes to 1 hour.

The tofu can now be cooked in the usual ways: griddled (see technique p. 92), fried, in sauces, etc.

Recipe ideas
Sautéed Red Cabbage with Smoked Tofu and Chestnuts, p. 319
Sautéed Spinach and Chanterelle Mushrooms with Tofu, p. 320
Chow Mein with Tofu, p. 324
Buddha's Delight: *Lo Han Chai*, p. 327

Making Vegan Tofu Mayonnaise ★

This vegan mayonnaise is excellent served as a dip for crudités, in burgers, as a salad dressing, to name but a few uses.

Ingredients
½ clove garlic
9 oz. (200 g) silken tofu
1 teaspoon turmeric
2 teaspoons mustard
2 tablespoons (25 ml) olive oil
1 teaspoon cider vinegar
Fine salt and freshly ground pepper

Peel and remove the green shoot from the garlic (see technique p. 29). Chop it in a mini-blender or small bowl of a food processor (1). Add the tofu, turmeric, mustard, olive oil, and cider vinegar and process on the highest speed (2). Transfer to a bowl and season to taste with the salt and pepper (3).

● **Chef's notes**

The mayonnaise will keep for 2 days in a sealed container in the refrigerator.
Remember to remix it to a smooth emulsion with a fork before serving.
As for all sauces, you can enhance it with finely chopped herbs: parsley, chives, tarragon (add tarragon at the last minute as it can make the mayonnaise acidic), etc.

❗ **Recipe ideas**
Portobello Burgers and Kale Chips, p. 347

Making Vegan Béchamel Sauce ★

A fail-safe recipe that is even easier to prepare than traditional béchamel, and without the fat content! Use it in soufflés and gratins in the usual way.

Ingredients
2 ½ cups (600 ml) soy milk
⅓ cup (2 oz./50 g) rice flour or cornstarch
Fine salt, freshly ground pepper, and nutmeg

Pour the milk into a pan and add the rice flour or cornstarch to the cold milk (1). Mix it in until dissolved, using a whisk (2).

Bring to a boil, whisking continuously, then simmer for approximately 2 minutes, until the mixture thickens.

Season to taste with the salt, pepper, and nutmeg.

❗ Recipe ideas
Lasagna (see Chef's notes), p. 220

Rehydrating Textured Soy Protein ★

These curious little "sponges" that come in all manner of shapes—chunks, flakes, granules, etc.—are made from soy flour. They are rich in protein and contain no cholesterol. They are a pantry staple and are handy for improvising a hearty, nutritious vegetarian meal. As they have a neutral flavor, they require plenty of seasoning.

Ingredients

4 cups (1 liter) vegetable, mushroom, or seaweed broth
2 tablespoons (30 ml) soy sauce
1 teaspoon white or brown miso
1 teaspoon cider vinegar
1 teaspoon spices of your choice, depending on your recipe: turmeric, *piment d'Espelette*, smoked paprika, curry, etc.
2 oz. (60 g) textured soy protein

Mix the broth, soy sauce, miso, vinegar, and chosen spices together in a measuring jug.

1 Put the soy protein in a large bowl and pour over the seasoned broth **(1)**.

Leave to swell for 30 minutes. Drain thoroughly using a fine-mesh sieve **(2)** and cook immediately: rehydrated soy protein does not keep.

● Good to know

Allow 1/3–1/2 oz. (10–15 g) of dried soy protein per person; this will give you approximately 2 oz. (50 g) when rehydrated.

Adding an acidic ingredient such as vinegar or lemon juice will help rehydrate textured soy protein more quickly.

Although it is extremely rich in protein (it contains twice as much as beef), soy protein is poor in other nutrients and should therefore be combined with other ingredients. It can be sautéed in a wok with vegetables or slow-cooked in a vegetable and tomato sauce; with its firm, dense texture that resembles chopped or ground meat, soy protein is easy to incorporate into many recipes.

❘ Recipe ideas

Two-Bean Chili Sin Carne (see Chef's notes), p. 307

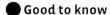

2

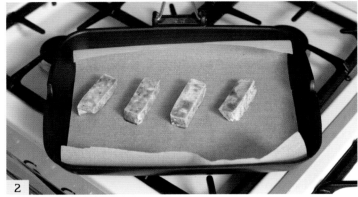

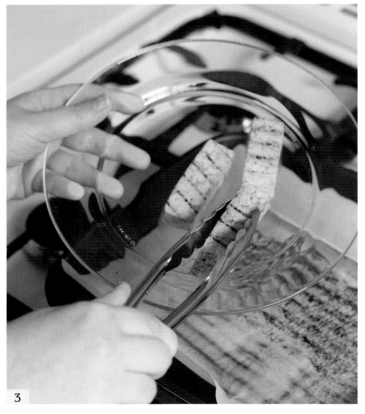

Griddling Tofu ★

The fragile texture of tofu can make it difficult to handle. This technique will give you perfectly griddled tofu every time!

Ingredients
Firm tofu (plain, smoked, or with herbs), preferably pressed
Soy sauce, *dengaku* sauce (see recipe p. 266), or a simple
  marinade of your choice

Equipment
Iron griddle pan

Pat the tofu dry with paper towel and cut into cubes or rectangles. Either marinate or coat with the sauce of your choice (1).

Lay a sheet of parchment paper on the griddle, put the griddle over a medium heat, and place the pieces of tofu on the paper (2). Griddle for 2 to 3 minutes, then turn the tofu pieces over using a pair of tongs (3) and repeat.

● Chef's notes
When handling tofu, use a pair of tongs to help limit breakage. Tongs are also handy for handling vegetables without damaging them—an indispensable tool for vegetarian cooking!

Cooking Tempeh ★

Whether you are preparing plain or marinated tempeh, gently steaming it improves its texture and tempers its flavor considerably. So before you say you don't like it, try this method!

Ingredients
1 block of tempeh
Water

Cut the tempeh into large pieces and put them in a steamer basket.

Bring a reasonable amount of water to a boil in a pan large enough to hold the steamer. Put the steamer in the pan, making sure the water cannot penetrate it. Cover and let steam for 10 minutes.

Serve the plain tempeh pieces either warm or cold, or marinate them.

● Chef's Notes
Tempeh prepared this way tends to be more moist and will absorb more marinade.

● Good to know
Tempeh, which originates from Indonesia, is made by fermenting soybeans with a rhizopus mold to bind the soybeans into a compact cake.

❗ Recipe ideas
Herby Spring Rolls with Sesame Sauce, p. 315
Gado-Gado with Tempeh, p. 323
Buddha's Delight: *Lo Han Chai*, p. 327

Preparation

Cooking and Rehydration

Mushrooms and Seaweed

Making Mushroom Broth ★

This fragrant broth is used for cooking grains and to intensify the flavor of sauces.

Makes 6–7 cups (1.8 liters) broth
Preparation time: 20 minutes
Cooking time: 45 minutes

Ingredients
1 onion
2 carrots
1 leek
2 sticks celery
7 oz. (200 g) button mushrooms
2 cloves garlic
1 tablespoon olive oil
8 cups (2 liters) water
3 fragrant dried mushrooms (shiitake)
3 slices dried porcini (or 1 fresh porcini)
3 sprigs thyme
2 tablespoons (30 ml) soy sauce

Peel the onion and carrots, wash the white and green parts of the leek thoroughly. Chop them all finely, together with the celery. Slice the button mushrooms **(1)**; peel and crush the garlic.

Heat the oil in a large heavy-bottom pan. Gently brown all the vegetables. Add the water, then the fragrant dried mushrooms, porcini, and thyme. Bring to a boil **(2)**, cover, and simmer for 45 minutes.

Strain through a sieve **(3)** and press down firmly to extract as much liquid as possible **(4)**.

Stir the soy sauce into the strained broth, taste and season if necessary.

● Chef's notes
Although the mushrooms strained from the broth will have lost quite a bit of their flavor, they can still be used for sauces, stuffings, vegetable patties, veggie meatballs, or soups.

● Good to know
The broth will keep for 3 days in the refrigerator or for 3 months in the freezer.

❢ Recipe ideas
Barley and Mushroom Risotto, p. 282

Making Seaweed Broth (Dashi) ★

Dashi, a fundamental ingredient in Japanese cooking, can be made with or without dried tuna. This recipe uses only seaweed and mushrooms, and will give you a particularly savory vegetarian base for many dishes.

Makes 2 ½ cups (600 ml) broth
Soaking time: 8 hours

Ingredients
Small piece kombu (2 ½ × ¾ in./5 × 2 cm)
2 fragrant dried mushrooms (shiitake)
2 ½ cups (600 ml) water

In a covered container, soak the kombu and fragrant dried mushrooms in the water for 8 hours.

Strain, and use the broth to cook vegetables or make a soup, etc.

● Chef's notes
Don't throw out the kombu: slice it finely and include it in a dish of stir-fried vegetables, noodles, or fried rice.

● Good to know
The broth will keep for 4 to 5 days in the refrigerator.
Combining these two foods rich in umami (savory taste) results in a delicious broth with a unique flavor.

❙ Recipe ideas
Japanese Tea and Rice with Sea Spaghetti and Enoki Mushrooms, p. 334
Vegetable *Maki* with Miso Soup, p. 336

Desalting Seaweed ★

Certain seaweeds are sold preserved in salt; they need to be completely desalted before use.

Ingredients
Salted seaweed (sea lettuce, dulse, nori, wakame, etc.)

Place the seaweed in a large quantity of water to rinse (1) and stir with your hand: the salt will sink to the bottom of the bowl.

Squeeze the seaweed gently in your hands (2) to remove the excess water (or drain in a sieve). Rinse a second time in plenty of water. Taste, and if it is still too salty, rinse a third time. The rinsing water should look clear at the end.

● Chef's notes
If you prefer your seaweed with very little salt, leave it to soak for 10 minutes in the water from the final rinse.

● Good to know
Once desalted, brown seaweeds such as wakame can be steamed. This restores their green color but will soften their texture and slightly alter the taste.

❙ Recipe ideas
Seaweed Tartare, p. 335

Sautéing Mushrooms ★

For golden-brown mushrooms, cook them in two stages.

Serves 4
Preparation time: 5 minutes
Cooking time: 6 minutes

Ingredients
1 lb. 2 oz. (500 g) fresh mushrooms
Generous pinch fine salt
1 ½ tablespoons (20 g) butter, or 1 tablespoon oil of your choice

Slice the mushrooms. Heat a skillet and add the sliced mushrooms (1).

Sprinkle over the salt and cook the mushrooms briskly for 3 to 4 minutes to draw out the water they contain (2). Drain, reserving their juice (3).

Dry the skillet, then melt the butter or heat the oil in it. Fry the drained mushrooms until golden brown and cooked (4).

● Chef's notes
Use the reserved cooking juices to flavor sauces or marinades.

❘ Recipe ideas
Fried Rice with Shiitake, Bok Choy, and Cashew Nuts, p. 242
Barley and Mushroom Risotto, p. 282
Sautéed Spinach and Chanterelle Mushrooms with Tofu, p. 320
Mushroom and Apricot Polenta, p. 339
Indian Mushroom Hotpot, p. 340

Rehydrating Dried Mushrooms ★

Soaking time: 15 to 30 minutes

Ingredients
Dried mushrooms of your choice (see p. 165)
Hot water

Put the mushrooms in a large bowl: they will swell as they soak. Pour over enough hot water to cover (1).

Leave shiitake and porcini to swell for 15 minutes; morels should be left for 30 minutes.

Drain them over a bowl (2), pressing down gently.

Strain the soaking liquid again before using in sauces or a broth, to ensure any grit is eliminated.

● Good to know
Mushrooms can also be soaked in cold water: this will take 8 to 10 hours at room temperature.

❙ Recipe ideas
Fried Rice with Shiitake, Bok Choy, and Cashew Nuts, p. 242
Chinese Tofu and Black Mushroom Dumplings, p. 316
Buddha's Delight: *Lo Han Chai*, p. 327

Rehydrating Dried Seaweed ★

It may be sold as flakes, ready to be sprinkled, but dried whole leaf seaweed has much more flavor.

Soaking time: 10 to 30 minutes

Ingredients
Dried seaweed of your choice
Water

There are many varieties of dried seaweed: sea lettuce, wakame, dulse, sea beans, sea spaghetti, kombu, to name but a few. They are all prepared in the same way:

Soak in a large quantity of cold water. The soaking time will vary: 10 minutes for sea lettuce, wakame, and dulse; up to 30 minutes for kombu, sea spaghetti, and sea beans, as they have a firmer texture. Once the seaweed has swelled, drain thoroughly.

Kombu and sea spaghetti both need rinsing after draining; all the others can be used directly in your recipe.

● Chef's notes
Rehydrated seaweed should be used within 24 hours.

● Good to know
Drying seaweed tends to break up its fibers, making it more tender and easier to digest when soaked than fresh seaweed.

❙ Recipe ideas
Japanese Tea and Rice with Sea Spaghetti and Enoki Mushrooms, p. 334
Seaweed Tartare, p. 335
Dulse Croquettes with Asparagus Salad, p. 343

Roasting Nori Seaweed ★

A quick and simple way to enhance the flavor of nori seaweed.

Ingredients
Sheets of nori seaweed

Carefully hold the sheet of nori over a gas flame. It will shrivel up almost instantaneously **(1)**.

Crumble it into a bowl **(2)** and store in a dry place. Use it to sprinkle over salads, rice, pasta, roasted vegetables, purees, or in soups, etc.

❗ Recipe ideas
Japanese Tea and Rice with Sea Spaghetti and Enoki Mushrooms, p. 334
Japanese-Style Soy Balls with Wakame-Cucumber Salad, p. 344

1

Gelling with Agar-Agar ★

Known as *kanten* in Japan, this red seaweed has a gelling capacity that is eight times higher than gelatin.

Preparation time: 5 minutes
Cooking time: 2 to 3 minutes

Ingredients
½ teaspoon (2 g) agar-agar powder
2 generous cups (500 ml) of the preparation to be gelled:
  pureed fruits, nondairy milk, etc.

Sprinkle the agar-agar over the cold or lukewarm preparation to be gelled (**1**).

Bring to a boil, stirring continuously (**2**). Boil steadily for 30 seconds.

Allow to cool: the mixture will thicken as it cools (**3**).

● Chef's notes
Agar-agar is often recommended as a substitute for gelatin, but it is not always the perfect alternative. Although you can use it in aspic, terrines, panna cotta, etc., their texture will not be the same: it will be firmer and the surface more likely to split. You can process mixtures containing it in a blender or food processor to obtain a softer texture when gelled.
Agar-agar is ideal for gelling low-sugar jams: for 4 ¼ lb. (2 kg) fruit, use 2 ½ cups (1 lb. 2 oz./500 g) granulated sugar and add ½ teaspoon (2 g) agar-agar. The low sugar content means they need to be kept in the refrigerator and eaten within 3 months.

● Good to know
Avoid agar-agar sold in solid form: it is much harder to measure than powder.
The acidity in certain fruits can affect how they gel: double the quantity of agar-agar is needed for preparations with lemon, pineapple, or black currants, etc.
Do not freeze foods containing agar-agar; they will give out water when they defrost.

▮ Recipe ideas
Vanilla Flans with Peach Coulis, p. 348

2

3

Mushrooms and Seaweed

Eggs and Dairy Products

Hard-Boiling Eggs ★

Cooking time: 11 to 12 minutes

Ingredients
Hens' eggs (allow one or more per person)
2-3 drops of vinegar

Put enough water to cover the eggs in a saucepan and bring to a boil. Add the vinegar and immerse the eggs (**1**). Let them boil for 11 to 12 minutes, from the moment the water comes back to a boil.

Remove the eggs from the pan and stop them cooking by running them immediately under cold water (see Chef's notes), then roll them on a work surface to crack their shells (**2**).

Immerse them again in a pan of cold water for a few minutes, then shell them (**3**). Rinse to remove any remaining pieces of shell and dry.

● Chef's notes
Always take your eggs out of the refrigerator 1 hour before cooking them, so they are at room temperature, otherwise their shells may crack when immersed in the boiling water, due to the change in temperature.
Adding vinegar to the water allows any leaks from the shell to coagulate quickly.
To avoid overcooked eggs and therefore prevent the telltale green ring forming around the yolk, stop the cooking immediately by placing them under cold running water.

● Good to know
Depending on the size of the eggs, the cooking time can vary by 1 to 2 minutes.
For soft-boiled eggs (with runny yolks but fully set whites), allow 5 to 6 minutes boiling, depending on their size.
For perfectly soft soft-boiled eggs (with runny yolks and whites that are not quite fully set) 3 to 4 minutes is enough, depending on their size.

❙ Recipe ideas
Ful Medames, p. 300

Baking Eggs *au Plat* ★

As its French name indicates, the eggs in this recipe are baked in a dish (*plat*) in the oven. However, they can also be cooked in a skillet.

Cooking time: 8 minutes

Ingredients
2 eggs per person
½ teaspoon olive oil (or oil of your choice) per person
Fine salt and white pepper

Preheat the oven to 350°F (180°C/Gas Mark 4).

Break an egg into a small bowl, taking care not to break the yolk (1).

Lightly brush a small ovenproof dish for each person with the oil (2) and season the bottom of this dish with the salt and white pepper.

Gently slide the egg into the dish (3). Repeat with the remaining eggs, putting two in each dish.

Bake for 8 minutes. The whites should set and the yolks remain runny.

● Chef's notes
Add any spices or herbs to the warm eggs after cooking to pre-serve their flavor.

❙ Recipe ideas
Shakshuka, p. 359

Scrambling Eggs ★

Prepare your scrambled eggs by the book and you'll achieve a perfect soft and creamy texture every time.

Ingredients
2 eggs per person
1 tablespoon water or milk for every 2 eggs
Garnish: 1 tablespoon chopped fresh herbs; chopped cooked mushrooms; or peeled, seeded, chopped tomatoes, etc.
Fine salt and freshly ground pepper

Break the eggs into a heatproof round-bottomed bowl. Add the water or milk, season with salt and pepper, and mix together thoroughly with a fork; the mixture should not be frothy. Add the herbs or garnish of your choice.

Place the bowl over a pan of gently boiling water to create a bain-marie (1). Cook until scrambled, stirring the mixture continually to achieve a soft, creamy consistency (2).

● Chef's notes
It is best to make scrambled eggs for a maximum of four people at a time. If you are preparing this dish for more people, cook it in batches rather than trying to make a large quantity at once.

● Good to know
The eggs will continue to cook in the bain-marie even when removed from the heat, so serve them as soon as they are ready.

Baking Eggs *en Cocotte* ★

This is the perfect way to serve eggs for brunch or at large get-togethers. Baked eggs *en cocotte* are as soft as soft-boiled eggs and can be generously garnished.

Cooking time: 6 to 8 minutes

Ingredients
½ teaspoon melted butter per ramekin
Eggs (as many as you have guests/ramekins)
1 tablespoon cream per ramekin
Garnish per ramekin: 1 tablespoon sautéed chopped mushrooms, tomato sauce, etc., or 1 teaspoon chopped herbs
Fine salt and freshly ground pepper

Preheat the oven to 350°F (180°C/Gas Mark 4).

Lightly brush the ramekins with the butter and put a tablespoon of cream and the garnish in each one. Break an egg into each ramekin, taking care not to break the yolk (1). Season with salt and pepper.

Place the ramekins in a roasting pan or gratin dish, then pour in sufficient boiling water to come halfway up the outside of the ramekins (2). Bake for 6 to 8 minutes, checking frequently to ensure the yolks remain runny. Serve immediately.

● Chef's notes
To prevent the boiling water splashing the contents of the ramekins, place a sheet of parchment paper on the bottom of the roasting pan or gratin dish before filling it with water.

● Good to know
If you do not have ramekins to hand, you can use a well-greased muffin mold. The cups are an ideal size.

Making Omelets ★

Whether an Italian frittata, Spanish tortilla, or French omelet, this method of cooking eggs in a skillet to form an omelet of varying thicknesses is used in many countries.

Ingredients

2 eggs per person
3 generous tablespoons (50 ml) cow milk or soy milk
1 ½ tablespoons (20 g) butter, or 1 tablespoon oil, for cooking
Garnish: 1 generous tablespoon finely chopped herbs; diced cheese; or sautéed mushrooms, etc.
Fine salt and freshly ground pepper

Break the eggs into a large bowl. Add the milk and season with salt and pepper, then beat everything together with a fork. The mixture should not become frothy. Add your chosen garnish and mix in with a few stirs of the fork (1).

Heat the oil or butter in a skillet over medium heat, making sure it coats the bottom evenly by tilting the pan in every direction. Pour in the egg mixture to cover the bottom of the skillet (2).

Stir the mixture with a wooden spatula, drawing the egg around the edges, which will set more quickly, toward the center (3).

Loosen the edges of the omelet by going round with the spatula, tilting the pan a little to let any egg that is still liquid slide underneath and finish cooking. Finally, fold it over with the spatula (4).

If you prefer your omelet well cooked, you can slide it onto a plate, then flip it back into the pan to cook on the other side–it is all a matter of taste!

● **Chef's notes**

You can add other garnishes to the omelet just before folding it over: ratatouille, roasted vegetables, etc. The heat of the omelet will warm them through.

❗ **Recipe ideas**
Provençal Layered Omelet, p. 353

Poaching Eggs ★★

Poaching eggs directly in boiling water or in a sauce takes a little practice, but can be mastered in no time at all.

Cooking time: 3 minutes

Ingredients
1 egg per person
2-3 drops white vinegar or lemon juice

Break an egg into a ramekin or small bowl. In a shallow pan, bring water to a simmer and add the vinegar or lemon juice just before adding the egg. Stir the water round with a spoon to create a small whirlpool, then slide the egg into it (**1**).

Wait for 5 seconds, then using two tablespoons draw the white around the yolk to enclose and seal it (**2**).

Let cook for approximately 3 minutes. Meanwhile, fill a bowl with cold water. Using a skimmer, take the egg out of the water and transfer to the bowl of water to stop it cooking (**3**). Remove the egg and drain, trim it to an even shape with scissors if necessary, and serve.

● **Good to know**
Adding vinegar or lemon juice to the water helps the proteins in the egg white to coagulate well, shortening the cooking time.

❙ **Recipe ideas**
One-Eyed Bouillabaisse, p. 363

1

2

3

4

Making Mayonnaise ★★

The trick for successful mayonnaise every time is to use one hard-boiled egg yolk and one raw yolk.

Ingredients
1 hard-boiled egg (see technique p. 104)
1 egg
Approximately 1 cup (250 ml) grape-seed oil
2 teaspoons mustard
2 teaspoons vinegar or lemon juice
A good pinch each fine salt and freshly ground pepper

Remove the yolk from the hard-boiled egg (1). Place it in a small bowl and crush it with a fork.

Separate the yolk from the white of the raw egg and add it to the bowl along with the mustard, vinegar, salt, and pepper. Mix together well with a fork (2).

Add the oil very gradually in a thin stream, mixing continuously to incorporate it into the egg mixture and form an emulsion (3). You may need a little more or less oil, depending on the consistency you prefer. Taste and adjust the seasoning.

The mayonnaise can be kept for 24 hours in the refrigerator.

● Chef's notes
If the mayonnaise curdles, add 1–2 tablespoons of hot water: the mixture should emulsify again.
Place your bowl on a folded dish towel to stabilize it and make mixing easier.

● Good to know
Traditionally, mayonnaise only contains eggs and oil; when mustard is added it becomes what is called rémoulade. However, the names are frequently used interchangeably and what most of us think of as mayonnaise is, more often than not, a rémoulade. Grape-seed oil, which does not congeal when chilled, allows mayonnaise to be kept in the refrigerator for a day without losing its fine, glossy appearance. If you are serving it immediately, you can use different oils according to taste.

❙ Recipe ideas
Portobello Burgers and Kale Chips, p. 347

Making Fresh Curds and *Paneer* ★★

It is easy to form curds from milk by adding an acidic ingredient of vegetable origin, such as lemon juice or vinegar. Just by draining them a little, you can obtain a delicious, fresh curd-cheese spread, which can then be flavored as you wish. By pressing them thoroughly, you get a firm cheese known in India as *paneer*, which can then be sliced or cut up.

Preparation time: 15 minutes
Resting time: 6 hours

Ingredients
4 cups (1 liter) fresh, whole milk
1 tablespoon lemon juice or ½ tablespoon white vinegar

Bring the milk to a boil. Remove from the heat and add the lemon juice or vinegar (1). Leave to stand for 10 minutes: the curds will form and float in the whey (2).

Line a sieve with a piece of fine cheesecloth, or use a nut milk bag, and drain the curds (3). Let drain for 10 minutes in the sieve (4). At this stage, if you wish to use the curds as they are, you can put them in the refrigerator for 2 hours before serving them plain, with honey or freshly chopped herbs, etc. They can be kept in a sealed container for 4 to 5 days in the refrigerator.

To transform the curds into *paneer*, squeeze them firmly in the cheesecloth to extract as much whey as possible (5). Leave the curds wrapped up in the cheesecloth and press for 6 hours between two chopping boards (6), placing a weight on top for greater effect (a can of food, carton of milk, etc.) if you wish.

Carefully unwrap the *paneer*, remove it from the cheesecloth, and cut into cubes to be used according to your recipe (7).

If you are not going to use the *paneer* immediately, place it in a sealed container filled with cold water. It will keep for a maximum of 2 days in the refrigerator.

● Chef's notes
Fresh milk will have more flavor and form better curds than UHT pasteurized milk.

● Good to know
4 cups (1 liter) of milk will give you 1 cup (9 oz./250 g) of curd cheese or 1 ⅓–1 ½ cups (6–7 oz./170–200 g) of paneer.
Paneer must be kept in water and used quickly. Adding ¼ teaspoon of fine salt to the milk before boiling will help it stay compact and reduce crumbling.
Don't throw out the whey; use it in soups, smoothies, and for cooking pulses (it will help to soften them).

▎Recipe ideas
Paneer and Spinach Curry, p. 360
Popovers with Herb Cream Cheese, p. 367

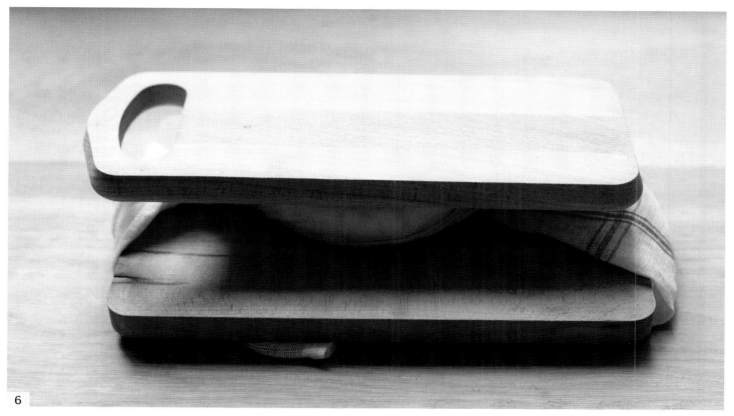

6

7

Making Greek-Style (Strained) Yogurt or Fromage Blanc ★★

There are several ways of making strained yogurt, depending on whether you use a lactic acid starter or not, and the type of rennet used. The final texture will also vary according to the way it is drained and pressed.

Preparation time: 20 minutes
Resting time: 24 to 36 hours

Ingredients
4 cups (1 liter) fresh, whole cow milk
Lactic acid starter of your choice: lactic acid powder, yogurt, etc.
Rennet

Equipment
Thermometer
Pierced mold for making curd cheese (see photo above), of the size and shape of your choice

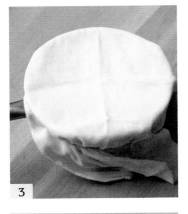

The lactic acid starter gives the strained yogurt its sour taste and changes its texture; it is possible not to use it, if you so wish. It exists in powdered form (see photo above, in the foil sachet), but you could also just use 3 tablespoons (50 ml) of a store-bought yogurt or the whey from making curd cheese (see p. 110). Be sure to buy products with the furthest expiration date possible.

Rennet is available from pharmacies in a dropper bottle. Most often, it is an extract of the gastric juices from the fourth stomach of ruminants (cows, goats, and sheep). This is why many vegetarians do not eat certain cheeses, such as Parmesan. However, you can also find vegetable enzyme coagulants or bacteria (vegetarian rennet) sold as pastels or in liquid form in specialist stores.

Heat the milk to 85°F (30°C), using a thermometer to check the temperature (1). If you are using powdered lactic acid, take a little of the heated milk, put in a glass, dilute the powder in it (2), and pour back into the pan; otherwise add yogurt or whey directly to the pan. Cover with a clean dish towel and set aside for 4 to 6 hours in a warm place (3).

The milk will have thickened and separated; it should smell sour. Add the rennet according to the quantity indicated in the package instructions (4) and stir well.

Cover and set aside for at least 8 hours in a warm place. The following day, the curds will have formed into a firm block:

cut them up roughly and you will see the whey at the bottom of the pan (5).

Put the curds in the molds (6). Set aside to drain to obtain the consistency you require: 5 to 10 hours for smooth, creamy yogurt; or just 2 hours, then beaten with a fork in a bowl for a lighter, whisked style of yogurt.

You can keep strained yogurt for 5 days in a sealed container in the refrigerator, removing the whey as you use it if you like a firmer consistency. Otherwise, leave some in the bottom of the container to keep the yogurt soft and moist.

● Good to know
The curds may take up to 18 hours to form in cold weather, so try to make it in a warm, well-heated place.
Use fresh, whole milk for the best taste and a dense texture.

Making Clarified Butter and Ghee ★★

Eliminating the water and casein from butter through cooking removes the components that cause it to burn and turn rancid. The result is a clear fat that can be heated to high temperatures (up to 480°F/250°C). Extending the cooking time to make ghee is also an effective method of conservation and allows it to be stored for longer, unrefrigerated.

Cooking time: 20 minutes

Ingredients
4 sticks (1 lb./500 g) unsalted butter

Cut the butter into pieces. Melt it in a small pan over low heat for 10 minutes, stirring from time to time: a white foam will rise to the surface (1). If you are just making clarified butter, remove the foam with a spoon.

If you wish to make ghee, continue to cook it for an additional 10 minutes: the foam will gradually subside, thin out, and bits of milk solids will fall to the bottom of the pan. These will color little by little; watch carefully and remove the pan from the heat as soon as this residue turns brown: the "grilled" smell is characteristic of ghee that is done.

For both preparations, carefully strain the butter through a fine-mesh sieve into a glass jar (2). The residue should be white for clarified butter and amber for ghee. You will have an oily substance suitable for all types of cooking, particularly in woks or skillets (3).

Ghee will solidify at room temperature (4). It will keep for at least 3 months and does not require refrigeration. However, clarified butter must be stored in the refrigerator and used within 3 months.

● Chef's notes
It is much simpler to prepare clarified butter or ghee in large quantities: the butter burns less readily and you can control the cooking process more easily. Always make at least 10 oz. (300 g) at a time.

● Good to know
The main objective of clarified butter is to eliminate the risk of burning when used for cooking; ghee has the added advantage of prolonging the product's shelf life and doesn't need to be stored in the refrigerator.

❙ Recipe ideas
Chickpea Curry with Cauliflower, Sweet Potatoes, and Coconut Milk, p. 219
Biryani, p. 245
Spicy Potato *Dosas*, p. 297
Urad Dhal with Mango and Pomegranate Raita, p. 303
Indian Mushroom Hotpot, p. 340
Paneer and Spinach Curry, p. 360

Preparation

Cooking

Nuts and Seeds

Why Soak Nuts and Seeds?

To prepare nuts and seeds correctly, it is important to remember that, just like pulses, they were naturally made to germinate. When in dry conditions unsuitable for sustaining a new plant, they are protected by growth inhibitors (in the form of enzymes) and phytic acid. If you eat them without soaking them first, you will ingest these substances, which can prevent the absorption of nutrients and make them difficult to digest.

This is why it is recommended to soak nuts and seeds in a large volume of water to reduce or eliminate these substances, before eating or cooking with a substantial quantity—there is no need to soak small amounts, such as a pinch of sesame seeds to be sprinkled over your rice!

However, some nuts may already have had their phytic acid removed when you buy them (macadamias or cashews, for instance). In this case, soaking them just serves to soften their texture.

After soaking, rinse thoroughly. They can be kept for 2 to 3 days in the refrigerator.

Once soaked, nuts and seeds can be eaten whole, chopped, made into nut milk, etc.

TYPE OF NUT/SEED	RECOMMENDED SOAKING TIME
Almonds	8–12 hours
Brazil nuts	Unnecessary (except to soften and make easier to grind)
Cashew nuts	Unnecessary (except to soften and make easier to grind)
Hazelnuts	8–12 hours
Linseeds	Unnecessary
Macadamia nuts	Unnecessary (except to soften and make easier to grind)
Pecan nuts	4–8 hours
Pine nuts	Unnecessary (except to soften and make easier to grind)
Pistachios	Unnecessary (except to soften and make easier to grind)
Pumpkin seeds	2–3 hours
Sesame seeds	8 hours
Sunflower seeds	4–8 hours
Walnuts	4–6 hours

Peeling Almonds ★

To peel almonds you just need a little water—and patience!

Soaking time: 15 minutes to 8 hours

Ingredients
Almonds
Hot or cold water

If you are in a hurry: Put the almonds in a large bowl and cover with boiling water. Let soak for 15 minutes. Drain, then peel by making a slight incision at the base of each one and squeezing: the skin will just slip off.

If you have the time: Soak the almonds for 6 to 8 hours in water at room temperature. Peel them by squeezing at their base: the skin will slip off.

● Chef's notes
Unpeeled almonds keep longer and turn rancid less quickly than almonds that are bought ready peeled.

● Good to know
This method is not suitable for hazelnuts. To peel whole hazelnuts, roast them at 350°F (180°C/Gas Mark 4) for 10 to 12 minutes, stirring them every 5 minutes. Let them cool down, then rub gently between your fingers: the darkened skin rubs off easily.

❚ Recipe ideas
Ajo Blanco, p. 372
Mediterranean Vegetable Tartlets, p. 375
Nut and Maple Syrup Tart, p. 384

Making a Nut Paste ★

A simple means of transforming nuts into a soft, smooth paste to spice up sandwiches, sauces, or tart doughs and enrich purees and soups.

Ingredients
10 oz. (300 g) unsalted nuts: peeled or unpeeled almonds, skinned hazelnuts, cashews, pistachios, etc., soaked according to the table on p. 116
1 teaspoon vegetable oil (optional)

Preheat the oven to 350°F (180°C/Gas Mark 4). Roast the nuts for 10 minutes, stirring them regularly. Let cool, then put them in a powerful blender, making sure they cover the blade. Break them down into small pieces on low speed (1).

Scrape down the sides with a rubber spatula to ensure the nuts have maximum contact with the blade to enable the paste to form (2).

Continue to blend, scraping down the sides regularly: the blade should always be in contact with the nuts. The nuts will gradually release their oil, turning first into a stiff paste, then into a smoother one (3). This can take 10 minutes or longer. If necessary, add the oil to help the process along.

● Chef's notes
Use a powerful blender if possible, otherwise you will need to pause the blending frequently to prevent overheating.
Roasting the soaked nuts removes excess moisture so the paste will keep for longer. If you have a food dehydrator you can dry them out at a low temperature after soaking.
Use at least 8 oz. (250 g) of nuts to make this paste, so there is a sufficient quantity to blend correctly.

● Good to know
Nut pastes will keep for 2 months, preferably in the refrigerator. However, walnut paste goes rancid very quickly, so make it in small quantities.
It is particularly difficult to make a homemade sesame paste with a smooth and creamy texture; if you like it really smooth, use a store-bought tahini.

Making *Gomasio* ★

This Japanese condiment, made popular through the rise of Japanese and macrobiotic cuisine, provides a means of flavoring and seasoning food that is both tasty and healthy.

Ingredients
¾ cup (3 ½ oz./100 g) sesame seeds, hulled or whole (see Good to know)
1 tablespoon gray, unrefined sea salt (if unavailable, use kosher salt)

Toast the sesame seeds over medium heat for 10 seconds in a nonstick skillet or completely dry, cast-iron pan **(1)**: they will then release their oil more easily when they are ground.

Add the salt and shake the pan to mix, tilting it in all directions for 5 seconds **(2)** as the salt warms a little, then immediately transfer to a cold plate to stop the mixture cooking **(3)**.

Blend briefly in a mini-blender or coffee grinder **(4)**, until you can only distinguish approximately 20 percent of the sesame seeds; they should not be ground finely.

Store *gomasio* in a glass jar **(5)** and use within a month.

● Chef's notes
A mortar with a rough interior known as a suribachi is tradition-ally used to grind sesame seeds. It has been replaced by more modern equipment, but it is a juice extractor that gives the clos-est result to the mortar: go ahead and try it!
This seasoning can be used as a base for numerous flavorings: add crumbled, roasted nori (see p. 100), hemp seeds or linseeds (grind them with the salt and sesame), dried herbs, spices (pepper, curry, etc.), dried celery leaves, and so on.

● Good to know
From the Japanese goma (sesame), this condiment offers all the advantages of sesame's rich mineral content while enabling the salt to be more easily absorbed.
Hulled white or yellow sesame has a milder flavor than whole (unhulled) sesame, which can give the mixture a hint of bit-terness. Nevertheless, whole sesame seeds are twice as rich in calcium—a valuable nutritional asset.
It is best to add gomasio just before serving, rather than during cooking. Remember that it is seasoning your dish with salt.
Sprinkle gomasio on eggs, on vegetable dishes—on all sorts of foods, in fact!

1

2

3

4

5

Making Uncooked Vegan Heavy Cream ★

Cashew nuts, with their soft texture, are best suited to make this vegan substitute for heavy dairy cream.

Soaking time: 4 hours
Chilling time: 1 hour

Ingredients
¼ cup (1 oz./30 g) cashew nuts
1 generous tablespoon (20 ml) water, for blending
2-3 drops lemon juice

Soak the cashew nuts in plenty of water for 4 hours (1). Drain and rinse them.

Put them in a blender with the generous tablespoon (20 ml) water. Blend on low speed, then on maximum speed for approximately 10 seconds (2).

Add the lemon juice to taste (3) and place in the refrigerator for at least 1 hour before serving.

The cream can be kept for 2 days, covered, in the refrigerator.

● Chef's notes
Adjust the quantity of water you add, depending on the desired thickness of the cream.
You can also make this cream with almonds instead of cashew nuts; they will give the cream a more pronounced taste.

● Good to know
Adding lemon juice gives the nut cream the slightly acidic taste that is characteristic of yogurt and crème fraîche made from dairy milk. It is optional, so omit if you prefer a milder, more neutral flavor.

Recipe ideas
Carrot Cake with Caramelized Hazelnuts, p. 227
Two-Bean Chili Sin Carne, p. 307

Making Béchamel Sauce with Almond Puree ★

One hundred percent vegan, this sauce has a delicate flavor and can be used in gratins or to add creaminess to stuffings.

Ingredients

Scant 1 cup (200 ml) broth of your choice: vegetable, mushroom, etc.
1 heaping tablespoon (⅓ oz./10 g) thickening of your choice (potato flour, cornstarch, arrowroot starch)
1 heaping tablespoon (1 oz./15 g) peeled almond puree
Fine salt, freshly ground pepper, and nutmeg

Put the thickening in a small bowl (1); add 3-4 tablespoons (50-60 ml) of water and mix to a smooth cream with no lumps (2).

Bring the chosen broth to a boil. Pour the diluted thickening in slowly (3) and cook over low heat, whisking continuously, until the mixture thickens.

Add the almond puree (4) and stir until completely incorporated (5).

Season with salt and pepper, and add nutmeg to taste.

● Chef's notes

This sauce can be used as a substitute in all recipes that call for traditional béchamel sauce. It provides a neutral base to be flavored with spices, herbs, etc.
It reheats well and can be kept for 2 days in a sealed container in the refrigerator.

1

Making Almond Milk ★

Although almond milk is readily available in food stores, the homemade version has an incomparable flavor and is very economical to make. It also allows you to sweeten it, or not, according to your personal taste.

Makes 3 scant cups (700 ml)

Ingredients
½ cup (2 ½ oz./75 g) almonds, peeled or unpeeled
Scant 3 cups (700 ml) water, preferably filtered, plus extra for soaking
1 pinch fine salt
A splash of malted rice, agave, or maple syrup (optional)

Soak the almonds for 8 hours in a generous amount of cold water to cover (1). Rinse, and discard the soaking water. Put the almonds in a food processor and process with the scant 3 cups (700 ml) filtered water, salt, and syrup if using (2). Strain the liquid obtained through a nut milk bag or fine-mesh sieve lined with cheesecloth or a clean dish towel (3). Squeeze firmly to extract as much liquid as possible (4); the pulp should look dry (5). If you use unpeeled almonds, you will have more pulp remaining than if you use peeled ones. The flavor will nevertheless be more pronounced with unpeeled almonds.

Pour the milk into a bottle that you can seal (6) and keep in the refrigerator for up to 3 days.

● Chef's notes
The remaining pulp can be used to enrich vegetable patties, gratins, smoothies, etc.

● Good to know
Should you run out of almond milk, you can dilute nut paste (see technique p. 118) in water to produce an instant nut milk.

❙ Recipe ideas
Vanilla Flans with Peach Coulis, p. 348
Chia Pudding with a Green Smoothie, p. 383

2

Recommended quantities for nut milk:

TYPE OF NUT	SOAKING TIME	QUANTITY FOR 4 ¼ CUPS (1 L) WATER
Almonds	8 hours	2 ¾–3 ½ oz. (80–100 g)
Cashew nuts	4 hours	2–2 ¾ oz. (60–80 g)
Hazelnuts	8 hours	2 ½ oz. (70 g)

3

4

5

6

Making Linseed Gel ★

In recipes where eggs are used to bind ingredients (cookies, croquettes, etc.), linseed gel is an effective replacement, due to the viscous substance produced by linseeds.

Ingredients
1 tablespoon linseeds
3 tablespoons water

Put the linseeds in the small bowl of a food processor, a mini-blender, or an electric coffee grinder and process until fine (1). Transfer to a bowl (2) and add the water; mix together, then wait for 10 minutes to allow the gel to form (3).

● **Chef's notes**
Use these quantities to replace approximately 1 egg.

● **Good to know**
You can also make this gel with chia seeds, using these proportions, as they produce the same viscous substance as linseeds.

Making Vegan "Parmesan" ★

All the taste of the famous Italian cheese, in a totally vegan version! Use it in sauces or sprinkled on pasta.

Ingredients
Generous ½ cup (3 oz./100 g) cashew nuts, or a mixture of
   blanched almonds and cashew nuts in equal quantities
2 tablespoons malted yeast flakes
2 teaspoons yellow sesame seeds
1 teaspoon fleur de sel

Roughly chop the cashew nuts in a mini-blender or electric coffee grinder. Add the other ingredients (1) and process briefly to avoid heating up the ground mixture (2).

Use immediately (3) or keep in a sealed jar for 6 weeks in the refrigerator.

● **Good to know**
Malted yeast, a microscopic fungus, is rich in proteins and, above all, in vitamins from the B group—notably B12, which is often lacking in a vegan diet.
With its unique, cheesy flavor, this "Parmesan" can be added as a final touch to numerous dishes; avoid cooking it in order to preserve its nutritional benefits.

❘ **Recipe ideas**
Lasagna, p. 220
Gnocchi *alla Romana*, p. 261
Cauliflower Mac and Cheese, p. 265

Making *Tarator* Sauce ★

This vegan, tahini-based sauce is usually served with falafels, but it can also be used as a dressing for crudités, mixed into vegetable purees, and so on.

Ingredients
1-2 cloves garlic
4 tablespoons tahini (sesame seed puree)
Juice of 1 lemon
½ teaspoon fine salt
Water (quantity according to desired texture and taste)

Peel and chop the garlic.

Put the tahini in a bowl and add the garlic, lemon juice, and salt; mix together.

Pour the water in gradually, until you obtain the desired texture (from a coating consistency to thick and creamy).

● Chef's notes
The tarator sauce can be kept for 4 days in a jar in the refrigerator. You can adjust the quantity of garlic, according to your preference.

❚ Recipe ideas
Falafel and Tabbouleh, p. 304

Making Olive Puree ★

In the south of France, in Italy, and in Greece, this aromatic, fundamental recipe makes a tasty addition to sandwiches, savory tarts, and pizzas.

Ingredients
1 ½ cups (8oz./250 g) pitted black olives
Scant ½ cup (2 oz./50 g) salted capers, well rinsed
1 teaspoon cognac
1 tablespoon olive oil
2 teaspoons dried thyme
Pepper

Put all the ingredients in a food processor, except the olive oil. Reduce to a puree, then gradually pour in the olive oil to form an emulsion. Taste and adjust the seasoning as necessary.

● Chef's notes
To make a green olive puree, use the same quantity of olives, but replace the capers with 2 tablespoons of ground almonds.

● Good to know
This puree can be kept in the refrigerator for 2 weeks. Put it in a jar and cover the surface with a thin layer of olive oil, then seal it. The Provençal version, known as tapenade, also contains anchovies. The name comes from the Provençal word tapeno, *meaning "caper."*

❚ Recipe ideas
Mediterranean Vegetable Tartlets, p. 375

1

Making Praline ★★

This delicious preparation, used frequently in dessert-making, combines the rich flavor of nuts with the delectable sweetness of caramel.

Ingredients
3 oz. (100 g) nuts of your choice: pecan nuts, hazelnuts, almonds, or a mixture of two
⅓ cup (2 ½ oz./70 g) granulated sugar
1 teaspoon oil (preferably oil from one of the nuts being used)

Caramelize the nuts (see technique p. 131).

Let the caramelized nuts cool, then chop roughly with a large knife (1).

Grind them in a powerful blender or electric coffee grinder (2): you will obtain a fine powder at first that will gradually liquefy due to the friction and heat during grinding. Continue, using the pulse setting, for as long as is necessary for the mixture to turn completely liquid (3); pause at regular intervals to prevent the blender or grinder overheating.

Praline will keep for 1 month in a sealed jar in the refrigerator.

● Chef's notes
Traditionally, praline is made from hazelnuts or almonds, or an equal mix of the two.

● Good to know
Add praline to your chocolate recipes, mix it into pastry cream or a yogurt, or pour it on rice pudding like a coulis—wherever you use it, praline will always bring a touch of gourmet sweetness.

2

3

1

2

Making Coconut Whipped Cream ★

This nondairy version is just as easy to prepare as traditional whipped cream.

Ingredients
One 13 ½ fl. oz. (400 ml) can coconut milk
Sugar and vanilla extract to taste (optional)

A day ahead, place the can of coconut milk vertically in the refrigerator.

The following day, take the can from the refrigerator, open it carefully, and spoon out the layer of thick cream floating on the surface into a metal bowl (1). Take out as much of the thick cream as possible, stopping when you see a clear liquid appear. (Reserve this "whey": see Chef's notes.)

Using an electric beater, whip the coconut milk just as you would for traditional whipped cream (2). Whip until it has a firm, mousse-like consistency. If using, add sugar and vanilla extract to taste.

● Chef's notes
Do not try to use coconut milk in cartons. Check the can's label to ensure the milk is 100 percent coconut, without any thickeners or emulsifiers.
You can use the reserved "whey" to make curries, sauces, smoothies, or soups.

● Good to know
The coconut whipped cream can be kept for 2 days in a sealed container in the refrigerator. You will need to whip it again briefly before serving.

❙ Recipe ideas
Red Berry "Torn Pancake" with Coconut Whipped Cream, p. 403

1

2

3

Extracting Coconut Water ★

A preliminary step before using the flesh of ripe coconuts.

Ingredients
1 coconut

Find the three small indents–known as "eyes"–that are situated at the base of the coconut **(1)**.

Pierce the softest of the three "eyes" with a knife or other sharp implement (tip of a screwdriver or drill bit, etc.) **(2)**. It will be easy to penetrate. Select a second "eye" and pierce it more firmly.

Hold the coconut over a large glass, a bowl, or other container **(3)**. The liquid, called coconut water, will dribble out naturally; shake the coconut regularly so that it empties completely. If you wish, you can use a fine-mesh sieve or tea strainer to filter the liquid as it runs into the container.

● Chef's notes
Coconut water collected this way tastes better chilled for an hour in the refrigerator. It will keep for 48 hours in a sealed bottle. Drink it plain, use it in a smoothie or marinade, mix it with fruit juice, or use it for soaking muesli and cereal.

❗ Recipe ideas
Chia Pudding with a Green Smoothie, p. 383

1

2

3

Opening a Coconut ★★

Once the coconut has been emptied of its water (see technique p. 128), it needs to be opened in order to obtain its flesh.

Ingredients
1 coconut, emptied of water

With the back of a large, heavy knife, tap the coconut several times along its circumference, turning it as you do so (1). Repeat as necessary; it will gradually weaken and crack (2), then split in two (3).

Using a small knife, remove the flesh from the shell of the coconut (4). Either chop up the flesh or grate it, depending on the intended use or your recipe.

● Chef's notes
Once removed from the shell, the coconut flesh will keep in a sealed container in the refrigerator for 4 to 5 days.

● Good to know
It is not essential to extract the water from the coconut first, but doing so ensures that you collect as much of it as possible.
It is sometimes recommended that you split the coconut with a hammer, which can be quicker, but there is a risk of splintering the shell.

▌ Recipe ideas
Indonesian Bean Salad, p. 380
Fluffy Coconut with Grapefruit and Creamed Avocado, p. 391

4

Opening a Young Coconut ★★

Young coconuts can sometimes be found in stores; they are very rich in coconut water and are still surrounded by woody fibers. Here's how to prepare them.

Ingredients
1 young coconut

Peel away the white, woody outer layer of the coconut with a sharp knife (1). If necessary, and depending on the size, you can lay it on its side. Peel until you get to the husk.

Cut out a lid from the husk, using a larger knife if needed (2); if the husk is really tough, tap the knife lightly with a hammer.

Pour the contents of the coconut into a large bowl (3): there will be a large quantity (approximately 2 cups/500 ml) of water, much more than inside a mature coconut.

Scoop out the flesh inside with a spoon or a rubber spatula (4). Use it in vegetable or fruit salads.

● Chef's notes
Select coconuts that are heavy (they should be full of water) and white all over, including the base. Avoid those with bases that have turned brown.
The coconut water should be pale and transparent: if it is at all red or brown do not drink or use it.

● Good to know
These coconuts are also sold as Thai coconuts.

Caramelizing Nuts ★★

Whether you're making praline or a gourmet garnish for desserts, caramelizing is a useful technique that can be used for any type of nut.

Ingredients
3 oz. (100 g) nuts of your choice: pecans, hazelnuts, pine nuts, cashew nuts, almonds, pistachios, etc.
⅓ cup (2 ½ oz./70 g) granulated sugar
1 teaspoon oil (preferably oil from one of the nuts being used)

Lightly toast the nuts in a dry skillet over medium heat (pecan nuts are used in this recipe) (1).

Add the sugar, sprinkling it over the entire contents of the skillet (2). Let caramelize over medium heat without stirring, but shake the skillet back and forth so the nuts can all be coated with sugar. Let them cook until they give off an aroma of caramel and have begun to color to the degree you require: either golden or brown.

Watch this process carefully and remove the skillet just before the nuts are ready–the heat of the skillet will continue to caramelize the nuts, even when removed from the heat.

Turn off the heat, add the oil, and stir the nuts to separate them (3).

Lay a sheet of parchment paper on a flat surface (chopping board, wide dish) or marble slab (4).

Leave to cool in a dry place until the mixture hardens (5). Separate the nuts if necessary and either chop or crush them, depending on the intended use or your recipe.

● **Chef's notes**
Once caramelized, the nuts should be used quickly, as any humidity will soften them and cause the caramel to melt.

● **Good to know**
These nuts form the base for making praline (see technique p. 126).

❙ **Recipe ideas**
Carrot Cake with Caramelized Hazelnuts, p. 227

5

Fruits

Preparing Pomegranates ★

When preparing pomegranates to collect their seeds, never cut them in half from top to bottom.

Ingredients
Very ripe pomegranates

Cut off the top of the pomegranates with a sharp knife. Make an incision along each section (indicated by thicker, white pith), starting at the top (1). Pull the sections apart (2). Fill a bowl with water and deseed each section directly into it (3).

Any bits of the bitter, white pith will float to the surface: remove them using a skimmer, then drain the pomegranate seeds through a fine-mesh sieve. They can now be eaten or used according to your recipe.

● Chef's notes
Pomegranate juice stains badly: peeling the fruit in water reduces the risk of being stained by squirting juice.

● Good to know
Pomegranate seeds extracted in this way will keep for up to 3 days in a sealed container in the refrigerator.

❙ Recipe ideas
Urad Dhal with Mango and Pomegranate Raita, p. 303
Iranian Herby Yogurt Soup, p. 354
Roasted Cauliflower, Red Tahini, and Preserved Lemon, p. 371
Passion Fruit and Pomegranate Pavlova, p. 399

1

2

3

Juicing Pomegranates ★

The delicately sharp taste of pomegranate juice makes it a useful flavoring for many dishes.

Ingredients
Pomegranates

Cut the pomegranates in half horizontally and juice them with a manual juicer, pressing down firmly and stopping before you reach the white pith (1).

Carefully pour the juice into a glass, leaving behind any seeds or pips (2).

● Chef's notes
Avoid using an electric juicer, which has a tendency to juice the fruit right to the pith, giving the juice an unpleasantly bitter taste. Use the juice to deglaze a skillet, add flavor to a fruit salad, or spice up a smoothie: anything you might do with lemon juice, in fact.

● Good to know
Freshly pressed pomegranate juice can be kept for 2 days in a sealed bottle in the refrigerator. You could also freeze it in an ice-cube tray for up to 2 months.
To make homemade grenadine—a syrup originally made from pomegranate juice, but more often from red fruits nowadays, used in cocktails and other drinks—reduce equal volumes of sugar and pomegranate juice for 10 minutes over medium heat. Remove from the heat and add a few drops of lemon juice to taste. Serve diluted.

1

2

Preparing Mangoes ★★

The trick for removing the juicy flesh is to leave the fruit unpeeled.

Ingredients
Ripe mangoes

Cut each mango into three pieces: slice as close as possible to one side of the pit, then repeat on the other side. You should now have two thick outer sections and a thinner central section containing the pit (1).

Cut around the pit to extract the flesh surrounding it (2). Peel by slicing around between the flesh and the skin. Use this small section, which may be in pieces, in a salad or to make a coulis.

Mark the flesh of the other two sections into squares with the tip of a sharp knife (3), making sure you do not cut through the skin.

Press on the outer skin, in the center of the section, and it should turn inside out easily, with the cubes of flesh protruding from the skin (4).

Serve as it is, or detach the cubes into a bowl using a knife (5).

● Chef's notes
Like avocados, mangoes continue to ripen after they have been picked. Buy several at a time and use them as they ripen.

● Good to know
From Indian mangoes to those from South America, this fruit can vary greatly in size and flavor. An average mango is said to weigh approximately 14 oz. (400 g) (gross weight).

❙ Recipe ideas
Urad Dhal with Mango and Pomegranate Raita, p. 303

1

2

3

4

5

Preparing Pineapples ★★

Pineapples can be cut into quarters and their skin removed in the same way as a melon, but the following method is more spectacular and allows you to cut the fruit into attractive slices.

Ingredients
1 pineapple

Remove the pineapple's tough skin by cutting off thick strips from top to bottom with a large, sharp knife (1).

Rotating the pineapple, remove the "eyes" with a sharp knife, cutting at an angle in long, parallel grooves on either side of each strip of "eyes" (2).

Lay it flat and cut into slices (3).

● Chef's notes
If possible, use a chopping board with a groove to collect the juice that will run during the preparation.
The "eyes" can also be removed with a melon baller or a potato peeler with an eye remover.

● Good to know
These pineapple slices will keep for 2 days in a sealed container in the refrigerator.

❗ Recipe ideas
Pineapple with Molasses, Lime, and White Chocolate Sauce, p. 396

1

2

3

Preparing Rhubarb ★

The leafstalk from a thicker stem, rhubarb is actually a vegetable. But as it is most often cooked in desserts, it has come to be considered as a fruit—and a well-loved one!

Resting time: 2 to 3 hours

Ingredients
1 lb. 2 oz. (500 g) stalks of rhubarb
2 tablespoons (1 oz./30 g) golden cane sugar

Use a sharp knife to pull off the fibers from the rhubarb stalks (1). If it is young, there may be very few or even none at all. The thicker the stalk is, the more fibrous it is likely to be: if this is the case, cut it into short lengths and remove the fibers from each, one at a time.

Chop the rhubarb into pieces, put them into a large bowl, and sprinkle with the sugar (2). Leave for 2 to 3 hours for the water contained in the rhubarb to be drawn out.

A syrup will form (3), softening the rhubarb's acidity; this means you can use less sugar when cooking it.

Cook it according to your recipe: it can be stewed, poached in a syrup, used in a tart or pie, etc.

● **Chef's notes**
Enhance the taste of rhubarb by adding a star anise or a few grains of aniseed when you cook it.

● **Good to know**
Be sure to remove any leaves left at the end of the leafstalks, as they are toxic.

Recipe ideas
Rhubarb, Red Currant, and Ginger Parfait, p. 407

Peeling Soft Fruit ★

The simplest method for peeling soft, thin-skinned fruits, with little waste, is to immerse them in boiling water.

Ingredients
Peaches, tomatoes, nectarines, etc.

Make a cross at the base of the fruit with a sharp knife (1); this will enable you to detach the skin easily while preserving the fruit's shape.

Immerse the fruit in boiling water using a spoon (2).

After 10 seconds, remove the fruit with a skimmer (3). Let cool for a few moments, then carefully remove the skin, beginning at the base where you made the cross.

● Chef's notes
To gain time, the fruit can be immersed in ice water immediately after it is removed from the boiling water: the skin will come off almost on its own, due to the change in temperature. This is a useful technique if you have a large quantity to peel but there is a risk of damaging the fruit; bear this in mind if you are planning to serve the fruit whole and wish to retain its original shape as much as possible.

▌ Recipe ideas
Solaris, p. 209
Peach and Red Currant Cobbler, p. 288
Shakshuka, p. 359
Mediterranean Vegetable Tartlets, p. 375
Tomato and Berry Salad with Balsamic Vinegar, p. 394

Removing the Peel and Pith from Citrus Fruit ★

This technique allows you to remove the thin layer of white pith beneath the skin of citrus fruit along with the peel, in order to avoid an unpleasant bitter taste.

Ingredients
Citrus fruit of your choice: lemon, orange, grapefruit, etc.

Cut off each end of the citrus fruit (a pomelo is shown here) to stabilize it **(1)**.

Place it on a chopping board, ensuring it is flat and stable, and slide the blade of a sharp knife between the pith and the flesh **(2)**. Follow the curve of the fruit to conserve as much flesh as possible.

● Chef's notes
Use a chopping board with a groove to collect the juice that will run during the preparation.

● Good to know
To remove the peel and pith from small citrus fruits like clementines, place them in the freezer for 1 hour first: the skin will harden and be much easier to remove.

Recipe ideas
Citrus Beet and Sprouted Buckwheat Salad, p. 278
Orange and Pistachio Loaf, p. 328
Fluffy Coconut with Grapefruit and Creamed Avocado, p. 391

1

2

1

2

Segmenting Citrus Fruit ★

Once the peel and pith have been removed, a citrus fruit can be used whole, sliced, or, as shown in this technique, divided into segments.

Ingredients
Citrus fruit, peel and pith removed

Holding the fruit over a bowl to collect the juice, slide the blade of a small, sharp knife between the flesh and the fine membrane separating each segment (1).

Gently angle your knife when you reach the center: this should be sufficient to detach the segment, without having to cut the other side of the membrane (2). Repeat, going round the fruit and detaching each segment.

● **Chef's notes**
When the whole fruit has been segmented, squeeze what remains of the fruit to obtain the last of the juice.

● **Good to know**
A knife with a thin, flexible blade, such as those traditionally used for filleting fish, is particularly useful for this technique.

❙ **Recipe ideas**
Citrus Beet and Sprouted Buckwheat Salad, p. 278
Fluffy Coconut with Grapefruit and Creamed Avocado, p. 391

Fruits

Making Jam ★

To enjoy the delights of seasonal fruit throughout the year.

Preparation time: 30 minutes
Cooking time: 10 to 20 minutes

Ingredients
2 ¼ lb. (1 kg) fruit (net weight, peeled and ready to cook)
Generous 4 ½ cups (2 lb./900 g) granulated sugar
Juice of ½ lemon

Sterilize the pots and lids by submerging them in boiling water for 10 minutes (1). Drain on a clean dish towel while you prepare the jam.

Mix the fruit with the sugar and lemon juice in a wide, shallow pan. Bring gently to a boil to create a syrup (2). Depending on how much time you have, you can either remove the pan from the heat and let the fruit marinate for several hours in the syrup (giving the jam more flavor) or proceed directly to the next step: cooking over high heat.

Place a candy thermometer in the pan and boil the fruit mixture until it reaches 220°F (105°C): this takes approximately 5 to 10 minutes from the moment a full boil is reached, depending on the type of fruit, its ripeness, its acidity, etc.

You should be able to see when the jam is ready: any foam will have disappeared, the bubbling will be less intense, and the fruit will stay immersed in the syrup. If you do not have a thermometer to check the temperature has reached 220°F (105°C), check the setting point by placing a teaspoon of jam on a cold plate: it should form a soft gel (3).

As soon as the jam is ready, fill the pots to the top through a jam funnel, using a ladle (4). Seal hermetically with the lids and turn the pots upside down until completely cold. Store them away from light.

● Chef's notes
When you open a pot of jam there should be a pronounced "click," which indicates that the pot is sterile. A bulging lid, the smell of alcohol, or traces of mold are all signs that the jam should not be eaten.
Lemon juice highlights the jam's flavor, helps to preserve the fruit's color, and encourages the jam to set while preventing the recrystallization of the sugar: be sure to add it!

● Good to know
You can also use less-refined sugars: golden cane sugar, muscovado, panela, etc. However, they will darken the color of the jam noticeably and, with their hints of licorice, they do not suit every fruit. Panela sugar helps jams to set: use it with acidic fruits such as rhubarb or plums.
Jams do not improve with aging. Even if they will keep for 3 years, it is better to use them in the year they are made. Once opened, keep them in the refrigerator.

Soaking Dried Fruits ★

An essential step for recovering dried fruits' softness and sweetness.

Soaking time: 1 hour

Ingredients
Dried fruits
Hot water, tea, herbal infusion, water with added liquor (commonly rum), etc.

Put the dried fruits in a large bowl: they will swell, so allow plenty of space. Pour over the hot liquid of your choice, to cover the fruit generously. Leave for 1 hour, then drain and use according to your recipe.

● Chef's notes
When cutting dried fruit after soaking, use scissors: the fruit has a tendency to stick and using scissors will save you time.

❗ Recipe ideas
Dried Apricot Flan, p. 400

Practical
Guide

A Brief History of Vegetarianism

Vegetarianism, far from being a recent trend, has origins that stem back to antiquity. Its evolution can be traced through a brief survey of the history of religions and of philosophy around the world.

In the Old Testament, God said to Adam and Eve before they left the Garden of Eden, "Behold, I have given you every plant yielding seed that is on the surface of all the earth, and every tree which has fruit yielding seed; it shall be food for you."[1]

It was only after the Flood that humankind was allowed to eat meat. "Every moving thing that is alive shall be food for you; I give all to you, as I gave the green plant."[2] As early as the seventh century BCE, we find traces of "ahimsa"—nonviolence and respect for life—in India. This philosophical concept emerges again in Hinduism, Jainism, and Buddhism, whose followers are vegetarian.

In the sixth century BCE, Pythagoras, the Greek mathematician and philosopher, developed the concept of transmigration of souls, and forbade his students to consume animal flesh and eggs, or to wear wool. For centuries afterward, the vegetarian diet was called the "Pythagorean diet." Greek and Latin thinkers continued to reflect on the subject: Hesiod, Plato, and Ovid considered vegetarianism as emblematic of the Golden Age, while Plutarch condemned the eating of flesh.[3]

In the first century CE, vegetarian philosophy extended through Asia Minor, through Apollonius of Tyana and then the Neoplatonist philosopher Porphyry, who, in the third century, wrote prolific comments on Plutarch's philosophy.[4]

When Europe was Christianized, vegetarian practice and thought regressed; it was adhered to only by religious minorities who were considered heretics, such as the Bogomils and Cathars. Vegetarianism expanded only in Asia, with several offshoots. Hindus consume plant and dairy products, but certain Brahmins avoid red vegetables, such as beets and tomatoes, because they are the color of blood. Jains do not eat eggs, honey, root vegetables, garlic, and onions. Taoism, Confucianism, and Buddhism all integrate vegetarianism into their practices.

During the Renaissance, some personalities—most notably (although disputably) Leonardo da Vinci—spoke out in the West. However, they were a tiny minority. Certain religious orders followed these practices (Trappists are vegetarians, while Cistercians and Carthusians followed a vegetarian diet with the exception of fish), although not due to moral objections, but because they had taken vows of poverty.

With British involvement in India, **beginning in the seventeenth century**, vegetarianism once again became a subject of concern in Europe, thanks to Thomas Tryon (1634–1703), a pacifist who advocated animal rights, and John Oswald (1760–1793), who served in the army in India and then wrote a fervent appeal for compassion toward animals.[5] This had a strong influence on romantic writers like Shelley and, later, George Bernard Shaw. It was only in 1847 that the British Vegetarian Society was founded in London. Its nineteenth-century members were what we would call "vegans" today. The American Vegetarian Society was set up a few years later, in 1850.

During World War II, food shortages and rationing meant that the British were encouraged to grow their own fruit and vegetables, and a large part of the population survived on a predominantly vegetarian diet.

Mahatma Gandhi—for whom vegetarianism was an integral part of his life and who wrote extensively on the subject— emphasized in a speech to the Vegetarian Society in London the moral foundation of vegetarianism, saying, "the basis of my vegetarianism is not physical, but moral. If anybody said that I should die if I did not take beef tea or mutton, even on medical advice, I would prefer death. That is the basis of my vegetarianism. . . . I think that what vegetarians should do is not to emphasize the physical consequences of vegetarianism, but to explore the moral consequences."

Whether the motives are ethical, religious, or cultural, there has never been a shortage of reasons to advocate a vegetarian diet. More recently, the increase in the global population as well as problems caused by global warming have brought a heightened awareness of vegetarianism by emphasizing how our dietary choices impact the environment.

Different Types of Vegetarianism

There are various kinds of vegetarianism today, each with its own particularities.

Vegetarian

The Vegetarian Society's definition of a vegetarian is "someone who lives on a diet of grains, pulses, nuts, seeds, vegetables, and fruits with, or without, the use of dairy products and eggs. A vegetarian does not eat any meat, poultry, game, fish, shellfish, or by-products of slaughter."

---

1. New American Standard Bible, Genesis, Chapter 1, verse 29.
2. New American Standard Bible, Genesis, Chapter 9, verse 3.
3. *De esu carnium*, "On the Eating of Flesh."

4. *De abstinentia*, "On Abstinence from Killing Animals"
5. *The Cry of Nature or An Appeal to Mercy and Justice on Behalf of the Persecuted Animals*, 1791.

When eggs (with the exception of fish roe, for which the animal has to be killed) and dairy products are included, the diet is sometimes referred to as **lacto-ovo vegetarian** (although with veganism on the upswing, this term is beginning to fall into disuse). Although these are animal products, no slaughter is involved. An **ovo vegetarian** eats eggs but not dairy products, and a **lacto vegetarian** diet includes dairy products but not eggs. It's worth noting that the vegetarianism practiced in India excludes eggs, and thus is lacto vegetarian.

Pescatarians—those who follow a vegetarian diet, usually lacto-ovo, but eat fish and seafood—are often considered non-vegetarians. In many Asian countries, notably in Thailand (but excluding India), vegetarian dishes may include shrimp paste and fish sauce (*nam pla*). In the Middle Ages, the Cathar sect ate fish, as their doctrine held that fish did not have souls.

Flexitarianism, or **semi-vegetarianism**—a relatively recent phenomenon—is the practice of following a mostly vegetarian diet, but eating meat occasionally.

Vegan

The Vegan Society defines veganism as "a way of living which seeks to exclude, as far as is possible and practicable, all forms of exploitation of, and cruelty to, animals for food, clothing or any other purpose." Vegans therefore eat no animal flesh or animal products—eggs, dairy products, honey, gelatin, and rennet are excluded from their diet. The word "vegan" was coined in 1944 to distinguish those who abstain from eating animals from those who reject all products derived from animals.

Vegans refuse all exploitation of animals, which means that they not only eat a vegan diet, but also choose not to purchase or use products involving animal testing or products of animal origin, such as leather, silk, and wool. They also avoid all forms of entertainment that exploit animals, including zoos, aquariums, and horse or dog racing.

It is difficult to ascertain just how many vegetarians there are worldwide, as there are no reliable figures, only respondents to open surveys who classify themselves as vegetarians. Estimates put the figure at **450 million**, a number that includes 375 million in India (approximately 40 percent of the nation's population). Within Europe, Germany, Italy, and Great Britain have the highest percentage of vegetarians among their populations (ranging from 6 to 10 percent). In North America, 2 to 4 percent of the population is vegetarian, while in Brazil the figure is 6 percent. And, of course, there are communities such as the Rastafarians for whom vegetarianism is a historical tradition.

How Can I Balance My Diet?

The American Academy of Nutrition and Dietetics has officially been favorable to a vegetarian diet since 1987. The benefits of a vegetarian diet have been proven in combatting heart disease, type II diabetes, and certain cancers. The risk of food deficiencies is minimal if sensible guidelines are followed. For those on a vegan diet, vitamin B12 supplements are strongly recommended.

Generally speaking, there are concerns about three food groups:
• **Protein:** a balanced diet should include 5 ½ oz. (155 g) of protein foods per day at the 2,000-calorie level.[6] But, of course, protein is not only found in meat.

Animal proteins contain the nine amino acids that all humans require, while most sources of plant protein are considered incomplete, with the exception of hemp seeds, quinoa, soybeans, buckwheat, and amaranth. The best solution is to combine pulses with grains—as many dishes do, such as Italian *pasta fagioli* and Indian rice and lentils—to obtain complete proteins. In fact, the two do not need to be eaten simultaneously; it is enough to eat them on the same day. According to the Academy of Nutrition and Dietetics, "Protein consumed from a variety of plant foods supplies an adequate quantity of essential amino acids when caloric intake is met."

• **Calcium:** found in dairy products, but is also supplied by the cabbage family, almonds, leafy vegetables, tofu, seaweed, and more. Many commercially available nondairy milks contain supplements.

• **Iron:** the iron found in plants, such as pulses, tofu, quinoa, walnuts, and leafy vegetables, is less easily assimilated than the heme iron contained in meat. The body absorbs iron better when vitamin C is also present. Vitamin C, of course, is plentiful in fruits and vegetables, and so available in abundance in a vegetarian diet.

A vegetarian diet is naturally rich in fiber, vitamins, and micronutrients. If followed sensibly, it is a diet that allows you to meet the official nutritional recommendations easily, avoiding the intake of excess protein, saturated fats, and salt. By alternating nuts, seeds, grains, vegetables, root vegetables, pulses, fruits, oils, and dairy products as much as possible, many beneficial nutritional associations can be obtained. Quality and diversity are the keys to achieving a balanced diet effortlessly.

FOOD	PROTEIN CONTENT PER 3 ½ OZ. (100 G)
Spirulina (seaweed)	2 to 2 ½ oz. (55 to 70 g)
Malted (brewer's) yeast	1 ⅔ oz. (48 g)
Soybeans (seeds)	1 ⅓ oz. (37 g)
Ham	1 ¼ oz. (36 g)
Skimmed milk powder	1 ¼ oz. (35 g)
Peanuts	1 oz. (30 g)
Almonds	1 oz. (30 g)
Steak (beef)	1 oz. (27 g)
Hard cheeses (e.g. cheddar, Gruyère)	⅞ to 1 oz. (25 to 27 g)
Chicken (white meat)	⅞ oz. (26 g)
Pulses (e.g. lentils, chickpeas)	⅔ to ⅞ oz. (20 to 25 g)
Sunflower seeds	¾ oz. (23 g)
Amaranth	½ oz. (15 g)
Tofu	½ oz. (13 g)
Quinoa	½ oz. (13 g)
Wheat	½ oz. (12 g)
Millet	⅓ oz. (11 g)

6 "Dietary Guidelines for Americans 2015–2020," on health.gov/dietaryguidelines/2015/guidelines/chapter-1/a-closer-look-inside-healthy-eating-patterns/#food-groups.

Eggs

Whether you buy your eggs from a supermarket or a farmers' market, go for a place with rapid turnover so that the eggs are as fresh as possible. Fresh eggs taste better, are more nutritional and, for poaching, will hold their shape better. Try the classic test: place the whole egg in a bowl of water, the older it is the more likely it will float.

Choose organic—where the hens are given organic feed and anti-biotics are allowed only when strictly necessary—or free-range, where the hens must have access to the outdoors (precise standards differ between countries).

Size definitions vary country to country. When making the recipes in this book use "large" eggs (US), "medium" eggs (UK), unless specified otherwise.

Egg Substitutes

There are many ways to replace eggs in recipes. It all depends on the role the egg plays. If the recipe calls for one egg only, it is often possible to do without it and simply substitute a little water, non-dairy milk, or nut puree (notably blanched almond puree). This is the case for a pastry dough or shortbread cookies.

Linseeds (6) and chia seeds (7) are viscous. When combined with a liquid, they swell and form a heat-resistant gel. Prepare them ahead of time by combining them with water, processing, and allowing the mixture to rest for 10 minutes (see technique p. 124). Then simply incorporate them following the recipe. To give a nice golden topping to a pie or tart, a little soy milk or other nondairy milk works perfectly.

To make an alternative to an omelet or scrambled eggs, the best ingredient is silken tofu (1).

If you are baking, there are several options. For cakes and loaves, use 2 oz. (50 g) of silken tofu for each egg listed in the recipe, or the same quantity of apple puree (8) or mashed banana (3).

Experimenting with the dry ingredients also allows you to substitute eggs while retaining a moist texture. This is relatively easy for recipes that use a large quantity of liquid, such as crêpes, pancakes, flans, and clafoutis.

Lupin flour (4), made from a pulse, has just the properties needed to emulsify baked goods such as brioches or chocolate rolls, and other leavened doughs.

Starches (5) also give very good results. Cornstarch (UK cornflour), potato starch, or arrowroot should be thoroughly combined with a cold liquid to prevent lumps. For example, for the filling of a savory tart, dissolve a generous ½ cup (3 oz./90 g) of starch with ¾ cup (200 ml) of nondairy milk for the entire amount of batter. To make creamy desserts, heat the mixture gently until thickened for a velvety texture.

Agar-agar (2), a seaweed from Japan, is excellent in mousses and other creamy desserts. Sprinkle it over a hot liquid, bring to a boil, and simmer for 1 minute. As the mixture cools, it will gel and hold the preparation together (see technique p. 101).

For raised doughs that call for beaten egg whites, vegan baking combines nondairy milk, cider vinegar, and baking soda—a mixture that works effectively.

Cheese

To the surprise of many, cheese is not always vegetarian. Cheese is made by coagulating milk to produce curds (solid) and whey (liquid)—a process known as curdling—which are then separated so the curds can be processed into cheese. Rennet is used for curdling, and most often it is animal rennet—an extract of the gastric juices from the fourth stomach of ruminants (cows, goats, and sheep)—that is used. Certain cheeses with Appellation of Protected Origin status always use animal rennet, such as Parmigiano Reggiano (Parmesan). However, some cheeses are made without animal rennet, for example *paneer*, and vegetarian versions of many cheeses are now widely available; they use rennet from either fungal or bacterial sources, or genetically modified microorganisms.

Cheese Substitutes

Cheese imparts both taste and texture to dishes. By combining several ingredients, it can be easily replaced in vegan cooking.

To enhance texture, **silken tofu (1)** is ideal, particularly to replace cream cheese and ricotta, strained yogurt, or fromage blanc.

Malted (brewer's) yeast (2) is a microscopic fungus, rich in vitamin B12 and proteins. Its cheese-like flavor makes it perfect for incorporating into sauces and salads, and it can be used to enhance mixtures for sprinkling (see technique p. 124).

The fermented taste of **miso (3)**, whether white (rice-based) and milder, or red (barley- or soybean-based), brings umami to your preparations and is a sure way of enhancing taste.

For books on vegan cuisine and nondairy products, consult the bibliography at the end of this book (pages 414–15).

Zucchini
(Courgettes)

This summer squash, like all squash, originated in the Americas and was brought back to the Mediterranean by Christopher Columbus. However, the vegetable we know as zucchini, or courgette, was developed in the nineteenth century in Italy, by the Milanese. Most likely introduced to the United States by Italian immigrants, the earliest records of the vegetable there date from the 1920s.

1. **Cocozelle Italian, also known as Cocozelle di Napoli:** a green non-trailing (bush) variety. For sautéing and stuffing. Peel if the skin is thick or tough.

2. **One Ball golden round zucchini:** ideal for stuffing.

3. **Grey or opal zucchini:** thin-skinned and tender; the skin can be slightly bitter. Best when cooked.

4. **Yellow zucchini (varieties include Taxi or Gold Rush):** very tender with a delicate flavor. Serve raw and unpeeled.

5. **Rond de Nice:** round and green, French heirloom variety. Ideal for stuffing.

6. **Verde di Milano, also known as Green Zucchini of Milan:** should be cooked.

7. **Zephyr:** a bicolored sweet variety containing very few seeds. Can be served raw or cooked.

Tomatoes

A botanical fruit or a culinary vegetable? No matter, the golden rule for preserving the fragrant flavor of tomatoes is never to put them in the refrigerator.

1. Black Zebra: an heirloom variety of black tomato with firmer flesh than the Black Krim (see no. 12), but not as flavorsome.

2. Jaune Saint Vincent: a yellow tomato of French origin with a good balance of sweetness and acidity. Best served raw.

3. Rose de Berne: a round, pink-red variety, sweet and fragrant and very juicy. Serve in a salad or cooked in a sauce.

4. Andine Cornue, also known as Horn of the Andes: a red, elongated, plum-shaped tomato with dense flesh and very few seeds. Ideal for coulis and candied tomatoes.

5. Yellow plum tomato: very fruity and sweet. Perfect for serving with aperitifs.

6. Orange Bourgoin: full of sweetness and makes delicious sauces.

7. Red Zebra: from the same family as the Green Zebra (see no. 9). Rarely weighs more than 3 oz. (100 g).

8. Beefsteak tomato: identifiable by its characteristic ribbed, pointed shape. Dense flesh with very few seeds. Can be served raw or preserved, as it keeps its texture well.

9. Green Zebra: a medium-size variety that turns slightly yellow when fully ripe. Fairly thick skin with fresh and fruity flesh. Perfect served raw or in chutney.

10. Vine tomato: firm and crisp texture. The fragrance of the stalks can be misleading; the tomato itself has a mild flavor.

11. Pineapple tomato: the largest orange tomato—can weigh up to 2 lb. (900 g). Serve in thick slices for a salad.

12. Black Krim, also known as Black Crimea: very few seeds and mild acidity. Can be used in a salad or stuffed.

Eggplants
(Aubergines)

This vegetable is a popular ingredient in Indian and other Asian cuisines, as well as many Italian and Provençal dishes.

1. Graffiti: well-balanced with a subtle flavor.

2. Ronde de Valence: firm, dense flesh. Ideal for gratins and fritters.

3. Black Beauty: a deep purple–black eggplant that's very fragrant and sometimes bitter.

4. Japanese White Egg: white creamy flesh, no seeds, and a delicate flavor.

5. Thai Long Green: mild, sweet, and fragrant. Cook in sauce or sauté with chili.

6. Fengyuan Purple, also known as **Chinese eggplant:** one of the longest eggplants (up to 24 in./60 cm). Thin-skinned and mild, with no bitterness. Good for grilling or adding to stir-fried dishes.

Squashes

1. **Galeux d'Eysines:** pink, lumpy skin but sweet, delicate, and tender flesh.

2. **Butternut squash:** popular for its family-friendly size and its flavor, which lends itself to all uses. Can be used in both sweet and savory dishes.

3. **Spaghetti squash:** when cooked, its pulp separates into long spaghetti-like strands, hence its name (see technique p. 17).

4. **Pomme d'Or:** a distinctive, sweet-flavored small squash. Good for stuffing and its fibrous texture is suitable for soups and gratins.

5. **Chayote, also known as mirliton, christophene, choko, or vegetable pear:** thin-skinned and very tender, this pale green, pear-shaped squash can be used like zucchini (peeled and grated, raw or cooked, in gratins, soups, etc.).

6. **& 9. Pattypan (white and yellow), also known as scallop or sunburst squash:** a small, scallop-edged squash that exists in white, yellow, and green varieties. Can be miniature or weigh up to 6 ½ lb. (3 kg). The flavor is not distinctive; scoop out the flesh and stuff them, or use the flesh as for zucchini.

7. **Rouge Vif d'Étampes:** this "vivid red" French squash has moderately sweet orange flesh. Delicious in soups or in pumpkin pie.

8. **Red kuri squash, also known as orange Hokkaido, potimarron, or onion squash:** dense, sweet flesh, with a delicate chestnut flavor and a thin skin that does not need peeling. Has become very common in recent years due to its many uses.

10. **Kabocha, also known as Japanese pumpkin:** a small squash that's copper-green on the outside and yellow-orange on the inside. Can be cooked in tempura or poached in broth.

11. **Sweet Dumpling squash:** green or orange with green flecks, the flesh is particularly sweet with only a mild musky flavor, making it suitable for jams and tarts.

12. **Acorn squash:** identifiable by its oblong heart shape. Its nickname "pepper squash" comes from its pronounced flavor.

Leaf Vegetables and Salad Greens

1. Swiss chard, also known as leaf beet or silverbeet: can have white, red, yellow, or purple ribs of varying thickness depending on the variety. Has green leaves with a flavor similar to spinach.

2. Radicchio di Chioggia, also known as Rossa di Treviso: part of the chicory family, radicchio is of Italian origin and has a distinctly bitter flavor. Serve raw and thinly sliced, or braised the same way as chicory.

3. White chicory, also known as Belgian endive, and red chicory: a variety of chicory cultivated by force-growing in sand, which is how it remains white. Has a slightly bitter flavor.

4. Lamb's lettuce, also known as corn salad or mâche: one of the richest vegetables in omega-3 essential fatty acids. Usually served in salads, but also very good sautéed like spinach or in a green juice.

5. Arugula, also known as rocket: hot and peppery, to varying degrees depending on the variety; it comes from the Brassicaceae, or mustard, family, hence its flavor. Makes a particularly tasty pesto.

6. Mesclun, or mixed-leaf salad: its name comes from the Provençal word for mixture. Typically Niçoise, it is made up of a selection of five varieties of young leaf vegetables (Swiss chard, spinach, etc.) and baby salad greens (lettuce, arugula, chicory, etc.).

7. Sorrel: its sharp, tangy flavor comes from the high level of oxalic acid that it contains. It is preferable to serve it cooked (in omelets, sauces, etc.).

8. Spinach: young leaves can be eaten raw; simply sauté fully grown leaves. Despite its reputation, spinach is not particularly rich in iron.

9. Watercress: peppery and aromatic. Good in salads, soups, and purees, or as an aromatic herb—chop finely and sprinkle over dishes to garnish and season.

Salad Greens

1. Little Gem: a small lettuce with crinkly leaves, originally from southern Europe, notably Spain. Usually served in salads but can also be braised.

2. Butterhead lettuce: there are more than 1,500 known varieties of lettuce! This is one of the most popular, appreciated for its tender-leaved heart.

3. Escarole, also known as scarole, or Batavian or broad-leaved endive: a lettuce from the chicory family, hence its slightly bitter flavor. Popular in Italian cuisine, it is served braised in Naples, or as a garnish for pizza or savory tarts, with capers and pine nuts.

4. Dandelion: the young leaves are edible in the spring. The slightly bitter flavor goes particularly well with eggs (soft-boiled, fried, etc.). The flowers can be used in jam making.

5. Romaine, also known as Cos lettuce: a lettuce with large, firm-textured leaves and a thick center rib. Worth trying juiced for its mild flavor and revitalizing mineral content.

6. Batavia, also known as summer crisp or French crisp lettuce: a popular lettuce, available in green and red varieties.

Cabbages

1. Broccoli: usually only the florets are used, but the stalk can also be peeled, diced, and sautéed, or juiced.

2. Cauliflower: can be served raw or cooked. Its sulfurous smell begins to develop once it is picked, so use as quickly as possible after purchase.

3. & 6. Brussels sprouts: high in vitamins C and K. Care should be taken not to overcook them. There is also a purple variety with a more pronounced flavor.

4. Red cabbage: can also be white. Both are delicious raw, finely sliced in coleslaw or salads, or braised, sautéed, steamed, or even pickled.

5. Romanesco, also known as Roman cauliflower: named after its place of origin. Is prepared in the same way as broccoli or cauliflower.

7. Savoy cabbage, also known as curly cabbage: its textured leaves make it more resistant to the cold than other varieties.

8. Purple pointed cabbage, also known as hispi, hearted, or sweetheart cabbage: can also be green. Has a sweeter flavor than red cabbage and can be used in the same recipes.

1. **Bok choy, also known as pak choi:** resembles Swiss chard with its white ribs, but is a cabbage. Has a delicate, mildly sweet flavor, perfect for stir-frying.

2. **Kai-lan, also known as Chinese broccoli:** used in Cantonese and Vietnamese cuisine, often steamed or stir-fried.

3. **& 4. Kohlrabi:** can be purple or green, with no difference in taste between them. The leaves are delicious stir-fried, the bulb can be served raw and grated, or braised.

5. **Cavolo Nero, also known as Lacinato kale:** a Tuscan variety of leaf cabbage essential for making ribollita (Tuscan soup made with bread and vegetables) and winter minestrone.

6. **Kale (green and purple):** includes several varieties of leaf cabbage, traditional in Europe before World War II and now regaining popularity. Resistant to the cold and rich in nutrients. Use in soups, juices, or for making chips.

7. **Napa cabbage, also known as Chinese cabbage:** can be served raw in salads, stir-fried, or marinated with chili.

Root Vegetables
See p. 160

1. **Celeriac, also known as celery root:** can be used raw and grated in a remoulade, cooked and pureed, made into fries, etc. Keep the leaves to add flavor to broths or salt (see technique p. 34).

2. **Baby turnip, also known as Tokyo turnip:** Sweeter and tenderer than the larger variety. Can be served raw, in salads, or braised, sautéed, roasted, or boiled. The spicy greens can be eaten too, and are especially tasty sautéed or in soups.

3. **Chervil root, also known as turnip-rooted chervil:** must be cold-stored for 2 months to develop its delicate flavor that resembles chestnuts or potatoes, hence its high price. Its leaves are not edible.

4. **Yellow turnip:** mild and sweet. An essential ingredient for couscous.

5. Parsnip: resembles a carrot but has a sweeter flavor, particularly after cooking. Can be cooked like a carrot or potato (boiled, pureed, roasted, fried, steamed) and is especially good in slow-cooked dishes.

6. Parsley root, also known as turnip-rooted parsley: has a more pronounced flavor than parsnips and can be cooked in the same way.

7. Sand-grown carrot: has the most delicate flavor of the root vegetables.

8. & 9. Colored carrots: originally white, purple, or yellow, the orange carrot was cultivated at a much later date. Serve raw to fully appreciate the rainbow (they lose their color as they cook).

10. Bunched carrots: harvested with their greens to indicate their freshness, they only keep for 2–3 days.

11. Black radish: hot and spicy. Can be cooked or served raw and grated to be used as a condiment or in small quantities to spice up salads.

12. White radish, also known as daikon: very mild and crunchy. Can be eaten raw, in a broth, or made into tempura.

13, 14 & 15. Purple (aka plum), Red Meat (aka Watermelon), and Green Meat (aka Misato Green) radishes: winter radishes, to be peeled and finely sliced on a mandolin. Range from mild and sweet to spicy and are often brightly colored.

16. Red radish (varieties include French Breakfast or Fire and Ice): a salad favorite, most often eaten raw, but can also be glazed like a baby turnip. The greens can be used in soups.

1. Cassava, also known as manioc or yuca: originally from Brazil and a major staple food in Africa and Southeast Asia. There are bitter and sweet varieties and it is traditionally fried, boiled, or pureed. Can be poisonous if prepared incorrectly. Other products made from cassava include tapioca (cassava starch) and *garri* (flaky flour made from fermented cassava).

2. Rutabaga, also known as swede: a cross between the cabbage and the turnip, popular in cold countries (Finland, Canada, etc.). Good in soups, pureed, or in a gratin.

3. Jerusalem artichoke: can be eaten raw when young, otherwise steam or boil in their skin to peel them easily and reveal their delicate artichoke flavor.

4. White sweet potato: dense, firm, mild-flavored flesh, well suited for desserts.

5. Orange sweet potato: moist, meltingly soft, and fluffy when cooked. Richer in nutrients than the white variety. Can be cooked like a potato: fried, roasted, baked, in soups or stews, etc. The leaves can be eaten when cooked.

6. Scorzonera, also known as black salsify: this root vegetable and the common or white salsify (with pale brown rather than black skin), nicknamed the oyster plant, are both commonly referred to as salsify. Their fresh flavor is particularly delicate and they should be cooked in a *blanc* (see technique p. 43).

7. Yam: a tuber that is sometimes confused with sweet potatoes. Widely consumed in Africa and Oceania. Has a floury texture and chestnut-like flavor. Delicious fried or oven-baked.

8. Taro, also known as *dachine* or *eddoe*: a tropical tuber with edible leaves. Its flesh can be white or purple and has a starchy texture. Needs to be well cooked, preferably unpeeled, to dissolve the calcium oxalate crystals it contains. Can be cooked in the same way as a potato.

9. Beets (red, Chioggia [aka candy stripe beet], and yellow): varying degrees of sweetness. Differentiate between the winter beet—large in size and best served cooked or pickled—and the smaller spring beet sold in bunches, which can be served raw or cooked.

Potatoes

There are more than a thousand different varieties of potato—originally from Peru—in a wide range of colors, sizes, and textures. It is the world's fourth largest food crop, after corn, wheat, and rice.

1. Roseval: small, waxy potato with a firm and moist texture and a thin red skin. Does not break up as it cooks. Ideal for steaming or for use in salads.

2. Bleu d'Artois: very firm texture, excellent for making fries. Retains its blue color during cooking.

3. King Edward: one of the oldest European varieties, grown in the UK since 1902. Its floury, fluffy texture makes it suitable for most cooking methods: baking, roasting, sautéing, and for making fries.

4. Charlotte: retains its firm texture when cooked, ideal for sautéing or use in slow-cooked recipes.

5. Belle de Fontenay: firm, waxy, flavorsome flesh, suitable for salads, steaming, and sautéing.

6. Ratte: very firm texture and thin skin, good for steaming, although top chefs use it for purees.

7. Mona Lisa: waxy potato that turns meltingly soft when cooked, to be used in gratins or purees.

8. Bintje: floury texture, ideal for purees and fries.

9. *Grenaille*: the French name given to very small potatoes—less than 1 ½ inches (35 mm)—harvested before they are fully grown, whatever the variety. Traditionally steamed or braised in their skins to preserve their soft texture and sweet flavor; also delicious roasted. Fingerling or new potatoes can be prepared in the same way.

Mushrooms

See p. 164

1. **Shiitake:** fragrant, rich in vitamin D and antioxidants. Distinguished by its savory, umami flavor. Widely used in Asian cooking.

2. **Horn of plenty, also known as black trumpet, black chanterelle, or *trompette de la mort* ("trumpet of death"):** don't be put off by the names which just refer to its shape and color. It is perfectly edible and delicious when sautéed! Particularly good for drying and can then be reduced to a powder to be used as a natural flavor enhancer.

3. **Girolle, also known as golden chanterelle:** a wild mushroom with a fruity fragrance, belonging to the chanterelle family. Requires careful cleaning with a small brush to remove soil particles and other debris from its gills.

4. **& 8. Oyster mushroom (pink and yellow), also known as pleurotte:** can be pink or yellow but most often an off-white color (not shown on p. 164) and accounts for approximately 25 percent of all mushrooms cultivated in the world. Rich in fiber and vegetable proteins as well as antioxidants. Should be eaten thoroughly cooked. The pink variety is firmer with a slight bitter taste and loses its color when cooked.

5. **Chanterelle:** identifiable by its brown cap. Less fragrant than the girolle (see no. 3) but is prepared in the same way.

6. **& 7. *Shimeji* (brown and white):** native to East Asia and mainly cultivated in Japan. Must be cooked to remove the bitter taste. Rich in umami, with a delicate walnut flavor. Excellent stir-fried or slow-cooked in sauce.

9. **Enoki, also known as enokidake or golden needle:** cultivated essentially in Japan and Korea and used frequently in East Asian cuisine. Traditionally used in soups, it can also be served raw in salads or briefly sautéed. Cut off the base of the stalk and it is ready to use.

10. **Porcini, also known as cèpe or cep:** the best example from the flavorsome boletus family, with a firm texture and savory taste. Can be griddled, sautéed, dried, and even preserved.

11. **Common or cultivated mushroom (*Agaricus bisporus*):** the most widely cultivated and consumed mushroom in the world. Includes the button or white mushroom (small and young, with white flesh and a closed cap), the cremini or baby portobello (slightly older, with browner flesh and a cap that may be beginning to open), and the portobello (fully mature, with large open caps). White ones tend to have a milder flavor, and the pinkish brown ones (as pictured on p. 164) are more fragrant. Always choose mushrooms with the base of their stalk intact and uncut, so you can tell they are fresh.

Dried Mushrooms

See p. 165

1. **Porcini, also known as cèpe or cep:** always dried in slices, not whole, to ensure they dry out completely.

2. **Chinese snow fungus, also known as white tremella or white jelly mushroom:** traditional in Chinese cuisine, mainly used for thickening soups.

3. **Shiitake:** one of the rare mushrooms that greatly increase in flavor when dried. Use in soups and broths.

4. **Chinese black mushroom, also known as cloud ear, wood ear, or Judas' ear:** widely used in Chinese cuisine. Has little flavor but its surprisingly gelatinous texture is both elastic and firm.

5. **Morel:** although served fresh in spring, it is particularly good for drying. Must be cooked very thoroughly, at least 20 minutes, to prevent any risk of toxicity.

Rice

1. Jasmine rice, also known as fragrant Thai rice: the most exported rice in the world. Long, fine grains with a delicate jasmine flavor and a slightly sticky texture once cooked.

2. Glutinous rice, also known as sticky rice: rich in amylose and amylopectin. Forms the base for numerous Vietnamese, Japanese, Chinese, and Korean recipes, which use its texture to full advantage. Traditionally cooked in a banana leaf or steamed in a special steamer pot and wicker basket.

3. Broken rice, also known as cracked rice: the more the grains are broken, the more starch they release. An economical way to make thick soups and desserts, particularly used in Africa and Asia.

4. & 5. Basmati rice (brown and white): a highly prized rice originally from India and Pakistan. Is matured for a year after harvest to develop its flavor (in Hindi "basmati" means "queen of fragrance"). The very fine grains grow longer when cooked and do not stick together.

6. Precooked or parboiled rice: mainly produced in the United States. Is precooked by steam, which gelatinizes the starch in the grain so it remains whole, firm, and does not stick when cooked. It has a neutral flavor.

7. Bomba rice: essential for making classic paella. Its short grains can double in size when cooked, without sticking. Look for the appellation Calasparra when choosing bomba rice.

8. Sushi rice: *Oryza sativa Japonica* is cultivated essentially in California and Italy; Japan's production is almost entirely for domestic consumption. Has short grains that easily absorb water and release their starch.

9. Risotto rice: one of the secrets to successful risotto. Grown in the Po valley, varieties include *arborio, carnaroli,* and *vialone nano* (shown on p. 167) which has the smallest grains and the most flavor. Has short grains that easily absorb water and release their starch.

10. Red Camargue rice: protected by Product of Geographical Indication status, it is only cultivated organically. Has firm grains and is particularly tasty cooked using the pilaf method.

11. Black rice, also known as forbidden or *venere* rice: originally from China and reserved for the Emperor (hence its names); now also cultivated in Italy. Retains its firm texture and is slightly sticky when cooked.

12. Wild rice: an aquatic grass that does not belong to the rice family, grown in the United States and Canada. Traditionally harvested by Native Americans. Particularly rich in protein.

Derivatives of Rice

See p. 168

1. Rice flakes: parboiled rice, chopped and flattened into flakes, to be used in rice porridge, rice cakes, etc.

2. Puffed rice: used in granola and other breakfast cereals.

3. Rice cakes: plain or mixed with sesame or corn, they make a tasty snack or bread substitute.

4. Rice-paper wrappers: wafer-thin sheets of rice to be rehydrated (see technique p. 54). Used for rolling up or wrapping around a filling, as for spring rolls, etc. Exist in several sizes and can also be square in Vietnam.

5. Tteok: Korean rice cakes. Soak for 30 minutes before cooking for 20 minutes in a well-seasoned sauce.

6. Black rice vinegar: strong and sweet. A by-product from the fermentation of sticky rice. Used as a seasoning and for serving with Chinese dumplings.

7. Rice vinegar: sweet and fragrant, essential for seasoning sushi rice. Also good for pickles.

8. Rice milk: a vegan drink made from raw or cooked rice, to which sweeteners can be added or not. Light and neutral in flavor, suitable for both savory and sweet dishes (see technique p. 58).

9. Rice cream: usually sold as a UHT product, rice cream (not to be confused with creamed rice, sometimes called rice cream) is made from rice flour, vegetable oils, and water, and is a substitute for dairy whipping cream.

10. Rice noodles: widely used throughout Asia. Come in varying shapes and widths. To prevent them sticking, soak in cold water for at least 30 minutes before cooking in boiling water.

11. Rice vermicelli: very simple to prepare—they just need soaking for 10 minutes in boiling hot water, off the heat. Use in salads, spring rolls, etc.

12. Rice macaroni: naturally gluten-free, rice is now used to make gluten-free Italian pasta.

13. Rice flour: white or semi-milled, it is naturally gluten-free. Ground rice is a slightly coarser version of rice flour.

14. Semolina: has many uses, including making a type of couscous in Africa.

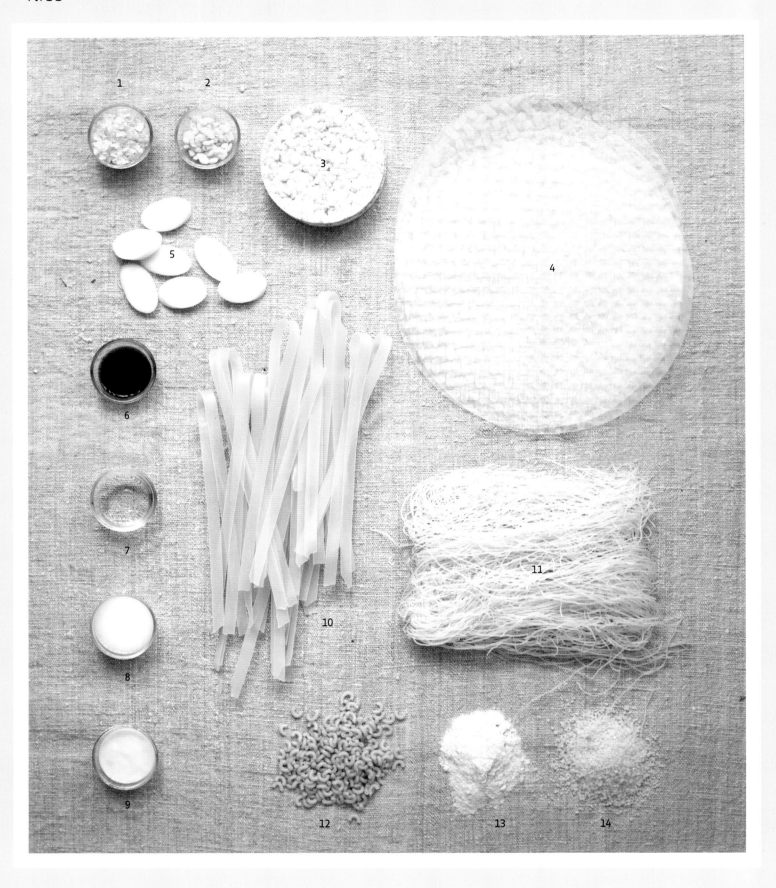

Wheat

1. *Freekeh*: grains of young green wheat roasted to give them a lightly smoked flavor. Traditional in North Africa and the Middle East.

2. Wheat berries: specifically used for sprouting.

3. Coarse-grain bulgur wheat: hard wheat precooked by steam, dried, and cracked. Sold in different grades (fine, medium, coarse), from whole or hulled grains.

4. Whole-wheat flour: rich in fiber. Always buy the organic variety.

5. Semi whole–wheat flour.

6. White flour.

7. Fine brown bulgur wheat (from whole grains): recommended for making kibbe.

8. Fine semolina: made from ground, sieved, and precooked wheat and comes in different grades. Fine semolina is used for gnocchi and pasta, for example. Can be steamed or mixed with boiling water until it swells, when it is precooked.

9. *Moghrabieh*: means "from Mashrek." Little balls of semolina used for making couscous in Lebanon.

10. *Fregola Sarda*: Sardinian pasta rolled by hand. Made from durum-wheat flour mixed with water, rolled into little balls, dried, and then lightly toasted in the oven.

11. Wheat germ: the part of the grain enclosing the embryo of the future plant, rich in minerals, trace elements, and vitamins. Available as wheat-germ oil or, as here, in flakes to be sprinkled over salads and soups, etc.

12. Seitan: a dough made from pure gluten with added seasonings, cooked in broth and then used as a meat substitute. Originally created by Buddhists, it has become part of the microbiotic diet (see technique p. 69).

13. Pure gluten: used for making seitan or can be added to certain flours with a low gluten content to enable them to rise better.

14. Lasagna sheets: pasta made from durum-wheat flour. Lasagna made from precooked sheets can be baked directly in the oven; the traditional sheets need blanching first in boiling water for 5 minutes, then should be drained.

15. Brown *torti* pasta: pasta made from whole-wheat flour releases energy more slowly and is richer in nutrients than pasta made from white flour.

Gluten-Free Grains

Gluten-free grains and pseudograins
The foods listed below are naturally gluten-free. However, they may have been contaminated by other grains, depending on how and where they were produced, transported, and handled. Where celiac disease is an issue, check the packaging to ensure the product has the gluten-free label with no "may contain traces of gluten" statement. Grouped together here are gluten-free pseudograins, as well as starches and semolinas that will enable you to cook without gluten.

1. 2. & 3. Quinoa (white, red, and black): a pseudograin from a plant from the same family as beets and spinach. Grows on the high plateaus of South America and was designated "the mother of all grains" by the Incas. Its high protein content (15 percent) makes it particularly beneficial in a vegetarian diet: it contains all the essential amino acids and is one of a very few plants, along with soybeans, hemp, amaranth, and buckwheat, that unites them all. The variety of colors reflects a diversity of flavors (see technique p. 75).

4. Buckwheat: belongs to the same family as rhubarb and sorrel and grows in cold countries. Gluten-free and easy to digest, it was long considered the cereal of the poor. Can be cooked simply in boiling water, whether whole (raw), as shown here, or toasted groats, like kasha in Eastern Europe, Russia, etc.

5. Japanese soba noodles: thin noodles made from buckwheat flour, served chilled with a dipping sauce or in hot soup, in Japan. Can also be made of a mixture of wheat and buckwheat (nagano soba) which makes them less brittle than those made from just buckwheat flour.

6. Buckwheat flour: has the flavor of hazelnuts and is used for making waffles and pancakes.

7. & 8. Millet (yellow and brown): a group of small-seeded grasses that grow predominantly in the dry zones of Africa and Asia. Used in soups or for making patties, the most common is pearl millet **(7)**, which is particularly easy to digest. Brown or red millet does not have its hull removed **(8)** and its texture therefore remains crunchy; it is especially rich in silica and revitalizing minerals.

9. *Fonio*: the grains are tiny (1/16 in./1.5 mm, or approximately 14,000 grains per 1/4 oz./2,000 grains per gram). Used for making soups or couscous in the same way as semolina.

10. Amaranth: highly prized in Aztec then Mexican cultures, this minuscule grain (less than 1/16 in./approximately 1 mm) has only recently become popular. When cooked, it becomes slightly gelatinous; it can also be prepared like popcorn. Rich in lysine, an amino acid absent in most grains, it is also rich in protein (13 percent).

11. Tapioca: a starch obtained from cassava (see p. 161, no. 1). Consists of small grains that take on a jellified texture when mixed with liquid. Used for thickening soups and desserts, particularly in Asia and Brazil. Tapioca pearls, sometimes known as *boba*, are little balls of tapioca added to soups, desserts, and sweet drinks.

12. Arrowroot: a starch extracted from the root of a tropical plant. Dissolves particularly easily in nondairy drinks and can replace eggs and flour for thickening mixtures.

13. & 14. Corn flour and white cornmeal: not to be confused with cornstarch, which is obtained from the endosperm of the kernel while corn flour and cornmeal are milled from the whole kernel. Corn (maize) can be purple, yellow or red; depending on how finely it is ground, it becomes cornmeal or flour. The flour gives cakes a buttery flavor, an appetizing yellow color, and a firm texture. Cornmeal can be white, as pictured here, or yellow and has a finer flavor; it is used for making polenta (see technique p. 71) and is usually sold precooked.

Grains with Gluten

1. Oat groats: oat grains with just their bran (see no. 3) removed. Their high-fiber content makes them particularly healthful, helping to lower blood cholesterol levels and to regulate the absorption of carbohydrates.

2. Oatmeal: can be precooked or not, with small or large flakes. Made of oat groats (see no. 1) that have been either crushed, ground, sliced (steel-cut) and/or rolled. Traditionally used to make porridge and also good for pastry, cakes, Irish breads, etc.

3. Oat bran: the hard, outer layer of oat grains, used for increasing the fiber content in certain recipes. Also has a cholesterol-lowering effect.

4. Vegan oat cream: cooked oats become creamy in texture when mixed with water, and can be used to make vegan milk or liquid cream.

5. Einkorn wheat, also known as small spelt: a rustic ancestor of wheat. Spelt (not shown) is a cereal grown in cold climates, whereas einkorn wheat can be found in regions with dry, marginal soils—such as Haute Provence, whose cuisine often makes use of it—where other types of wheat cannot grow due to climatic conditions. Its grain is enclosed in a fibrous husk that needs to be removed before consumption. Smaller than spelt and without its characteristic indent down the center of the grain, it has a distinctive hazelnut flavor. Both spelt and einkorn wheat can be cooked in the same way as wheat, although spelt is firmer.

6. *Farro*: Italian spelt from Tuscany, dating back to the Etruscans. Groups several types of ancient grains that are often mistaken for one another but are very similar in taste. Best soaked for 3 hours before cooking.

7. Spelt flakes: crunchy flakes to be used in granola or in breakfast cereals.

8. Spelt flour: richer in nutrients than wheat flour. Excellent for making bread and flavorful pasta (see no. 13).

9. Spelt bulgur: spelt takes a long time to cook, so cracking and precooking it to produce bulgur spelt allows the cooking time to be significantly reduced.

10. Barley coffee: certain grains such as barley and spelt, when grilled and finely ground, are used as substitutes for coffee, as they contain no caffeine. Particularly popular in Italy, Japan, and Korea.

11. Pearl barley: barley grains are surrounded by a fibrous husk that is removed to make them edible. When the outermost hull is removed but the bran is left intact, it is known as hulled barley, or barley groats. Pearl barley has been processed further, being polished to remove the bran layers. Although it takes less time to cook, it loses some of its fiber and nutrients when polished.

12. Malt vinegar: germinated barley can be used to produce malt, for the production of beer and whiskeys as well as for helping certain types of bread dough to rise. The juice from germinated barley can be fermented to produce a strongly flavored vinegar. Cereals' capacity to turn into vinegar is all too often forgotten!

13. Spelt pasta: pasta made from spelt flour (see no. 8).

14. & 15. Rye flour and rye grains: a rustic grain with less protein than wheat; its benefits lie in the amount of calcium and potassium it contains. Can be used to make flavorsome bread that keeps well, as well as tasty cakes with an original tang.

Dried Fava (Broad) Beans, Peas, and Chickpeas

Pulses are the dried edible seeds of plants from the legume family. A legume is a type of plant whose seeds grow in pods, such as peas or beans. The dried seeds from these plants are called pulses. The most common pulses are dried peas, beans, chickpeas, and lentils. In the US, the term "legume" is sometimes used to refer to the plant and the dried seeds.

Pulses are high in protein and fiber, low in fat, and rich in minerals such as iron, phosphorus, and zinc, as well as B-vitamins.

1. *Desi chana*, also known as *kala chana*: small, dark brown Indian chickpeas with very thick skin. Usually eaten with the skin removed and are sold split and skinned under the name *chana dhal*.

2. & 3. Chickpeas and black chickpeas: contain the most protein of all the pulses. Their size varies according to their origin and they can be white, cream, or black. Try sprouting them for 1–2 days before cooking them, as this renders them more easily digestible.

4. Dried fava beans, also known as broad beans: widely consumed in the Middle East, especially in Egypt and Lebanon, where they are enjoyed cooked whole for breakfast or in soups. Require a long cooking time. Peeled and split, they are also used for making falafel.

5. & 6. Small fava beans and skinned small fava beans: popular in North Africa and the Middle East. Can be soaked and then cooked like navy (haricot) beans; the skinned variety is used to make falafel.

7. Lima beans, also known as butter beans or *garrofón*: soft, creamy, buttery texture when cooked (hence the name butter bean), with a delicate flavor and thick skins which need to be removed after soaking. Essential ingredient for Spanish paella and also commonly used in Latin America and the West Indies in patties or croquettes.

8. & 9. Split peas and dried peas: harvested when fully grown, these peas are large and rich in starch. Can be yellow or green. Whole dried peas should be cooked like lentils. The split variety, which when skinned naturally separates in two, is easier to prepare; it breaks up easily when cooked, however, so suits soups or purees.

Navy (Haricot) Beans and Lentils

See p. 176

1. Adzuki beans: small beans of Japanese origin, usually red. Often steamed and then candied in a sugar syrup and used to fill pastries made from rice flour. Their taste is reminiscent of chestnuts.

2. *Toor dhal*, also known as pigeon peas or Indian yellow lentils: belong to the pea family, but often classed as a lentil because they are mostly found peeled and desprouted; are cooked in the same way as lentils. One of the most popular and tasty *dhals* in India.

3. Red lentils: as their hulls are removed, they have a short cooking time (15 minutes). Tend to break up when cooked and so are often used for purees and soups.

4. Lingot beans: medium-size navy beans similar to Italian cannellini beans. Used for baked beans and cassoulets.

5. *Borlotti* beans: an example of the bean family with red- or pink-tinged marbled skin. Have a particularly fine flavor.

6. Beluga lentils: small lentils with a firm texture and a spectacular deep black color that just turns slightly gray when cooked.

7. Flageolet beans: small beans harvested young, hence their green color and thin skins, and dried in the shade to retain the color. Firm and creamy texture when cooked. Originate from France.

8. Black beans: popular in South America, especially for making *frijoles* or served with rice. Also found in dishes from the Basque country.

9. Blonde lentils: the largest lentil of all, the least flavorsome, and the least expensive. For using in soups.

10. Black-eyed peas, also known as black-eyed beans or cowpeas: widely used from Europe to Africa, or from the south of the United States to Asia, particularly Vietnam. A small, tender bean that suits both sweet and savory recipes.

11. Kidney beans: firm-textured and retain their shape when cooked. Found throughout the northern hemisphere, often in slow-cooked stews.

12. Green lentils: thin-skinned with a hazelnut flavor, they remain whole when cooked. The best are those from Puy in France—the first pulse to be protected by Appellation of Controlled Origin status, in 1996.

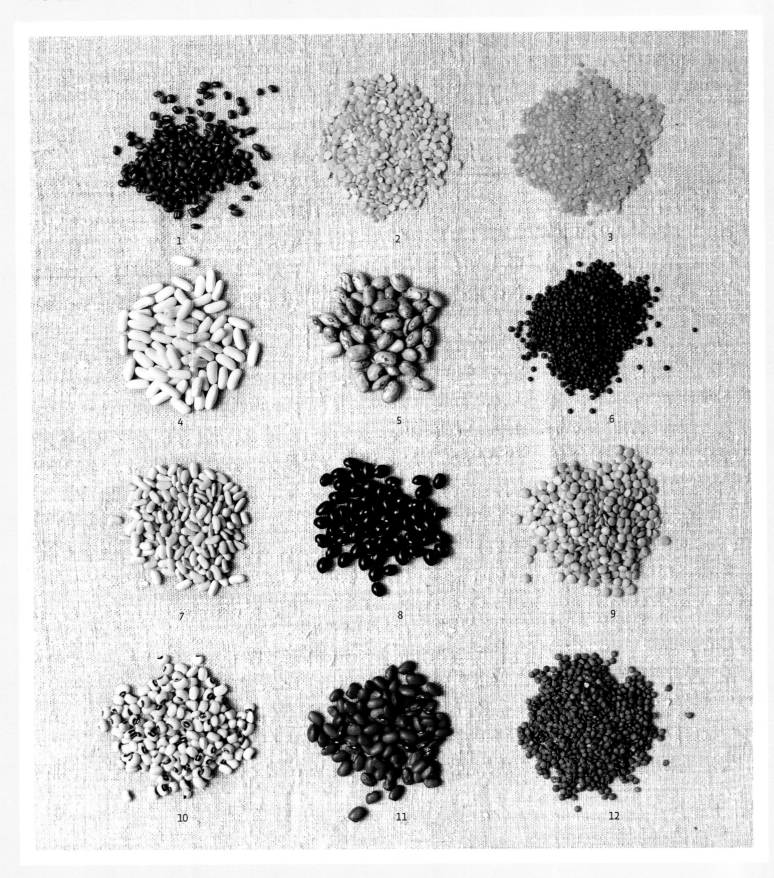

False Soybeans

Often mistakenly referred to as "soybeans," these pulses call for some clarification.

1. & 3. Mung beans, also known as moong beans or green gram, and mung bean sprouts: have long been referred to as green soybeans. The seeds do, in fact, resemble soybeans, but they do not belong to the same family. Used with their hulls removed or ground into flour, for Indian pancakes and *dhal*. Mung bean sprouts are commonly sold as "soybean sprouts," but they are not! (See also Glass noodles, no. 12, p. 179.)

2. Hulled *urad* beans, also known as white lentils: the whole *urad* bean is often called black soybean, as well as black gram, black lentil, or mungo bean, and is black in color. The hulled split bean (pictured here) is white. One of the most popular pulses in India, both for its color and slightly viscous texture when cooked, an advantage for making *dhals* and, in the form of flour, for making *dosas* and other pancakes.

Soybeans

1. Smoked tofu: firm-textured tofu smoked with beech wood or liquid flavoring. Good for winter dishes or in sandwiches. Its flavor is an ideal introduction to tofu.

2. Lacto-fermented tofu: made with fermented soy milk and is therefore richer in probiotics, with a more pronounced acidic, cheese-like flavor than firm tofu (see no. 3). Can be used plain, or with olives or tamari.

3. Plain firm tofu: drained and pressed (see technique p. 88), its firm consistency allows it to be cut up, fried, or marinated without crumbling. Also available flavored with mustard, herbs, etc.

4. Silken tofu: smooth, creamy texture, perfect for sauces, creams, and desserts. Has a more delicate flavor than firm tofu.

5. Soy milk: can be plain or vanilla-flavored and is often enriched with calcium or sweetened. Check the label to ensure it suits your requirements. (See technique p. 86 to make your own soy milk.)

6. Fried tofu pouches, also known as *aburaage*: from Japan. Need to be immersed in boiling water for 1 minute, then drained to remove any excess oil. When cut in two, they form a pouch that can be filled—with sushi rice, for example (*inari* sushi). Can also be cut up and added to soups, stews, noodles, etc.

7. Dried tofu skin (*yuba*): made from the fine skin that forms on soy milk when it is produced—just as it forms on cow milk when heated—which is then dried. Available in folded sheets (pictured here), tight little rolls, or frozen. Needs to be lightly soaked to rehydrate it, and can then be cooked briefly in soups and stews. Is also used in Buddhist monks' traditional cooking as a substitute for crisp meat skin when fried. Can also replace nori seaweed when preparing sushi.

8. Hulled yellow soybeans: whole yellow soybeans can be prepared in the same ways as dried navy beans, but it is hulled ones that are used to make soy milk, the base of many different vegan products.

9. Black soybeans: have thick black skins and are rich in polyphenols and antioxidants. In China and Japan, they are made into an aromatic, fermented paste for flavoring soups and marinades.

10. Textured soy protein: made from soy flour and particularly rich in proteins. Exists in various shapes and sizes (see preparation technique p. 91).

11. Edamame beans: immature green soybeans in their pods. Require boiling for 10 minutes before serving warm or cold. Readily available cooked and frozen. Can be shelled to serve with aperitifs or to jazz up fried rice dishes, soups, etc.

12. Glass noodles, also known as soybean vermicelli: these are not, in fact, made from green soybeans as is commonly believed, but from mung beans (see no. 1, p. 177), often mistakenly called green soybeans (see preparation technique p. 81).

13. *Kinako* (roasted soy flour): made from roasted soybeans ground into flour. Full of flavor but has a tendency to turn rancid. Use in pancakes, cookies, etc.

14. Soy cream: a vegan alternative to heavy cream, made from soy milk with added oil and thickeners.

15. Tempeh: cooked soybeans fermented using a fungi that forms white threads and binds the beans into a solid block. An Indonesian specialty that differs from tofu; dense in texture, with the flavors of mushrooms, hazelnuts, and cheese (see preparation technique, p. 93).

16. Soy sauce: various colors and flavors depending on the composition and the production and fermentation processes used. Chinese, Korean, and Japanese versions can therefore be very different. However, it is important to note the difference between tamari and shoyu: tamari is stronger and made only from soybeans; shoyu, more widely available, also contains wheat, so is not gluten-free—those with a gluten intolerance should therefore be vigilant. Shoyu can be light or dark. The light version is saltier and is used as a seasoning in sauces and soups. The darker shoyu is usually used in slow-cooked dishes.

17. & 18. *Shiro* miso (beige miso) and *hatcho* miso (red miso): product of the fermentation of soybeans, sometimes combined with a cereal (rice, wheat, barley, etc.), and *koji*, a culture of microscopic fungi. A smooth paste with an incredibly concentrated flavor, most commonly used in miso soup. The mildest, sweetest version is made from rice (*shiro* miso), and the strongest is *hatcho* miso, made only from soybeans. Rich in nutrients and used as a condiment in soups, marinades, etc. Is an excellent flavor enhancer, making it indispensable in vegetarian cooking.

Seaweed

1. Dulse: typically Celtic, mild, with only a little iodine and a delicate hazelnut flavor. Reasonably firm texture; serve raw, chopped, or steamed. Traditionally eaten in Brittany, Ireland, Scotland, and Iceland.

2. Wakame: the flagship seaweed of Japanese cuisine, which uses it in miso soup and salads. Also cultivated in Brittany, France. Rich in calcium and fiber; its soft texture and delicate oyster flavor give it widespread appeal.

3. Sea spaghetti: brown seaweed with a pronounced iodine flavor. Once soaked, it can be served raw in salads or steamed for 10 minutes like green beans. Rich in vitamin C.

4., 5. & 6. Japanese nori, Breton nori, and Japanese nori sheets: nori, also known as laver or *Porphyra*, is the most widely consumed seaweed in the world. Red when fresh, it turns black or purplish-blue when dried. Available as small flakes, chopped, or compressed into sheets. Its seductive flavor, combining smokiness and iodine, makes it a tasty addition to omelets, sauces, etc. Very common in Japan, it is also highly cultivated in Brittany, France. Contains 47 percent protein and is the seaweed used to make *maki* (see technique p. 56).

7. Spirulina: blue-green micro-algae that grows in fresh-water lakes with water rich in alkalines and sodium bicarbonate. Exceptionally rich in protein, it is classed as a superfood and is used more for its nutritional benefit than its flavor. Can be added to condiments (e.g. *gomasio*, see technique p. 119) or directly to smoothies, cold soups, etc.

8. Chlorella: microscopic, single-cell fresh-water seaweed, rich in proteins, chlorophyll, and omega-3 fatty acids, and reputed to aid detoxification. Use in small quantities in green smoothies.

9. Irish moss: red seaweed with strong gelling and thickening properties, used in the food industry for extracting carrageenans. Available in powder form, it is mainly used for making jellies, mousses, and desserts, especially in vegan recipes.

10. & 11. Agar-agar powder and agar-agar strands: red, microscopic Japanese seaweed in use since the seventeenth century. Often used to replace gelatin in cooking because of its gelling properties. The powder is simpler to use than the strands (see technique p. 101).

12. & 13. Japanese royal kombu and Finistère royal kombu: large, brown variety of seaweed sometimes called "Neptune's belt." Is the most important known source of iodine. Considered the most noble seaweed in Japan, though it is exploited by the food industry for making alginates. Both pulpy and crunchy, it is always cooked before use; it gives the Japanese broth dashi its characteristic flavor (see technique p. 97). When added to the cooking liquid its glutamate content shortens the cooking time for pulses, while also imparting flavor. Can be candied in soy sauce and sake to make a refined treat. When dried, it sometimes develops white marks known as "kombu flowers." Its high concentration of saccharides and glutamic acid define its quality. Kombu should never be washed before use, or it will lose some of its flavor.

14. Sea lettuce: known as *aosa* in Japan. Has a similar flavor to sorrel and its leaves can be left whole to wrap around food or chopped for using in sauces, soups, etc.

Nuts

1. **Almonds**: whether with their skins intact or removed, they are rich in protein and lipids. Can be used to make a delicious nondairy milk (see technique p. 122), as well as soups, cakes and pastries, etc.

2. **Cashew nuts**: cultivated in India, Africa, and Vietnam. Have an unpronounced flavor and a soft texture when raw. Widely used in vegan cooking as a substitute for dairy products (notably cream, see technique p. 120).

3. **Brazil nuts, also known as Amazonian nuts**: the nuts containing the most selenium. Occasionally they are bitter, in which case they should not be eaten.

4. **Pistachios in the shell**: red- or green-skinned, they are an essential ingredient in Greek and Asian cuisine. Come essentially from Turkey, Sicily (known for its fine pistachios from Bronte), and Iran (the most renowned). Can be roasted and salted to accompany aperitifs.

5. **Pecan nuts**: very rich in lipids (72 percent). Indispensable in the cuisine of the southern United States—in fact, the official state tree of Texas is the pecan tree and pecan pie is its official state pie!

6. **Peanuts, also known as groundnuts**: paradoxically, the peanut is not a nut, but a member of the legume family! However, it is not typical as it contains 49 percent lipids, and for culinary uses is generally considered a nut. Are cooked in their shells in boiling water and served in salads in Asia and Africa. Most often roasted, then salted, they can be chopped and sprinkled over salads and also make a very tasty nondairy spread.

7. **Macadamia nuts**: originally from Queensland, northeast Australia. Turn rancid easily and should be bought in small quantities. Avoid buying them in the shell as they are extremely hard and difficult to crack with domestic utensils.

8. **Walnuts**: French walnuts from Grenoble and Perigord have Appellation of Protected Origin status, but this type of nut is grown all over the world, including the United States. Certain varieties are cultivated for their oil, others for eating. As they turn rancid quickly, it is best to crack them yourself or buy the kernels in small quantities and keep them in the refrigerator.

9. **Hazelnuts, also known as filberts**: Turkey is the major producer, but Italian hazelnuts are most often used by pastry chefs, particularly those from Piedmont.

Seeds

See p. 184.

1. **Pumpkin seeds**: their flavor is surprisingly similar to that of pistachios. Are even tastier when lightly toasted.

2. **Hulled hemp seeds**: have a delicate and original flavor. Their high levels of omega-3 and omega-6 essential fatty acids, in perfect proportions to meet our needs, make them particularly beneficial. Very low amounts of psychoactive substances (tetrahydrocannabinol or THC) distinguish edible hemp from cannabis. Good for sprinkling over dishes or for making a vegan beverage.

3. **Sunflower seeds**: one of the least expensive seeds. Try sprouting them to sprinkle over salads. Avoid the roasted variety which will have lost its nutritional value.

4. & 5. **Black sesame seeds and whole sesame seeds**: contain phosphorus, magnesium, and proteins—it's not surprising they are a symbol of immortality! Brown in color when whole and white when hulled, but can also be black with a more earthy flavor. Form the base of the sesame-seed puree tahini, as well as the seasoning *gomasio* (see technique p. 119).

6. **Poppy seeds**: small blue-black seeds, very popular in Eastern Europe. Used to flavor or garnish bread and cookies, and are also ground into a paste for making traditional cakes in Austria, Poland, and Hungary.

7. **Linseed**: whether brown or yellow, their value lies in their omega-3 content. To obtain the maximum benefit, grind them just before use, to avoid them turning rancid. They form a viscous gel when in contact with water and can therefore be used to replace eggs in certain recipes (see technique p. 124).

8. **Chia seeds**: tiny brown or white seeds, originally from Central America. Contain 20 percent omega-3. Their viscosity when mixed with water makes them useful for thickening mixtures or replacing eggs.

9. **Tiger nuts**: not a nut, but a round tuber from the family of sedge grasses. Rich in fiber and naturally sweet. In Spain, it has been made into a drink called *horchata di chufa* for centuries; it can also be ground into a flour, common in North Africa.

Coconut and Its Derivatives

See p. 186.

An oleaginous plant with exceptional properties, the coconut is used in various ways and forms, particularly in vegan cooking.

1. & 2. Coconut chips and desiccated coconut: coconut flesh can be sliced and then oven-dried, lightly roasted, or simply grated and dried. These products can turn rancid due to their high fat content. Prepare or buy them in small quantities and always taste before using them.

3. Coconut butter: dry coconut pulp blended until it obtains the texture of butter, which can then be whisked or used as a spread.

4. Coconut oil: extracted by cold pressing and rich in saturated fatty acids. Remains solid up to 75°F (25°C); over that temperature it melts naturally. Is exceptionally stable and does not degrade when heated to high temperatures—it is the healthiest oil for cooking and frying. Used for wok cooking in Asia, and can replace butter in vegan pastry recipes.

5. Coconut: in its most mature form (see technique p. 129, for opening).

6. Coconut flour: produced from the dry pulp once all the oil has been extracted from it. Contains 60 percent fiber and 15 percent carbohydrate. Can be mixed with other flours to comprise a quarter of the total flour content to make cakes and bread, thereby reducing their glycemic index considerably.

7. Coconut palm sugar: produced from the sap of coconut palm flowers, this unrefined brown sugar contains zinc and potassium and has a low glycemic index (35). Can be used to make more wholesome cakes with a pleasant caramel flavor.

8. Coconut milk powder: dehydrated, just like dried cow milk. Can be used directly in sauces or reconstituted with water.

9. Young coconut: a coconut that has not yet hardened or become woody. Used for its water (see no. 10) and tender pulp (see technique for opening p. 130).

10. Coconut water: the liquid naturally contained inside a coconut. The quantity is considerable in a young coconut (up to 2 cups/500 ml). Contains no lipids or sugar and is particularly thirst-quenching and restorative, as it is rich in potassium, sodium, magnesium, calcium, and phosphorus.

11. Coconut milk: prepared from grated coconut pulp and water. The fat content varies depending on the brand.

12. Coconut cream: the thickest part of coconut milk with the highest fat content. Can be whisked to make coconut whipped cream (see technique p. 127).

Oils

See p. 187.

Depending on their essential fatty acid content, oils degrade at different temperatures. It is important for your health to respect their smoke point. Give precedence to extra-virgin, unrefined oils, and ways of using them without heating.

1. Peanut oil, also known as groundnut oil: virgin peanut oil should not be heated. The smoke point of the refined oil is 430°F (220°C), so it is adapted for frying.

2. Sunflower oil: unrefined sunflower oil can be heated up to 320°F (160°C). The smoke point of the refined oil, adapted for frying, is 430°F (220°C).

3. Unrefined canola oil, also known as rapeseed oil: its cabbage-like flavor can be surprising. To be used cold only. Refined canola (rapeseed) oil can be used for cooking.

4. Toasted sesame oil: its exquisite flavor is highly prized in Asian cuisine. Can be heated to 410°F (210°C), perfect for cooking in a wok.

5. Walnut oil: to be used cold only.

6. Pumpkin-seed oil: to be used cold only. Has a distinctive flavor of roasted pistachios.

7. Grape-seed oil: the only oil that does not congeal when chilled. Recommended for making sauces such as mayonnaise and for preserving.

8. Frying oil: traditionally produced from oleic sunflower oil, sometimes combined with olive oil, these oils are made specifically for shallow and deep frying and remain stable at very high temperatures.

9. Olive oil: can be heated to 465°F (240°C). The different types of fruitiness—from green or ripe (black) olives—can be distinguished by the strength and the depth of their aromas.

10. Margarine: solid fat consisting of an emulsion of several different oils, water, and emulsifiers. Choose those that do not contain palm oil.

11. Coconut oil: see Coconut and Its Derivatives, no. 4.

Sugars and Sweeteners

1. Agave syrup, also known as agave nectar: produced from the agave plant used for making tequila. Its sugar content is three times greater than conventional sugars and it is composed essentially of fructose. Often recommended as a replacement for honey in vegan recipes. There is currently controversy concerning its high fructose content and its effects on fats stored in the body.

2. Malted rice syrup: produced from the fermentation of brown rice. Acts like a slow sugar for blood sugar levels and liquefies when heated. Ideal cold for pouring over crêpes, in yogurt, etc.

3. Golden syrup: a typically British product, this amber-colored inverted sugar is made from molasses. Does not crystallize and can be used to replace honey in vegan recipes.

4. Maple syrup: produced from maple sap brought to boiling point. Its sugar content is 1.4 times higher than that of refined white sugar. Rich in vitamin B, proteins, and minerals such as zinc, calcium, potassium, and magnesium. Consists of 30 percent water: for the same volume, less sugar is absorbed by the body than with traditional sugar. Available as clear (the lightest in flavor), medium (a more pronounced and typical woody flavor, ideal for cakes), and dark syrup (reserved for marinades and savory recipes where its spiciness works wonders).

5. *Sirop de Liège*: a paste produced from a reduction of apple and pear juice. Used as a spread or for frosting or glazing rather than for cooking.

6. *Panela*, also known as *rapadura*: Spanish and Brazilian names for sugarcane juice that is dried then sieved, typical of Central and South America. Is unrefined and contains all the mineral salts and vitamins of sugarcane. Has a licorice flavor. Can be sprinkled on fruit or used for jam making, as it helps to set.

7. *Muscovado*: unrefined brown sugar, produced from sugarcane syrup cooked until it caramelizes and then crystallizes. Its color varies from light to very dark, corresponding to the flavor which ranges from caramel to aged rum.

8. Light brown sugar: produced from sugarcane with its molasses partially removed. Has 10 times more minerals than refined white sugar and is ideal for making cakes.

9. & 10. Refined white sugar and confectioners' or icing sugar: produced from cane or beets. Contains no minerals or vitamins, only sucrose. Confectioners' sugar can be made at home by grinding refined white sugar in a mini-blender.

11., 12. & 13. Lemon blossom, chestnut, and multi-flower honeys: produced by bees, and therefore not eaten by vegans. Composed of glucose and fructose; depending on the kind of honey, the proportion of these two sugars varies, explaining the differences in texture. Multi-flower honey is mild in flavor and liquid in texture, making it a useful all-purpose choice. Chestnut honey is dark in color with a strong woody flavor and goes well with cheeses. Lemon blossom honey has a delicate aroma; it is also an antiseptic and is often used in hot drinks.

14. Stevia-based sweetener: produced from the leaves of the stevia plant which have a sweet licorice flavor. The plant has long been used in South America for sweetening drinks. The principal sweetening compounds, 300 times sweeter than ordinary sugar, are extracted from the leaves to produce different sweeteners and sugar substitutes. Is heat-stable, but often leaves an aftertaste which some find unpleasant. Exists in powder and cube form.

15. Xylitol: a sweetener produced from birch wood. Gives an astonishing sensation of freshness in the mouth. Its sweetness is equivalent to that of refined white sugar, and its sweet flavor increases when cooked. Intake should be limited to no more than ¼ cup (1 ¾ oz./50 g) per day, as it can have a laxative effect.

16. & 17. Molasses and date molasses: sugarcane molasses is the juice remaining after the sugar has been extracted from the cane. Is syrupy, with a licorice flavor, and slightly bitter. Rich in vitamin B and mineral salts. The term "molasses" also refers to other dark-colored syrups produced by cooking concentrated fruit juice, such as date, grape, pomegranate, carob, and fig molasses.

18. Coconut palm sugar: produced from the sap of coconut palm flowers, this unrefined brown sugar contains zinc and potassium and has a low glycemic index (35). Can be used to make more wholesome cakes with a pleasant caramel flavor.

19. Palm sugar: produced from the sap of palm tree flowers, this unrefined brown sugar is rich in minerals and has a low glycemic index. It can be cooked.

20. Okinawa black sugar: produced from sugarcane cultivated on the islands of southern Japan. A raw sugar, rich in vitamins and minerals, made from the juice of boiled cane. Available in chunks that can be melted or grated. Its pronounced flavors of licorice and spice evoke *muscovado* sugar.

Apples

1. Reinette Clochard: a traditional French apple that is great eaten fresh, as well as in tarts and other desserts as slices hold their shape when cooked. Can be stored particularly well.

2. Canadian Reinette: despite its name, it is a French russet apple. Juicy with a perfect balance of sweetness and tartness. Recommended to be eaten fresh or used in tarts, notably *tarte tatin*, as it keeps its shape well.

3. Cox's Orange Pippin, also known as Cox: the classic English apple. Fragrant and slightly tart, with a flavor reminiscent of pears and sometimes melon, mango, and orange. To be eaten fresh, cooked (it is often used in baking or in preserves and chutney), or juiced.

4. Granny Smith: easily identifiable by its bright green color, it is particularly firm, tart, and crisp. Its flesh turns brown more slowly than other varieties when cut open. At its best when eaten fresh.

5. Gala: mild and very sweet, with little tartness, good eaten fresh or cooked in tarts. One of the most popular apples in the United States.

6. Golden Delicious: another hugely popular variety. A multi-purpose apple that is quite watery with a reasonably mild, sweet flavor.

7. Jonagold: a cross between the Golden Delicious and Jonathan apples, developed in the US. Juicy, sweet, yet tangy, its large size makes it very useful for cooking. Conserves its distinctive aromatic flavor when cooked.

8. Belle de Boskoop: Dutch cultivar that is rustic and firm textured. Best cooked and is excellent for baked apples.

9. Elstar: a Dutch cross between the Golden Delicious and Ingrid Marie apples, with sweet, white flesh. Good for eating fresh as well as for cooking, as it holds its shape well.

10. Rubinette: a cross between the Cox and the Golden Delicious, combining their flavor and fragrance.

11. Topaz: tart, spicy, and not too sweet. Best eaten fresh. Developed in the Czech Republic as a disease-resistant variety.

12. Nashi, also known as Asian pear: round like an apple, but is in fact a pear. Crisp, firm, and thirst-quenchingly juicy, with a surprisingly sweet, mellow flavor.

Pears

1. Beurre Hardy: French pear from the early nineteenth century, popular in the United Kingdom. Thick-skinned with very smooth, buttery flesh and an exceptional flavor.

2. Comice: Plump and very juicy multi-purpose pear, with sweet, meltingly soft flesh.

3. Guyot: meltingly soft, juicy, and refreshing. Particularly good in savory recipes.

4. Williams: white, juicy, and scented, sometimes grainy. Good eaten fresh or in tarts.

5. Louise-Bonne d'Avranches: very juicy and slightly spicy in flavor. Just as tasty fresh as cooked.

6. Conference: the most cultivated variety in Europe. An autumn and winter pear with smooth, juicy flesh and very little tartness. Excellent eaten fresh and holds its shape well when cooked.

Citrus Fruits

1. Yuzu: originally from Japan and made fashionable by pastry chefs. It has a mild acidity and its juice and zest evoke clementines and grapefruit.

2. Citron: its zest and white flesh are mainly candied for use. In Italy, it is served finely sliced in a salad with olive oil.

3. Bergamot orange, from Sicily: yellow when ripe. Its juice and zest are used fresh for making candies, cakes, etc., and its fragrance gives Earl Grey tea its distinctive character.

4. Buddha's Hand: easily identifiable by its distinctive form with "fingers." A variety of citron, usually served in thin slices and used as a condiment or candied.

5. Sudachi: a sour Japanese citrus fruit with a large number of seeds. Not eaten as a fruit; it is the juice that is used, for adding flavor etc., in the same way as lemon or lime.

6. Finger lime (*Microcitrus australasica)*: originates from Australia (often called Australian finger lime). The pulp is composed of crunchy little balls that provide an astonishing burst of flavors in the mouth when eaten.

7. Kaffir lime: both the leaf and the strange, lumpy little fruit are highly prized ingredients, especially in Southeast Asian cuisine. Only the zest of the fruit is used, finely grated and added to dishes just before serving, to preserve its flavor.

8. Limequat: a cross between a Mexican (key) lime and a kumquat. Can be eaten whole, as its skin is fragrant and sweet, although the flesh is somewhat sour. Yellow when ripe (as pictured here). Mainly used for the rich quantity of essential oil found in its zest.

9. Lime: refreshing and full of juice, which is used in numerous tropical dishes. Its zest is also very fragrant.

10. & 11. Sorrento lemon and Fino lemon: the Sorrento is protected by Italian Product of Geographical Indication status. Is appreciated for its mild-flavored flesh with few seeds, making it ideal for salads, juicing, and for making Limoncello. The thin-skinned Fino owes its popularity to its abundant, fragrant juice.

12. Grapefruit: often confused with the pomelo (which is frequently referred to as a grapefruit; see no. 13). Originated in Asia and is identifiable by its size (approximately 1 lb./500 g, but can weigh as much as 16 lb./8 kg) and its thick skin, numerous seeds, and dense pulp. Excellent in sweet or savory salads.

13. Pink pomelo: often called a grapefruit in error. Can be pink or white, and is thin-skinned and almost seedless. Appreciated for its slightly bitter flavor, whether used for its juice or in segments.

14. Kumquat: so thin-skinned that it can be eaten without peeling, but watch out for the seeds! Delicious when candied.

15. Clementine: a cross between a mandarin (small acidulous citrus fruit with lots of seeds) and a Seville orange (bitter orange). Very easy to peel, with mild, sweet flesh, it has become one of the most popular citrus fruits. Is rarely cooked.

16. Calamondin, also known as *kalamansi*: when unripe, the skin is green but the flesh is always orange. At once sweet, acidulous, and bitter, with an original, exotic note. Widely consumed in Southeast Asia, particularly in the Philippines.

17. & 18. Salustiana juice orange and navel orange: broadly speaking, there are two types of orange: juicing oranges, such as Salustiana—the quintessential juice orange, with soft flesh and abundant juice—and firm-fleshed ones, low in juice, for eating. The different varieties are available one after another during winter, juicing oranges being by far the most popular. Navel oranges (18) are so-called for the navel-like protrusion at their apex.

Plums

1. Mirabelles de Lorraine, also known as mirabelle plums: the name stems from the word *mirabilis* meaning "admirable," accurately describing the honeyed flavor of this tiny plum. Available for a short time when in season. Delicious eaten fresh or made into tarts, jams, and fruit brandies.

2. President: an end-of-season plum. Its sweet, juicy, and slightly acidulous flavor is delicious in tarts, compotes, and jams.

3. Greengage, also known as Reine-Claude: there are many varieties of this green plum with yellow tints. The most fragrant is the green or golden variety. For eating fresh or cooking.

4. Golden Japan: one of the earliest ripening varieties. Sweet but has a delicate flavor. Best eaten fresh.

5. Victoria: a popular English plum, with red or purple skin and sweet, golden-colored flesh. Good eaten fresh or used in preserves.

Tropical Fruits

1. Yellow Cavendish banana: the most widely consumed dessert bananas in the world.

2. Plantain: larger than dessert bananas and need to be cooked as their flesh is very firm. Purple or black when mature. Can be boiled whole or their flesh sliced and fried.

3. Lady Finger banana: these mini bananas are firmer in texture than traditional yellow bananas and more fragrant.

4. & 5. Green Thai mango and mature Thai mango: certain varieties of Thai mango are only eaten when green. Slightly acidulous with the flavor of fresh almonds, their flesh can be used for spicy salads. Asian mangoes are smaller in size than the African and Brazilian varieties and their flesh turns yellow rather than orange when ripe. Their flavor is more delicate and fragrant.

6. Kent mango: partially red when ripe, with a juicy, sweet texture that is not fibrous, making it particularly pleasant to eat.

7. Cayenne pineapple: by far the most cultivated in the world.

8. Sugarloaf pineapple: grown in Guadeloupe (and sometimes called Guadeloupe pineapple) and Benin. Its flesh can be white or yellow. A particularly sweet and fragrant variety.

9. Victoria pineapple: small in size and exclusively grown on the island of Réunion, east of Madagascar, in the Indian Ocean. Renowned for its intense flavor.

Fruits

1., 2., 3. & 4. Hass (aka Haas) avocado, Brazil avocado, bacon avocado, cocktail (aka baby) avocado: although a tropical fruit, the avocado is normally eaten in savory dishes, except in Brazil, where it is widely consumed as a dessert. The pit of the cocktail avocado is tender when the fruit is cut in two, as it is still forming: this variety can simply be peeled and eaten without having to remove the pit.

5. Pomegranate: indispensable in Middle Eastern cuisine, and is eaten dried in India, as well as in the form of tangy molasses. Was often used to provide the necessary note of acidity to balance flavors in certain recipes, for which lemon or lime juice is now usually used.

6. Kiwi: can be green, yellow, or red inside. Avoid blending or mixing in a food processor, as the seeds can cause a stinging sensation in your mouth.

7. Persimmon: soft-textured varieties should be eaten very ripe with a spoon; firmer ones can be cut into pieces more easily. Their flavor is an acquired taste, at once sweet and astringent. Can be used for making jam.

8. & 9. Lychee and rambutan: have a pearly appearance and delicate texture when peeled, and are very sweet. Keep better when bought in a bunch and are best eaten raw.

10. Physalis, also known as Cape gooseberry or ground-cherry: from the same family as the tomato and eggplant. Should always be eaten when fully ripe—indicated by a strong orange color—with its papery calyx removed once dried out. Can be sautéed, added to a compote, or simply used as a decorative and tasty garnish.

11. Mangosteen: originally from Southeast Asia. Its flesh is particularly rich in antioxidants. Good in fruit salads or sorbets.

12 & 13. Passion fruit: wrinkled when fully ripe. The pulp is most easily removed with a spoon. Can have brown or yellow skin (both shown here), with no change to their tangy flavor.

1. Sapodilla: very sweet, with a flavor reminiscent of peach, pear, and vanilla. Rich in fiber and potassium. Has a pit that needs removing before eating.

2. *Pitaya*, also known as dragon fruit: a cactus fruit. The interior can be white, yellow (the sweetest), or pink (the most flavorsome)—all three have flesh dotted with little black seeds, similar to a kiwi.

3. Papaya: when green, it is often grated and used in salads, particularly in Asia. Turns orange when fully ripe, and is sweet and bursting with flavor.

4. Star fruit, also known as carambola: when sliced, it has the form of a five-pointed star. Essentially decorative, as it is sharp with an unremarkable flavor.

5. Cherimoya, also known as sugar apple: a bumpy green exterior conceals fragrant, creamy-textured, white flesh. Avoid eating the seeds.

6. Guava: its green skin develops small black or red markings when ripe. Has orange flesh with a distinctive pronounced fragrance. Valued for its rich vitamin C and calcium content. Can be used for juices, sorbets, syrups, fruit jellies, etc.

7. Soursop: not to be confused with the durian, another tropical fruit with spiny skin. Sweet and tangy, its white flesh is similar to a lychee.

8. Jackfruit: can weigh as much as 66 lb. (30 kg), so typically sold in slices (as pictured here). Has a similar flavor to pineapple and mango. Its seeds are poisonous if consumed raw, but once cooked they can be ground and added to spicy sauces.

Dried Fruits

Good to know: dates and figs are sometimes sprinkled with flour to prevent them sticking together. Those with a gluten intolerance should check products carefully before purchasing or eating.

1. & 2. Banana chips and whole dried bananas: very rich in magnesium and potassium. Can be eaten as a snack, with aperitifs, or whole. Do not need to be rehydrated.

3. Pineapple.

4. Mango: drying tropical fruits, such as mango, allows you to enjoy them all year round! If you soak them, keep the liquid for adding to a smoothie or for sweetening a hot drink.

5. Agen prunes: very rich in antioxidants and fiber, prunes are the least known "superfruit" yet one of the most accessible. Those from Agen, in southwest France, are particularly fine.

6. Cranberries: when dried, they lose the sharpness that they have when fresh, and become even richer in nutrients.

7. Calabacita figs.

8. Andalusian *figuettes*: small, very sweet figs dried on the tree for an intense flavor.

9. & 10. Golden raisins (sultanas) and raisins: sweet, with an unremarkable flavor. Provide a good source of energy.

11. Griotte cherries: when dried, their acidity is tempered.

12. Goji berries: small Chinese berries, rich in antioxidants, with a sharp, bitter flavor.

13. White mulberries: originate from China where they are traditionally used, as well as in Middle Eastern cuisine. More commonly red or black, but the white variety is set to become the latest superfood, with its high levels of antioxidants and its low sugar content. Sweet but with a less pronounced taste than black mulberries.

14., 15. & 16. Medjool dates, Mazafati dates from Iran, and Deglet Nour dates: one of the sweetest and richest dried fruits. Rarely eaten fresh. Frequently used in vegan pastry-making and baking for sweetening and for binding ingredients.

17. Apricots: their dark color, as shown here, indicates the absence of preservatives—a sign of certified organic dried fruits.

Rhizomes

1. Galangal, also known as Thai ginger: used extensively in Thailand, Malaysia, and Indonesia. It is not essential to peel it. Hotter and spicier than ginger, with a camphorated flavor. Used to add fragrance to broths and curries.

2. Fingerroot (*Boesenbergia rotunda*), also known as Chinese ginger: from the same family as galangal and used in Thai curry pastes. Less hot and earthier than galangal, it also colors food a pale yellow.

3. Turmeric, also known as curcuma: has a spicy, slightly bitter flavor and is frequently used in curries; it also imparts a bright yellow color to dishes. Fresh turmeric stains, so avoid using white plastic utensils which will be discolored irredeemably, and rinse all utensils used immediately. The same applies to your hands: disposable gloves are recommended.

4. & 5. Ginger and young ginger: deliciously lemony and mildly spicy. Usually comes from Africa or Asia. When young, it has thin skin and white flesh with a more pronounced floral flavor. Grated, or sliced for infusions, it is a natural flavor enhancer, indispensable for vegetarian cooking. Can also be preserved in vinegar for serving with sushi, or candied to be enjoyed at the end of a meal. (See technique for peeling p. 29).

Vegetable Seasons

Type of Vegetable	Jan	Feb	Mar	Apr	May	Jun	Jul	Aug	Sep	Oct	Nov	Dec
Artichoke				N	N	N	N	N	N			
Artichoke, Jerusalem	N	N	N			S	S				N	N
Asparagus, green	S			N	N	N						S
Asparagus, white	S			N	N	N						S
Beans, fava (broad)	S	S	S			N	N	N		S	S	S
Beans, green	S	S				N	N	N	N	N	S	S
Beets (beetroot)	N	N	N	N	N	N	N	N	N	N	N	N
Bell pepper	S	S	S			N	N	N	N	S	S	S
Bok choy	N	N	N	N	N	N	N	N	N	N	N	N
Broccoli	N	N	N	N	N	N	N	N	N	N	N	N
Brussels sprouts	N	N	N						N	N	N	N
Cabbage, green	N	N	N	N	N	N	N	N	N	N	N	N
Cabbage, Napa (Chinese)	N	N	N	N	N	N	N	N	N	N	N	N
Cabbage, red	N	N	N	N	N	N	N	N	N	N	N	N
Cabbage, white	N	N	N	N	N	N	N	N	N	N	N	N
Carrot	N	N	N	N	N	N	N	N	N	N	N	N
Cauliflower	N	N	N	N	N	N	N	N	N	N	N	N
Cauliflower, romanesco	N	N	N	N	N				N	N	N	N
Celeriac	N	N	N						N	N	N	N
Celery	N	N	N	N	N	N	N	N	N	N	N	N
Chayote	S			N	N				S	S	S	S
Corn						N	N	N	N	S	S	S
Crosne (Chinese artichoke)	N	N	N							N	N	N
Cucumber	S	S	N	N	N	N	N	N	S	S	S	S
Curly endive & escarole	S	S	S			N	N	N	N	S	S	S
Eggplant (aubergine)	S	S	S			N	N	N	N	S	S	S
Endive (chicory)	N	N	N						N	N	N	N
Fennel	S	S	S			N	N	N	N	S	S	S
Garlic	N	N	N	N	N	N	N	N	N	N	N	N
Kale	N	N	N			S	S	S		N	N	N
Leeks	N	N	N	N					N	N	N	N
Lettuce	N	N	N	N	N	N	N	N	N	N	N	N
Marrow	S	S				N	N	N	N	S	S	S
Mushroom	N	N	N	N	N	N	N	N	N	N	N	N
Onion	N	N	N	N	N	N	N	N	N	N	N	N
Parsnip	N	N	N	N					N	N	N	N
Peas	S	S	S			N	N	N	N	N	S	S
Potato	N	N	N	N	N	N	N	N	N	N	N	N
Pumpkin			S	S	S				N	N	N	
Radish	N	N	N	N	N	N	N	N	N	N	N	N
Radish, black	N	N	N						N	N	N	N
Radish, red	N	N	N	N	N	N	N	N	N	N	N	N
Rutabaga (swede)	N	N	N						N	N	N	N
Scorzonera (salsify)	N	N	N						N	N	N	N
Shallot	N	N	N	N	N	N	N	N	N	N	N	N
Sorrel			N	N	N	N	N		S	S		
Spinach	N	N	N	N	N	N	N	N	N	N	N	N
Squash, summer	S	S	S			N	N	N	N		S	S
Squash, winter	N	N								N	N	N
Sugar snap peas	S	S		N	N	N				S	S	S
Sweet potato	N	N	N	N	N	N	N	N	N	N	N	N
Swiss chard	N	N	N	N	N	N	N	N	N	N	N	N
Turnip	N	N	N	N					N	N	N	N
Watercress	N	N	N	N	N	N	N	N	N	N	N	N
Zucchini (courgette)	S	S	S			N	N	N	N	S	S	S

Legend:
- N = Northern Hemisphere season
- S = Southern Hemisphere season
- blank = Not usually grown

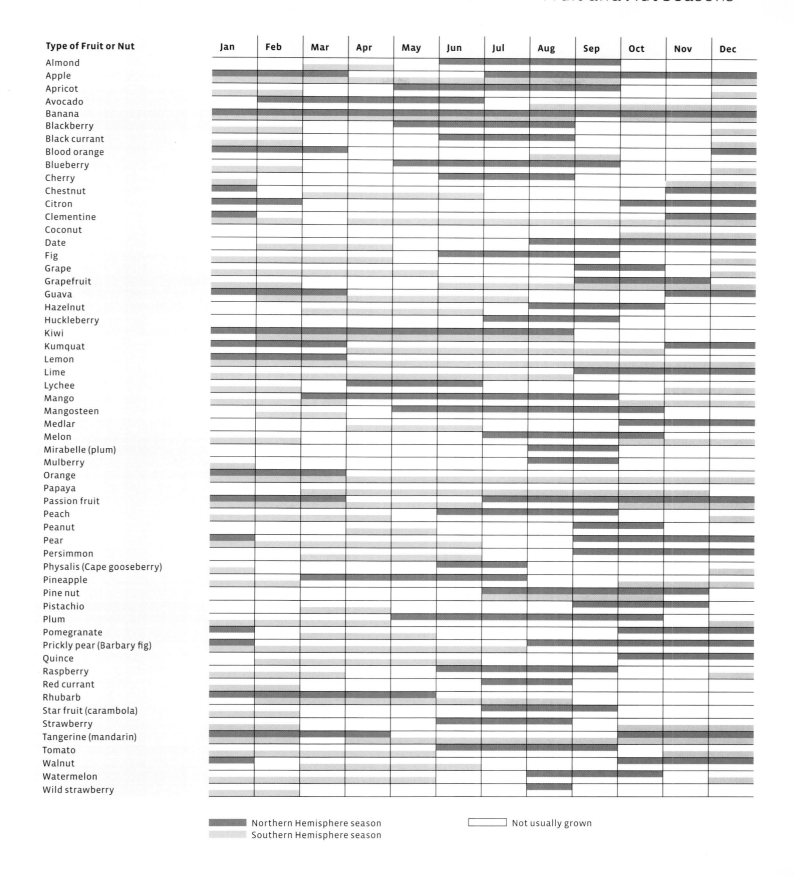

Type of Fruit or Nut	Jan	Feb	Mar	Apr	May	Jun	Jul	Aug	Sep	Oct	Nov	Dec
Almond												
Apple												
Apricot												
Avocado												
Banana												
Blackberry												
Black currant												
Blood orange												
Blueberry												
Cherry												
Chestnut												
Citron												
Clementine												
Coconut												
Date												
Fig												
Grape												
Grapefruit												
Guava												
Hazelnut												
Huckleberry												
Kiwi												
Kumquat												
Lemon												
Lime												
Lychee												
Mango												
Mangosteen												
Medlar												
Melon												
Mirabelle (plum)												
Mulberry												
Orange												
Papaya												
Passion fruit												
Peach												
Peanut												
Pear												
Persimmon												
Physalis (Cape gooseberry)												
Pineapple												
Pine nut												
Pistachio												
Plum												
Pomegranate												
Prickly pear (Barbary fig)												
Quince												
Raspberry												
Red currant												
Rhubarb												
Star fruit (carambola)												
Strawberry												
Tangerine (mandarin)												
Tomato												
Walnut												
Watermelon												
Wild strawberry												

Northern Hemisphere season
Southern Hemisphere season
Not usually grown

1

2

3

4

5

6

7

8

9

10

11

12

13

14

15

16

17

Basic Equipment

Graters and mandolins

These three items of equipment are indispensable for preparing vegetables.

Four-sided box grater (1): for grating root vegetables—carrots, parsnips, etc.—quickly and efficiently, and slicing potatoes thinly or thickly. It can also be used to grate tomatoes directly over dishes or into the pan—a very practical method from Spain!

Microplane® grater (2): for zesting citrus fruits precisely, without the bitter pith. Can also be used for Parmesan-style hard cheeses, nutmeg, chocolate, garlic, and ginger—it does everything! A kitchen tool that every chef has to hand.

Japanese mandolin (3): should always be used with a pusher to protect the tips of your fingers (see technique p. 40). It enables you to cut extra-thin slices or julienne vegetables in varying thicknesses, uniformly and with close precision. Light and easy to handle, it allows you to create a whole range of interesting shapes and textures from raw vegetables.

Fry cutter (4): some would call it a gadget, others consider it essential—it all depends on how many people you are cooking for! Can also be used for zucchini or pieces of celeriac.

Sprouting jars

There are sophisticated sprouters on the market with hydration and ventilation, but the simplest and most economical system is a jar with an open lattice top **(6)**. It should be slightly inclined to allow thorough draining, and it can be used to sprout alfalfa, radish, leek, etc. seeds easily.

For mucilaginous seeds such as flax, chia, cress, and arugula, and for wheat, it is preferable and much more practical to use a container fitted with a mesh **(5)**, which allows you to snip the shoots above it, leaving the roots below.

Blender (7)

Models can be more or less powerful, but it is preferable to choose one with a glass jar. Indispensable for making smoothies, soups, nut or grain purees, nondairy milks, etc. It is better to use the pulse setting when blending hard ingredients, or if possible buy one with an "ice crusher" function. Certain high-powered brands such as Vitamix are particularly well-suited for vegetarian mixtures and green smoothies, but they are a considerable investment.

Stand mixer (8)

Very useful for preparing doughs (pizza, brioche, etc.) and whisking egg whites to the perfect stiffness for meringues. It frees your hands to do other things, but this time-saving benefit is reflected in the price.

Juice extractor (9)

Fruit and vegetable juices are extracted with the aid of an Archimedes' screw turning at a minimum of eighty revolutions per minute, then filtered in the machine to obtain a pulp-free juice. It should not be confused with a centrifuge which works at high speed and oxidizes the juice. Particularly tasty and rich in nutrients, juice extracted in a juicer will keep for a day. The juice can also be used as a cooking liquid. Juice extractors can make ice cream from frozen fruits and grind ingredients in the same way as a pestle for hummus, pesto, etc., if the filter is removed first. Be sure to choose a model that is easy to clean and maintain—that's the key to using it frequently. (See technique p. 32.)

Equipment for dairy products and vegetable milks

Fine-mesh sieve (14): a multi-purpose utensil, essential for rinsing sprouting grains, washing quinoa, and draining pulses.

For draining curds when making strained yogurt or vegetable milks, a sieve lined with a **cheesecloth (10)** is used, or a **nut milk bag (13)** with strings to draw it up, making draining easier.

For tofu, a **wooden mold (11)** is traditionally used, lined with cheesecloth. However, it is now often replaced by **plastic molds (12)**, like the soft white cheese mold shown.

Mini-blender (15)

Useful for grinding in small quantities, blending freshly roasted spices, or making a quick dairy cream substitute. This small grinder is an essential piece of equipment, especially if it has several bowls and blades. The brand Personal Blender is a very simple model, but robust, and takes up very little space on a work surface.

Steamers

Bamboo baskets (16): traditionally used in Asian cuisine, it is the hardest to maintain. It is worth lining the base with parchment paper pierced in several places to protect it.

Metal steam basket (17): for placing in a pan over boiling water. It is the lightest and most practical piece of equipment for steaming many types of vegetables, gently reheating foods, or softening seitan (see technique p. 69).

Recipes

Solaris
by Pietro Leemann, 209

Vegetables

Pietro Leemann

Pietro Leemann was the first chef in Europe to be awarded a Michelin star (in 1996) for a vegetarian restaurant. After working with Freddy Girardet and Gualtiero Marchesi, he traveled through Asia, which was where he decided to become a vegetarian, at twenty-five years old. In 1989, he opened his own restaurant, Joia, in Milan, inspired by his discovery of the many vegetarian culinary traditions in cuisines from around the world.

His personal cooking style sums up both his travels and his philosophy: what we eat transforms us, and our food is a lifestyle choice that exerts an influence on our consciousness. Vegetarianism benefits our health, the climate, and animal welfare; it allows us to live in peace with the world and with ourselves, thus encouraging spiritual elevation.

Leemann, who founded the international cooking contest "The Vegetarian Chance"—in which non-vegetarian chefs are invited to prove their creativity by inventing vegetarian and vegan dishes—emphasizes that vegetarianism is not a constraint, but rather a boundless source of inspiration and a means to endless gastronomic discoveries.

Solaris, one of his signature dishes, is an ode to vegetables.

Joia
18 Via Panfilo Castaldi
Milan 20124
Italy

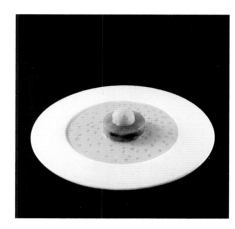

Serves 4
Preparation time: 1 hour
Cooking time: 2 hours 30 minutes
Resting time: 1 hour 15 minutes

Ingredients
5 oz. (150 g) red bell peppers
3 ½ oz. (100 g) yellow bell peppers
7 oz. (200 g) eggplant (aubergines)
3 ½ oz. (100 g) cherry tomatoes
1 oz. (30 g) tapioca
2 ½ tablespoons (40 ml) extra-virgin olive oil
1 g (approximately ¼ teaspoon) agar-agar
1 pinch saffron threads
3 ½ oz. (100 g) carrots
2 ½ tablespoons (40 ml) orange juice
2 teaspoons (5 g) oregano
Fine salt and freshly ground pepper

Melon sorbet
7 oz. (200 g) melon, such as cantaloupe
2 ½ tablespoons (1 oz./30 g) sugar
1 tablespoon plus 1 teaspoon (20 ml) lemon
  juice

To serve
1 tablespoon plus 1 teaspoon (20 ml)
  extra-virgin olive oil
²/₃ oz. (20 g) pureed raspberries

Equipment
Four 3-inch (8-cm) molds

Solaris

A refreshing composition of eggplants, tomatoes, peppers, and oregano from my vege-table garden, served with melon sorbet.

Place the peppers in a hot oven for 20 minutes, then peel off the skin. Cut the egg-plant into 1 ¼-inch (3-cm) slices and broil them. Dip the cherry tomatoes into boiling water, remove the skins, and dry them in a 175°F (80°C/Gas Mark ¼) oven for 2 hours.

Soak the tapioca in ²/₃ cup (150 ml) water for 3 minutes. Simmer gently over low heat for 25 minutes and season with salt and olive oil. Stir the agar-agar into 1 ¼ cups (300 ml) boiling water and cook for 2 minutes. Take ¹/₃ cup (80 ml) of the liquid (the remaining liquid will keep for up to 4 days) and combine it with the tapioca, then add the saffron to ¹/₃ of the tapioca mixture.

Soften the carrots well in a little olive oil. Blend them with the orange juice and season with salt. Blend the melon and add the sugar and lemon juice. Process in an ice-cream maker.

Combine the sliced vegetables with the remaining tapioca and oregano leaves. Spoon the saffron-flavored tapioca into the bottom of the molds and allow to set for 15 minutes. Fill the molds with the vegetable and tapioca mixture. Chill for at least 1 hour.

To serve
Turn the terrines onto four flat dishes and drizzle the carrot sauce around. Drip a little olive oil into each plate: the drops mirror the tapioca. Proceed in the same way with the raspberry puree. Top with a scoop of melon sorbet and serve.

● Good to know
During the Cold War, American Stanley Kubrick's movie 2001: A Space Odyssey *was released. (With hindsight, we now know its depiction of the future wasn't quite accurate; George Orwell was closer to the truth.) Russia responded with Andrei Tarkovsky's movie* Solaris. *It was also the era of the space race, a time of cultural and creative effervescence, one that left its mark on me. Here, Solaris is the sun—a symbol transformed into substance.*

Ingredients

Soup
2 ¼ lb. (1 kg) pumpkin (before trimming), of the variety of your choice
1 onion
1 tablespoon olive oil
1 clove garlic
3 ¼ cups (800 ml) vegetable broth
1 bay leaf
Grated zest of ½ unwaxed orange
½ teaspoon fine sea salt
²/₃ cup (150 ml) whipping cream or nondairy cream substitute, such as soy or oat
Freshly ground pepper

Tempura
¹/₃ cup (80 ml) water
1 handful ice cubes
Scant ½ cup (100 ml) peanut oil, or other oil for frying
½ cup (2 oz./60 g) all-purpose flour
12 large sage leaves, washed and well dried

Equipment
Blender
Chopsticks

Techniques
Preparing Squash, p. 17
Preparing Garlic, p. 29
Blending Soup, p. 32

Creamed Pumpkin Soup and Sage Tempura ★★

Serves 4
Preparation time: 20 minutes
Cooking time: 25 minutes

For the soup
Peel the pumpkin, remove the seeds, and cut the flesh into 1-inch (3-cm) cubes. Peel and dice the onion. Crush the garlic clove and peel it.

In a large pot over medium heat, heat the oil. Sauté the onion and garlic until lightly colored. Add the pumpkin cubes and sauté them. Pour in the vegetable broth and add the bay leaf, orange zest, and salt. Bring to a boil, cover with the lid, reduce the heat, and simmer for 20 minutes.

Discard the bay leaf and, with a slotted spoon or skimmer, transfer the pumpkin cubes to the blender. Add half of the cooking liquid and the cream and blend until smooth. Season with pepper and add salt if necessary. You can adjust the texture of the soup by adding more of the cooking liquid.

For the tempura
Combine the water and ice cubes. Allow 10 minutes for the water to chill well and the ice cubes to be almost melted.

Pour the oil into a pot or deep fryer, and heat.

Meanwhile, pour the chilled water into a soup plate and sift the flour directly into it. Using chopsticks, quickly incorporate the flour into the water; the aim is not to form a smooth batter. Dip the sage leaves into the batter and, working in batches of six, drop them into the oil. Fry until golden (about 1 minute) and remove with a skimmer. Place them on a plate and cover with a sheet of paper towel. Use the skimmer to remove any bits of batter floating in the oil and repeat the procedure for the remaining sage leaves.

Serve the soup, well heated, with the sage tempura.

● Chef's notes
Make sure that the sage leaves are completely dry before you dip them in the tempura batter: this prevents splashes of oil.
The tempura batter should be mixed as little as possible to retain its lightness and ensure it is crisp when fried. Combining the ingredients quickly with chopsticks ensures that the gluten in the flour does not develop its elasticity.

● Good to know
The soup can be frozen for up to two months.
You can also use other varieties of squash, or sweet potatoes.

Caesar Salad ★

Serves 4
Preparation time: 35 minutes
Cooking time: 3 minutes

A day ahead, prepare the garlic oil. Peel the cloves and remove the green shoots. Place the cloves in a jar. In a small saucepan over low heat, gently heat the olive oil until it is warm. Pour it over the garlic cloves, seal the jar, and leave to infuse at room temperature.

The next day, preheat the oven to broil. Grate 2 oz. (60 g) of the cheese. Filter the garlic-flavored oil. Remove the crust of the bread and cut it into chunks. Place them in a single layer in a large ovenproof dish or on a baking sheet. Drizzle with 3 tablespoons of the olive oil and sprinkle with 3 tablespoons of the grated cheese and some pepper. Combine with your hands to coat the bread chunks well. Toast them, stirring frequently, and keeping a careful eye on them, until nicely golden.

Pick off the leaves of the romaine lettuces, trimming them if necessary; wash and dry them carefully. Squeeze the lemon.

Cook the egg in boiling water for 3 minutes. Shell it and place in the bowl of the food processor fitted with a blade knife. Add the remaining grated cheese and begin processing, drizzling in the remaining garlic-flavored olive oil, Worcestershire sauce, lemon juice, and salt. Season with pepper and check if extra salt is required.

Pour the dressing into a salad bowl and add the lettuce and croutons. Combine carefully.

Make shavings with the remaining cheese and stir them carefully into the salad, ensuring that they do not break.

● **Chef's notes**
Garlic-flavored olive oil is a delicious base for seasoning. It keeps for up to 1 week in the refrigerator, so when you prepare it, make more than you need immediately and use it for other recipes.

● **Good to know**
The Caesar salad, invented on July 4, 1924, by Caesar Cardini at the restaurant of the Caesar Hotel in Tijuana, Mexico, was concocted on the spur of the moment using ingredients the chef had to hand. It was prepared in front of the restaurant's clients and was an immediate hit. Unfortunately, mayonnaise has often replaced the original sauce, but a lightly cooked egg makes all the difference in achieving a creamy texture for the dressing.
A traditional Caesar salad uses Parmigiano Reggiano, or Parmesan, which contains animal rennet so is not vegetarian. Non-vegetarians should feel free to substitute Parmesan.
Worcestershire sauce is another non-vegetarian ingredient, as it contains anchovies, but there are vegetarian and vegan versions available.

Ingredients
3 cloves garlic
Scant ½ cup (100 ml) extra-virgin olive oil
3 ½ oz. (100 g) vegetarian Parmesan-style hard cheese
3 ½ oz. (100 g) day-old or dried bread (sourdough bread, ciabatta, baguette, etc.)
2 romaine lettuces

Dressing
1 egg
2 teaspoons vegetarian or vegan Worcestershire sauce
1 lemon
½ teaspoon fine salt
½ teaspoon freshly ground pepper

Equipment
Food processor

Techniques
Preparing Garlic, p. 29
Hard-Boiling Eggs, p. 104

Ingredients

2 carrots

2 floury potatoes

7 oz. (200 g) pumpkin in winter, or zucchini
(courgettes) in summer

1 onion

2 stalks celery

14 oz. (400 g) Tuscan black kale

3 ½ oz. (100 g) green beans, fresh or frozen

3 tablespoons olive oil, plus a little more
for serving

6 cups (1.5 liters) water

1 bouquet garni

3 ½ oz. (100 g) fresh spinach or green part of
Swiss chard leaves

2 oz. (50 g) pasta for soup, such as *ditalini* or
elbow pasta

3 ½ oz. (100 g) freshly grated vegetarian
Parmesan-style hard cheese

Cannellini beans

¾ cup (5 oz./150 g) dried cannellini beans

6 cups (1.5 liters) water

1 onion

3 cloves

2 sprigs thyme

1 bay leaf

Minestrone ★

Serves 4

Soaking time: 12 hours or overnight

Preparation time: 30 minutes

Cooking time: 1 hour 30 minutes, plus 30 minutes

Twelve hours ahead, soak the cannellini beans. Drain and cook them according to the instructions on p. 82, adding the onion studded with the cloves, the thyme, and the bay leaf to the cooking water. Cook for 1 hour 30 minutes and drain.

Peel the carrots, potatoes, and pumpkin. Cut the vegetables into small cubes of the same size. Peel and dice the onion. Slice the celery stalks. Carefully wash the Tuscan black kale, remove any thick ribs, and slice roughly. Trim the green beans and cut them into small pieces.

In a pot over high heat, heat the olive oil. Soften the onion and celery. Add the pumpkin, carrots, potatoes, Tuscan kale, water, and bouquet garni. Bring to a boil, cover with the lid, reduce the heat, and simmer for 20 minutes. Stir, crushing the potatoes. Add the green beans, spinach, pasta, and cooked cannellini beans. Bring to a boil again and boil for 8 to 10 minutes.

Adjust the seasoning and serve with the grated cheese and a drizzle of olive oil.

● Chef's notes

For a version that's quick to prepare, use canned cannellini beans. Rinse them carefully and add them to the soup as above. Like all soups made with pulses, minestrone tastes even better when reheated gently the following day and served with large slices of toasted country bread.

● Good to know

In northern Italy, there are as many variations of minestrone—which literally means "substantial soup"—as there are regions. Tuscan black kale, as its name indicates, is typical of Tuscany, where ribollita *("reboiled") is a unique type of minestrone. In Genoa, pasta is added. In Lombardy and the Piedmont,* arborio rice, *the type used for risotto, is a typical ingredient. Elsewhere, ditalini pasta is added. Some cooks slip in some pork; others don't. It is all a question of season and local produce. Parmesan is traditionally used and its rind is included because it provides a concentrate of flavors; it thickens the liquid and gives the soup its unique taste, but you can make it without for a 100 percent vegetarian version.*

Techniques

Preparing Swiss Chard, p. 15

Making a Bouquet Garni, p. 30

Cooking Pulses, p. 82

Colcannon ★

Irish Mashed Potatoes with Cabbage and Parsnips

Serves 4
Preparation time: 30 minutes
Cooking time: 40 minutes

Peel the potatoes and parsnips and cut them into large cubes. Place them in a large pot of salted water over high heat and bring to a boil. Reduce the heat and simmer for 25 minutes, until tender.

Shred the cabbage and dice the white part of the scallions. In a skillet over low heat, melt half of the butter. Add the cabbage and diced scallion and sauté them gently (they should render their water but not color). Season with salt, cover with the lid, and continue cooking over low heat for 15 minutes, until the cabbage is tender.

Scald the milk. With a vegetable mill or fork, mash the potatoes and parsnips, gradually adding the warmed milk. Reserve some of it to adjust the texture, depending on how thick or creamy you like the mash. Stir in the cabbage and scallion. If necessary, add a little milk at this stage.

Slice the green stalks of the scallions. Dice the remaining butter and stir it into the mixture with the sliced scallion. Season with salt and pepper and stir again.

Serve with extra butter for the guests to add if they wish.

● Chef's notes
You can replace up to half of the quantity of the potatoes with extra parsnips.

● Good to know
In Ireland, it is custom to abstain from meat on All Saints'—or All Hallows'—Eve. Since the eighteenth century, this has been one of the traditional dishes eaten on that occasion.

Techniques
Preparing Parsnips, p. 21
Making Potato Puree, p. 28

Ingredients
1 ¾ lb. (800 g) floury potatoes
7 oz. (200 g) parsnips
¼ green cabbage (7 oz./200 g),
or equivalent weight in kale
3 scallions (spring onions)
7 tablespoons (100 g) butter,
plus a little extra to serve
⅔–¾ cup (150–200 ml) whole milk
Fine salt and freshly ground pepper

Ingredients

Spice mix

2 cardamom pods
1 ½ teaspoons coriander seeds
1 teaspoon fennel seeds
8 black peppercorns
1 clove
1 cinnamon stick
1 teaspoon ground turmeric

Curry

14 oz. (400 g) trimmed cauliflower
1 sweet potato (approximately 8 oz./250 g)
1 onion
1 ¼-inch (3-cm) piece fresh ginger
2 tomatoes or scant ½ cup (100 ml) *passata* (strained tomatoes)
2 tablespoons ghee or coconut oil
¾ cup (200 ml) coconut milk
2 cups (10 oz./300 g) cooked chickpeas

Chickpea Curry with Cauliflower, Sweet Potatoes, and Coconut Milk ★

Serves 4
Preparation time: 30 minutes
Cooking time: 45 minutes

For the spice mix

Slit the cardamom pods and take out the black seeds inside. Place all the spices with the exception of the turmeric in a heavy-bottom pan over medium-high heat. Heat the spices, stirring constantly. When the spices begin popping, transfer them to a plate and allow to cool. Add the turmeric to the mixture and use a coffee mill or spice grinder to grind them to a powder.

For the curry

Cut the cauliflower into florets. Peel and dice the sweet potato. Peel and dice the onion. Peel and grate the ginger. Roughly chop the tomatoes.

In a large skillet over high heat, melt the ghee. Add the spice mix and heat for 10 seconds, until fragrant, then add the onion and ginger. Sauté until very lightly colored for 2 minutes and add the cauliflower and sweet potato. Then stir in the tomato *passata*, coconut milk, and a scant ½ cup (100 ml) of water. Season lightly with salt.

Reduce the heat to low, cover with the lid and simmer for 20 minutes, adding a little water if necessary and stirring two or three times. Stir in the chickpeas and cook for an additional 5 minutes. Serve with rice and chopped cilantro (coriander leaves).

● Chef's notes

If you wish, replace the sweet potato with pumpkin. For a version suitable for vegans, be sure to use coconut oil.
You can replace the spice mix with 1 tablespoon of Bombay curry powder. If you are a fan of spicy food, add a chopped fresh chili pepper of your choice to the sauce (see technique p. 23).

Techniques

Peeling Fresh Ginger, p. 29
Dicing Onions, p. 39
Cooking Pulses, p. 82
Making Clarified Butter and Ghee, p. 113

Lasagna ★★

Serves 6
Preparation time: 30 minutes
Cooking time: 35 minutes

For the tomato sauce with vegetables
Peel and dice the winter vegetables. Peel the onion, garlic, and carrot and dice them finely. Chop the celery stalk finely. In a skillet over high heat, heat the olive oil. Add the onion, garlic, carrot, and celery to the pan and lightly color for 2 to 3 minutes. Add the other vegetables, stir, and pour in the tomato *passata* and red wine. Add the bouquet garni, peperoncino, salt, and pepper. Bring to a boil, cover with the lid, reduce the heat, and simmer for 20 to 25 minutes, depending on the type of vegetables used, until they are fairly tender but retain some firmness. If necessary, add a little water as they cook: the preparation should not become too dry.

For the spinach
If you are using fresh spinach, remove the stems. In a nonstick pan over high heat, cook the spinach for 1 minute, or until wilted. Drain well. If you are using frozen spinach, defrost and drain well. Peel and dice the onion. Sauté in the olive oil until lightly colored, add the spinach, and cook for 2 to 3 minutes. Remove from the heat and stir in the ricotta, cream, and nutmeg. Season to taste with salt and pepper.

To assemble and cook
Preheat the oven to 350°F (180°C/Gas Mark 4). Oil a rectangular or square ovenproof dish. Spread 2 to 3 tablespoons of the tomato sauce with vegetables over the bottom and cover completely with sheets of lasagna. Spread one third of the spinach mix over the lasagna sheets and cover this with another layer of lasagna sheets. Spread half of the tomato sauce with vegetables over the sheets and then cover with another layer of sheets. Repeat until you have used up all the ingredients, finishing with a layer of spinach mix. Sprinkle the top with the grated cheese.

Bake for 30 minutes. If necessary, brown the top very briefly under the broiler.

● Chef's notes

Root vegetables and other firm-textured vegetables, including squash, greatly improve when simmered in a sauce.
This lasagna dish can be prepared up to 2 days ahead of time and refrigerated without the cheese. Sprinkle with cheese just before placing in the oven.
To make a vegan version, simply replace the ricotta with vegan béchamel sauce (see techniques pp. 90 and 121) and the grated cheese with vegan "Parmesan" (see technique p. 124).

Ingredients
10 to 12 sheets of precooked lasagna, depending on the size of the ovenproof dish
1 teaspoon olive oil
3 ½ oz. (100 g) freshly grated vegetarian hard cheese (cheddar, Parmesan-style, etc.)

Tomato sauce with vegetables
1 lb. (500 g) winter vegetables of your choice, preferably firm-textured (pumpkin, sweet potato, turnip, celery, etc.)
1 onion
2 cloves garlic
1 carrot
1 stalk celery
2 tablespoons olive oil
2 ½ cups (600 ml) *passata* (strained tomatoes)
Scant ½ cup (100 ml) red wine
1 bouquet garni
1 pinch (or more, according to taste) ground peperoncino, or other ground chili pepper of your choice
Fine salt and freshly ground pepper

Spinach
2 lb. (1 kg) fresh spinach, or 1 lb. (500 g) frozen spinach leaves
1 onion
2 teaspoons olive oil
1 ⅔ cups (14 oz./400 g) vegetarian ricotta
3 tablespoons heavy cream or crème fraîche
1 small pinch nutmeg
Fine salt and freshly ground pepper

Techniques ❢
Making a Bouquet Garni, p. 30
Dicing Onions, p. 39
Making Vegan Béchamel Sauce, p. 90
Making Béchamel Sauce with Almond Puree, p. 121
Making Vegan "Parmesan," p. 124

Ingredients

7 oz. (200 g) einkorn wheat
2 cloves garlic
3 tablespoons olive oil, plus a little for the dish
1 eggplant (aubergine)
2 large tomatoes
1 zucchini (courgette)
1 red onion
3 sprigs thyme or summer savory
½ teaspoon fennel seeds
1 bay leaf, crumbled
Fine salt and freshly ground pepper

Equipment

7 × 10-inch (19 × 24-cm) earthenware
　ovenproof dish

Techniques
Using a Mandolin, p. 40

Ratatouille *Tian* with Einkorn Wheat ★

Serves 4
Resting time: 12 hours or overnight
Preparation time: 30 minutes
Cooking time: 1 hour 45 minutes

Soak the einkorn wheat for 12 hours in cold water. Rinse and transfer to a pot of boiling salted water for 10 minutes to precook. Drain again.

Preheat the oven to 300°F (150°C/Gas Mark 2).

Peel the garlic cloves. Lightly oil the ovenproof dish and rub it with one garlic clove, crushing it as you do so to extract as much flavor as possible. Chop the other garlic clove.

Rinse and dry the eggplant. Remove the stem and, preferably using a mandolin, cut it into slices ¼ inch (5-7 mm) thick. Remove the bases of the tomatoes and cut them into slices of the same thickness. Do the same with the zucchini and onion.

Spread the einkorn wheat over the bottom of the ovenproof dish. Season with pepper and mix to coat it with the garlic-flavored oil. Arrange the slices of eggplant, zucchini, tomato, and onion in a layer, packing them as closely together as possible–the vegetables will lose volume as they cook. Depending on the size of the dish, you may be able to make two layers of vegetables. Season with salt and pepper. Sprinkle with the thyme or summer savory, fennel seeds, and the crumbled bay leaf. Drizzle with olive oil.

Bake for 45 minutes. Remove the dish from the oven (do not switch it off) and press down lightly with a skimmer: this extracts the juices for the einkorn to cook in below.

Return the dish to the oven and cook for an additional 1 hour to 1 hour 15 minutes, until the vegetables are nicely browned and the einkorn wheat is cooked.

Serve hot or warm.

● Chef's notes
This dish is perfect for a picnic. It can be prepared ahead of time and also reheated. For a variation, use rice instead of einkorn wheat.

● Good to know
In Provençal dialect, tian refers to a varnished ceramic dish, oval or round, with sloping sides, generally about 4 inches (10 cm) high and 12–16 inches (30–40 cm) wide. It was used as a sink, to wash dishes or hands. Since it is glazed, it can be placed in the oven without any problem. Nowadays, tian refers to a glazed gratin dish, usually round and often with a smaller diameter (10 inches/25 cm).

Pea, Spinach, and Sprouted Seed Muffins ★

Makes 14 to 15 muffins
Preparation time: 15 minutes
Cooking time: 30 minutes

Preheat the oven to 350°F (180°C/Gas Mark 4). Line the muffin pans with the paper cases.

Grate the cheese. Pick the leaves off the parsley sprigs and chop them. In a pot of salted boiling water, blanch the peas for 1 minute and drain. Blanch the spinach leaves for the same time. Drain them well, pressing down hard, and chop them finely. Ensure that as much water as possible is discarded.

In a mixing bowl, whisk the eggs with the oil, milk, salt, and pepper. Fold in the flour, baking powder, and grated cheese. Finally, incorporate the peas, spinach, parsley, and mustard. Stop when just combined–do not overwork the batter, as it might become elastic.

Divide the batter among the prepared muffin pans and bake for 25 minutes, until well risen and golden on top and a cake tester inserted into the center comes out dry. Transfer to a rack and leave to cool.

To make the garnish, combine all the ingredients with the exception of the alfalfa seeds. Using a spatula, spread the tops of the muffins with the garnish, sprinkle with the sprouted seeds, and serve.

● Chef's notes
These muffins can be prepared up to 24 hours ahead of time. However, they should not be garnished more than 2 hours before they are served.
Instead of fresh peas, you can use the same quantity of frozen peas. If you are using frozen spinach, however, use only 3 ½ oz. (100 g), and blanch and drain the leaves by pressing hard to extract as much water as possible.

Techniques
Blanching, p. 41
Sprouting Pulses, p. 80

Ingredients
3 ½ oz. (100 g) vegetarian hard cheese
(cheddar, Parmesan-style, etc.)
About 10 sprigs parsley
5 oz. (150 g) peas
8 oz. (250 g) spinach leaves
3 eggs
⅓ cup (80 ml) olive oil
Scant ½ cup (100 ml) reduced fat milk
(cow or soy)
1 ⅔ cups (7 oz./200 g) all-purpose flour
2 ½ teaspoons (10 g) baking powder
2 teaspoons French mustard
Fine salt and freshly ground pepper

Garnish
Generous ½ cup (4 oz./125 g) cream cheese
⅔ cup (5 oz./150 g) mascarpone
2 teaspoons wasabi
2 handfuls sprouted alfalfa seeds
Fine salt and freshly ground pepper

Equipment
Muffin pans
Paper muffin cases

Vegetables

Ingredients

4 cloves garlic, unpeeled

3 ¼ lb. (1.5 kg) root vegetables of your choice
(chervil root [tuberous chervil], Jerusalem
artichokes, parsnips, multicolored carrots,
Chioggia beets, yellow beets, or Gold Ball turnips)

3 tablespoons olive oil

2 teaspoons dried thyme or oregano

½ teaspoon mild chili or paprika

1 teaspoon fleur de sel

1 bay leaf

¼ cup (1 oz./30 g) hazelnuts, crushed/coarsely
chopped

Sauce

1 small scallion (spring onion)

1 tablespoon white miso paste

2 tablespoons maple syrup

3 tablespoons water

Miso- and Maple-Glazed Roasted Root Vegetables ★

Serves 4
Preparation time: 30 minutes
Cooking time: 45 minutes

Preheat the oven to 425°F (225°C/Gas Mark 7).

Keeping the garlic cloves in their skins, crush them with the back of a knife. Wash and peel the vegetables. Cut them into large chunks along the lines of their shapes. Arrange the vegetable pieces and garlic cloves in one layer on a large rimmed baking sheet.

In a bowl, combine the olive oil, thyme, chili, and fleur de sel. Pour the mixture over the vegetables to coat them well. Bake for about 45 minutes, turning the vegetables once or twice, until they are roasted all over. You may need to adjust the cooking time, depending on the texture of the vegetables.

Sprinkle the crushed hazelnuts over the baking sheet and cook for an additional 5 minutes, until golden.

For the sauce
Dice the scallion very finely. In a small mixing bowl, mix the miso, maple syrup, and water until thoroughly combined–they should form an emulsion. You may need to add a little water. Stir in the diced scallion.

You can either combine the sauce with the vegetables or serve it on the side, for dipping.

● Chef's notes
It's important to cut the different vegetables into pieces of the same thickness, so that they cook evenly.
This recipe is practical if you have a large number of guests. Perfect when hot, it can also be cooled to make a salad and combined with arugula, baby spinach leaves, or mixed salad greens, and seasoned with the miso sauce.

Techniques
Roasting Vegetables, p. 46

Carrot Cake with Caramelized Hazelnuts ★★

Serves 6
Preparation time: 30 minutes
Cooking time: 30 minutes for the cake, plus 3 minutes for the hazelnut garnish

For the carrot cake
Preheat the oven to 350°F (180°C/Gas Mark 4). Lightly oil the cake pan.

Peel the carrots and grate them finely. In a mixing bowl, whisk the eggs with the peanut oil and hazelnut oil. Whisk in the sugar. With a flexible spatula, stir in the rye flour, all-purpose flour, baking soda, and salt, until just combined. Lastly, stir in the grated carrots and chopped hazelnuts. Do not overmix.

Pour the batter into the prepared pan. Bake for 25 to 35 minutes, until a knife tip inserted into the center comes out dry. Allow to cool slightly in the pan. Turn out onto a rack when still warm.

For the icing
Whisk the cream cheese with the heavy cream until smooth. Whisk in the honey and place in the refrigerator.

For the caramelized hazelnuts
Lightly oil a baking sheet or other flat surface in readiness for the hot hazelnuts. In a nonstick pan over high heat without any added fat, toast the hazelnuts for 1 minute, swirling them around constantly. Add the sugar and continue swirling the pan. As soon as the hazelnuts are coated in golden caramel, pour the contents of the pan onto the prepared oiled sheet. Allow to cool for a few minutes and then unstick them.

To assemble
With a round-tipped knife or metal spatula, spread the icing over the cake. Sprinkle with caramelized hazelnuts, cut into squares, and serve.

● Chef's notes
You can replace this icing with uncooked vegan heavy cream (see technique p. 120), adjusting the quantity of water to obtain a denser texture. Sweeten it with honey, rice syrup, or maple syrup.
This cake keeps well for 3 days, un-iced and covered in plastic wrap.

❙ Techniques
Making Uncooked Vegan Heavy Cream, p. 120
Caramelizing Nuts, p. 131

Ingredients
10 oz. (300 g) carrots
4 eggs
3 tablespoons (50 ml) peanut or sunflower oil
3 tablespoons (50 ml) hazelnut oil
Scant ⅔ cup (4 oz./120 g) light brown sugar
½ cup plus 1 tablespoon (2 oz./60 g) rye flour
½ cup (2 oz./60 g) all-purpose flour
1 ½ teaspoons baking soda
¾ cup (1 ½ oz./40 g) chopped hazelnuts
1 good pinch fine sea salt

Icing with caramelized hazelnuts
⅔ cup (5 oz./150 g) cream cheese
2 tablespoons heavy cream or crème fraîche
1 tablespoon runny honey
2 tablespoons (⅔ oz./20 g) hazelnuts
3 ½ tablespoons (1 ½ oz./40 g) sugar

Equipment
8-inch (20-cm) square cake pan

Ingredients

1 teaspoon oil (sunflower, grape-seed, coconut, etc.)

½ lb. (250 g) raw beets

1 organic orange

7 oz. (200 g) bittersweet chocolate, 70 percent cocoa

4 eggs

¾ cup (5 oz./150 g) light brown sugar

1 ¼ cups (4 oz./120 g) ground almonds

2 tablespoons unsweetened cocoa powder

1 teaspoon baking powder

1 good pinch fine sea salt

Equipment

8-inch (20-cm) diameter cake pan

Disposable gloves

Chocolate, Beet, and Orange Cake ★

Serves 6 to 8
Preparation time: 30 minutes
Cooking time: 50 minutes

Preheat the oven to 350°F (180°C/Gas Mark 4). Lightly oil the cake pan.

It is advisable to wear disposable gloves to work with the beets. Peel and grate them. Grate the zest of the orange and squeeze the juice.

Melt the chocolate over a hot water bath. Separate the eggs. Whisk the yolks with the sugar for 5 minutes, until pale and thick. Incorporate the melted chocolate, ground almonds, cocoa powder, baking powder, and salt. When combined, stir in the grated beets and the orange zest and juice.

Whisk the egg whites until they hold soft peaks. Carefully fold them into the batter, taking care not to deflate the mixture. Pour the mixture into the cake pan, smooth the surface, and bake for 45 to 55 minutes. A knife tip inserted into the center should come out dry when the cake is done.

Allow to cool slightly before turning out of the pan. Serve plain or with chocolate sauce.

● Chef's notes

This cake can be stored for 3 days, well covered in plastic wrap. If you make it ahead of time, add 1 tablespoon of an alcoholic beverage, such as vodka, rum, or triple sec, to the batter—it will keep even better.

Rice

Armand Arnal

Armand Arnal, born in the city of Montpellier in the southwest of France, trained with legendary pastry chef Pierre Hermé and then with the renowned Alain Ducasse, with whom he worked for seven years, mainly in New York and Tokyo. In 2006, he settled in the center of the Camargue region, which is famous for its rice. His restaurant is near Arles, at La Chassagnette, on the road to Sambuc. Nestled in the heart of a 7 ½-acre lush organic vegetable garden, the restaurant follows the rhythm of the seasons: 98 percent of its products are locally sourced. In this paradisiacal vegetable garden, some 180 botanical varieties provide the chef with endless inspiration.

Fundamental to La Chassagnette's objectives is reconciling organic farming, gastronomy, and sustainable development. Arnal's cuisine is now 100 percent gluten-free. It draws on all the resources of the Camargue region and brings together healthy eating, pleasure, and ecological awareness in a cuisine that is fresh, contemporary, and inspired by the shores of the Mediterranean. "I don't impose my cuisine on an ingredient," he likes to say. "I wait for the ingredient to give me the best it's got to cook it."

For Arnal, it was only natural to propose a recipe here using Camargue rice as its main ingredient.

La Chassagnette
Le Sambuc
Arles 13200
France

Serves 4

Preparation time: 25 minutes
Cooking time: 30 minutes

Ingredients

1 ½ cups (9 oz./250 g) organic
   red Camargue rice
4 scallions (spring onions)
3 new turnips
3 new carrots
½ head broccoli
2 oz. (60 g) organic tofu
3 tablespoons canola oil
2 teaspoons gluten-free soy sauce
3 ½ oz. (100 g) soy sprouts
1 bunch cilantro (coriander), chopped

Thai-Style Sautéed Organic Red Camargue Rice, with Spring Vegetables and Tofu

Twelve hours ahead, cook the red rice using the pilaf method (see technique p. 51). Cool and refrigerate.

To proceed, peel the scallions. Separate the white part from the green part and dice both very finely. Peel the turnips and carrots and slice very finely. Cut the half-head of broccoli into florets and cook in salted boiling water for 5 minutes. Refresh and drain well. Cut the tofu into small dice. Set aside all the ingredients, keeping them separate.

Heat the oil in a wok or skillet until it smokes. Sauté the tofu, add the remaining vegetables, and cook them for 3 minutes.

Add the cooked red rice. Stirring constantly, sauté for 3 minutes. Deglaze with the soy sauce. Add the white parts of the scallion and the soy sprouts. Just before serving, sprinkle with chopped cilantro and the scallion greens.

Avgolemono Soup with Zucchini ★ ★

Serves 4

Preparation time: 15 minutes
Cooking time: 15 minutes

Gently bring the broth to a boil with the unpeeled garlic clove and bay leaf. Remove the ends of the zucchini and, with a sharp knife or mandolin, cut them into slices about $1/16$ inch (2-3 mm) thick.

Rinse the rice and pour it into the broth. Cook for 12 minutes, add the zucchini slices, and cook for an additional 3 minutes. Meanwhile, finely grate the zest of one of the lemons. Squeeze the juice. In a mixing bowl, whisk the eggs, lemon juice and zest, and cold water together.

Pour a ladleful of hot broth over the egg mixture, whisking as you pour. Add a second ladleful to ensure the mixture is warm. Remove the broth from the heat and drizzle in the egg-broth mixture, whisking constantly, until it thickens slightly.

Season with salt and pepper and serve immediately with lemon wedges cut from the remaining lemon, so guests can adjust the tanginess.

● Chef's notes

This soup cannot be reheated because the fragile egg liaison would coagulate.

● Good to know

This soup, traditionally made without the zucchini, is known in Greek as avgolemono, which literally means "egg with lemon." It can be prepared with small pasta or tapioca instead of rice. With varying degrees of thickness, it's the tricky cooking of the eggs that determines the consistency, resulting in a velvety creaminess—or a broth full of strings! This type of dish is also found in Sephardi cuisine, as well as in Turkey and in the Balkans, sometimes as a sauce.

Techniques

Preparing Vegetable Broth, p. 31
Using a Mandolin, p. 40

Ingredients

Broth

6 cups (1.5 liters) vegetable broth
1 clove garlic, unpeeled
1 dried bay leaf

Garnish

2 small zucchini (courgettes)
Scant ½ cup (3 ½ oz./100 g) long grain parboiled rice
2 organic or unwaxed lemons
3 organic or free-range eggs
1 tablespoon cold water
Fine salt and freshly ground pepper

Ingredients

½ cup (2 oz./50 g) dried cranberries

4 Jack Be Little squash (or Sweet Dumpling, mini Hubbard, etc.)

2 tablespoons olive oil, plus a little extra to cook the squash

1 generous cup (7 oz./200 g) wild rice, such as Zizania

4 cups (1 liter) vegetable broth

1 clove garlic

2 oz. (50 g) nuts of your choice (almonds, hazelnuts, macadamia, or Brazil nuts)

2 leeks, pale and white parts only

2 teaspoons sherry vinegar

½ teaspoon *piment d'Espelette* or other mild chili pepper

Fine salt and freshly ground pepper

Wild Rice–Stuffed Jack Be Little Squash ★

Serves 4

Preparation time: 20 minutes

Cooking time: 40 minutes

Soak the cranberries in a little hot water until plump. Preheat the oven to 350°F (180°C/Gas Mark 4).

Scrub the squash under cold running water. Slice the tops off (these will form the caps) and scoop out the seeds with a spoon to form a cavity inside each one. Season the cavities lightly with salt and pepper and drizzle in a little olive oil.

Place the squash and caps, cut side downward, in an ovenproof dish and cook for 30 to 40 minutes, or until just tender; they should retain their shape.

Meanwhile, rinse the rice. Bring the broth to a boil with 1 teaspoon of fine salt. Pour in the rice and cook for 35 to 45 minutes, keeping a careful eye on it to ensure that the grains do not burst. Drain well. Peel and dice the garlic clove. Roughly chop the nuts.

Prepare the leeks and chop them finely. Sauté in the olive oil with the garlic until softened. Season with salt and pepper and combine with the rice, cranberries, nuts, sherry vinegar, and *piment d'Espelette*.

Divide the mixture among the squashes, replace the caps, and return to the oven to heat through for 10 minutes. Allow to cool to warm before serving.

● Chef's notes

Wild rice can be eaten without cooking if you allow it to sprout (this is called "blooming") for 3 to 4 days, until the grains burst. This stuffing can be made with sprouted rice, in which case it should not be baked to ensure that it retains all its nutritional value.

Techniques

Cleaning Leeks, p. 24

Preparing Vegetable Broth, p. 31

Soaking Dried Fruits, p. 143

Spring Vegetable Risotto ★★

Serves 4
Preparation time: 30 minutes
Cooking time: 25 minutes

Shell the peas and rinse the pods, reserving them for the broth. Rinse the asparagus, trim the bases, and peel them, reserving the peelings. Trim the ends of the zucchini, cut them in two lengthwise, and chop them into small dice.

Add the garlic clove and bay leaf to the broth and gently bring it to a boil. Add the pea pods and asparagus trimmings, cover with the lid, and simmer for 10 minutes, then strain. Set aside but keep warm; you will need to have the broth hot to prepare the risotto.

Peel the onion and carrot. Rinse and dry the celery stalk. Cut these vegetables into small dice. Pour the olive oil into a skillet or pot over high heat. When it is hot, stir in the onion, carrot, and celery, and soften for 2 minutes (do not allow to color), then add the rice. Sauté briefly, stirring constantly, until the rice is translucent and well coated with the oil. Pour in the wine. Stirring constantly, allow the wine to evaporate. Pour in half of the broth (3 ¼ cups/800 ml), season with salt, and cook for 12 minutes, stirring constantly.

Stir in the peas, asparagus, and zucchini. If necessary, add a little more broth and continue cooking for an additional 6 to 8 minutes, stirring constantly. The texture of the risotto should still be slightly liquid at this stage.

Remove from the heat and stir in the butter and cheese. Stir briskly so that the starch contained in the rice forms an emulsion with the butter and cheese–this creates the creamy texture of risotto. Adjust the seasoning if necessary by adding freshly ground pepper.

Serve immediately in soup plates, with extra grated cheese on the side.

● Chef's notes

The remaining vegetable broth will keep for 5 days, well chilled.
Risotto recipes often advise that the broth be added to the rice a ladleful at a time, as you stir constantly. However, pouring half of it in at once, and then more if needed, will give you the same result—albeit straying from the traditional technique!
If there is any leftover risotto, allow it to cool. Mix in an egg, some grated cheese, and shape into patties. Roll them in bread crumbs and fry in a skillet with a little oil until golden.

Techniques

Preparing Vegetable Broth, p. 31
Peeling Asparagus, p. 36
Dicing Onions, p. 39
Making Risotto, p. 52

Ingredients
Risotto
1 onion
1 carrot
1 stalk celery
3 tablespoons olive oil
1 ¼ cups (9 oz./250 g) round rice for risotto
(*arborio, carnaroli,* or *vialone nano*)
⅔ cup (150 ml) dry white wine
5 tablespoons (3 oz./80 g) butter,
chilled and diced
2 oz. (60 g) vegetarian Parmesan-style hard
cheese, grated, plus extra to serve
Fine salt and freshly ground pepper

Garnish
1 lb. (500 g) fresh peas
12 green asparagus
2 small zucchini (courgettes)

Broth
6 cups (1.5 liters) vegetable broth
1 clove garlic, unpeeled
1 dried bay leaf

Ingredients

1 onion

3 cloves garlic

12 spears green asparagus

4 baby artichokes

Juice of ½ lemon

3 large tomatoes

4 cups (1 liter) vegetable broth, divided

6 saffron threads

¼ cup (60 ml) olive oil

2 teaspoons smoked *pimentón* (Spanish paprika)

1 ¼ cups (9 oz./250 g) bomba rice

1 generous cup (7 oz./200 g) cooked lima (butter) beans

Fine salt and freshly ground pepper

Techniques

Preparing Baby Artichokes, p. 14

Preparing Vegetable Broth, p. 31

Peeling Asparagus, p. 36

Dicing Onions, p. 39

Cooking Pulses, p. 82

Peeling Soft Fruit, p. 139

Asparagus and Lima Bean Paella ★★

Serves 6

Preparation time: 30 minutes

Cooking time: 20 minutes

Peel and dice the onion and garlic. Trim the bases of the asparagus spears and peel them with a vegetable peeler. Cut off the tips and reserve them. Cut the asparagus stems into 1 ¼-inch (3-cm) lengths.

Remove the outer leaves of the artichokes, scoop out the choke, and cut them into quarters. Place the quarters in a bowl of water with lemon juice. Peel and roughly chop the tomatoes and place them in a bowl.

Heat the broth with the asparagus pieces. Remove from the heat, cover with the lid, and allow to infuse for 10 minutes, then strain. Set aside the asparagus pieces and the broth separately.

Place the threads of saffron on a small piece of aluminum foil and fold it into a packet that encloses them completely. Heat a large skillet over medium-high heat and place the foil containing the saffron on it. Heat for 10 to 15 seconds. Remove and allow to cool on a plate.

Heat the olive oil in the skillet over high heat. Sauté the onion and garlic for 5 minutes. Reduce the heat to medium. Drain the artichoke pieces and add them with the sliced asparagus to the skillet. Sauté for 5 minutes. Add the tomato, *pimentón*, and some salt. Pour in 2 ¾ cups (700 ml) of the broth and bring to a boil over high heat. Reduce the heat to medium, add the rice to the skillet to form a cross shape and leave to cook for 10 minutes.

Add the lima beans and asparagus tips. Pour in a scant ½ cup (100 ml) of the broth and crumble the saffron threads into the skillet. Shake the skillet from side to side to spread the contents evenly; do not use a spatula or spoon to stir.

Continue cooking for an additional 10 minutes or so. Taste to check if the rice is properly cooked. If necessary, add a little more broth and cook for a little longer. Serve immediately.

● Chef's notes

If you wish, add flat beans that have been blanched for 1 minute in salted boiling water, or use them instead of one of the vegetables in the list of ingredients.

● Good to know

The crust that forms at the base of the skillet is known as the socarrat, *a choice morsel that should be shared equally between guests. A* socarrat *is the sign that the paella has been correctly prepared.*

Fried Rice with Shiitake, Bok Choy, and Cashew Nuts ★

Serves 4
Resting time: 12 hours or overnight
Preparation time: 15 minutes
Cooking time: 20 minutes, plus 8 minutes

A day ahead, rinse the rice. Cook it, seasoned with salt, using your favorite method (creole, pilaf, or in a rice-cooker). Drain if necessary, allow to cool, and place in the refrigerator for 12 hours.

When you are ready to proceed, peel the garlic and remove the green shoot, then chop it. Peel and dice the onion. Peel and grate the ginger. Roughly chop the cashew nuts and slice the scallion. Using a damp cloth, clean the shiitake mushrooms. Cut off the ends of the stems, and then cut them into four or eight pieces, depending on their size. Rinse, dry, and roughly chop the bok choy.

In a dry skillet over medium heat, toast the cashew nuts until lightly colored. Transfer to a plate. Place the wok over high heat, drizzle in some of the toasted sesame seed oil, and add a good pinch of salt. Sauté the shiitake mushrooms until done and remove from the wok.

Sauté the bok choy with a drizzle of sesame oil and 1 pinch of salt for 2 to 3 minutes, until wilted. Transfer to a dish.

Pour the remaining oil into the wok and lightly brown the onion, garlic, and ginger until golden. Add the rice and lightly brown for 2 minutes. Stir in the shiitake mushrooms and bok choy and season with soy sauce.

Sauté for an additional 2 minutes, mix in the scallion, and serve immediately.

● Chef's notes
When making fried rice, you should use rice that has cooled completely, preferably rice that has been cooked and chilled for 12 hours. This ensures that it does not stick. You can also use frozen rice that has thawed in the refrigerator.

❙ Techniques
Peeling Fresh Ginger, p. 29
Making Creole Rice, p. 50
Making Slow-Cooked (Pilaf) Rice, 51
Cooking Rice in a Rice Cooker, 59
Sautéing Mushrooms, p. 98

Ingredients
1 ¼ cups (7 oz./200 g) semi-milled long grain Thai rice
1 clove garlic
1 onion
¾-inch (2-cm) piece fresh ginger, or more, according to taste
Scant ½ cup (2 oz./50 g) unsalted cashew nuts
1 scallion (spring onion)
14 oz. (400 g) fresh shiitake mushrooms
2 bok choy
2 tablespoons toasted sesame oil
2 tablespoons gluten-free soy sauce, or more, depending on your taste
Fine salt

Equipment
Wok

Ingredients

1 cup (6 oz./175 g) basmati rice

¼ cup (2 oz./50 g) yellow split peas (*toor dhal*)

2 cups (500 ml) water

2 cardamom pods

5 tablespoons ghee

3 cloves

1 small stick cinnamon, crushed into pieces between your fingers

2 cloves garlic

¾-inch (2-cm) piece ginger

1 small green chili pepper

2 carrots

1 turnip

1 large potato

1 handful green beans (about 10), fresh or frozen

A few cauliflower florets

2 tomatoes

2 onions

10 sprigs cilantro (coriander)

3 sprigs fresh mint

Scant ½ cup (100 ml) whole milk plain yogurt

2 teaspoons garam masala

1 teaspoon fine sea salt

1 handful cashew nuts

Techniques

Preparing Chilies, p. 23

Preparing Garlic, p. 29

Peeling Fresh Ginger, p. 29

Preparing Fresh Herbs, p. 38

Blanching, p. 41

Making Clarified Butter and Ghee, p. 113

Biryani ★ ★

Serves 4

Resting time: 30 minutes

Preparation time: 40 minutes

Cooking time: 40 minutes

In two bowls of water, soak the split peas and rice separately for 30 minutes. Drain and rinse. Bring the water to a boil and keep it simmering.

With a mortar and pestle, crush the cardamom pods. Discard the pods and keep only the black seeds. Heat 2 tablespoons of the ghee in a skillet over medium heat. Sauté the cloves, cardamom seeds, and cinnamon stick for 1 minute, until fragrant. Add the rice and split peas, stir to combine, and sauté for 2 minutes. Pour in the boiling water, season with salt, and bring to a boil. Reduce the heat to low, cover with the lid, and cook, stirring from time to time, for about 20 minutes, or until the water has evaporated completely.

Peel the garlic and ginger and grate them both. Seed the chili pepper and chop it finely. Peel the carrots, turnip, and potato and dice them. Trim the beans and cut them into three slices each. Blanch the cauliflower florets in salted boiling water for 3 minutes. Remove the base of the tomatoes and chop them roughly. Peel the onions, setting aside the outer layer, and dice them finely.

Wash, dry, and pick the leaves off the cilantro and mint and chop roughly. In a skillet over medium heat, heat 2 tablespoons of the ghee. Sauté the onions in the ghee for 5 to 7 minutes, until golden, and add the garlic, ginger, and chili pepper. Soften for 2 minutes and stir in the tomatoes, yogurt, and garam masala.

Add the carrots, turnip, and potato, and pour in ¾ cup (200 ml) water (cold or room temperature). Cover with the lid, bring to a boil, reduce the heat, and simmer for 15 minutes. Add the green beans and blanched cauliflower. Cook for an additional 10 minutes.

Carefully combine the rice with the vegetables and place in a warm oven, covered with foil. Slice the outer layer of the onion and fry in the remaining ghee until golden. Remove from the skillet. In the same skillet, sauté the cashew nuts until golden. Scatter the *biryani* with the sliced onion and cashew nuts and serve.

● Chef's notes

You can replace the split peas with garden peas, and simply add them at the same time as the green beans.

Biryani can be made with many other vegetables. Experiment with whatever is in season. For a festive meal, you can also add saffron diluted in a tablespoon of hot water as a final flourish.

Pad Thai ★

Serves 4
Soaking time: 45 minutes
Preparation time: 25 minutes
Cooking time: 10 minutes

For the sauce
Combine the tamarind paste, palm sugar, and soy sauce. Mix well and set aside.

For the *pad Thai*
Soak the noodles in a bowl of hot water for 45 minutes. Peel and finely dice the shallots. Peel the garlic cloves, remove the green shoots, and dice. Peel and grate the ginger. Finely dice the scallions. Seed the chili pepper and chop it finely. Rinse, dry, and chop the cilantro. Break the eggs into a bowl and beat them lightly with 1 tablespoon of water. Pat the tofu dry with paper towel and cut it into large dice.

In the wok over high heat, heat the peanut oil. Fry the shallots and drain them on sheets of paper towel. Add a little more oil to the wok and sauté the tofu pieces until golden all over. Transfer to a dish.

Place the garlic, ginger, chili pepper, and half of the chopped scallions in the wok and soften for 1 minute. Drain the rice noodles and add them to the wok with the sauce. Cook for 2 minutes.

Push the noodles to the edges of the wok and pour the eggs into the center with the dried ground bird's eye chili. Stir with a spatula or wooden spoon, just as you would to make scrambled eggs. When they are lightly set, incorporate them into the noodles. Lastly, add the tofu and heat through for 1 minute.

Remove from the heat and stir in the mung bean sprouts, cilantro, and peanuts. Divide among four bowls, sprinkle with the fried shallots, and serve with lime for the guests to squeeze.

● Chef's notes
It is impossible to make a pad Thai *for more than four people at a time without having it all stick together! Use a large wok, and, for best results, work in batches. The peanut oil can be replaced by coconut oil.*

● Good to know
*This dish was created in the 1940s, when the Kingdom of Siam became Thailand. Initially comprising typically Thai ingredients, the recipe did not call for carrots, cabbage, sesame oil, or lemongrass—all the ingredients we're so used to seeing in this dish. But as it became increasingly popular across the world, it was modified, notably with the addition of cilantro. Non-vegetarian versions contain fish sauce (*nam pla*), dried shrimp, pork fat, and chicken. There are, however, numerous vegetarian takes on this now iconic dish. Many vegetarian festivals are held annually in Thailand, where the definition of vegetarianism usually allows for the consumption of fish.*

Ingredients
Sauce
3 tablespoons tamarind paste
2 tablespoons grated palm sugar (jaggery)
2 tablespoons gluten-free soy sauce

Pad Thai
7 oz. (200 g) wide rice noodles
(*sen-lek* or *banh pho*)
3 shallots
2 cloves garlic
½-inch (1-cm) piece ginger (or galangal)
4 scallions (spring onions)
1 small red chili pepper, according to taste
12 sprigs cilantro (coriander)
2 eggs
8 oz. (250 g) firm tofu
About 2 tablespoons peanut oil
3 tablespoons unsalted peanuts
Dried ground bird's eye chili, to taste
3 ½ oz. (100 g) mung bean sprouts
2 limes in wedges, to serve

Equipment
Wok

Techniques ┃
Preparing Chilies, p. 23
Preparing Garlic, p. 29
Peeling Fresh Ginger, p. 29

Ingredients

Cream
½ cup minus 1 tablespoon (2 ½ oz./70 g) cream
  of rice (coarse rice flour)
½ cup plus 1 tablespoon (4 oz./120 g) sugar
3 ¼ cups (800 ml) whole milk
2 tablespoons orange flower water

Garnish
6 dried apricots
Scant ½ cup (100 ml) hot tea
3 tablespoons granulated sugar
3 tablespoons shelled, unsalted pistachios

Milk Flan with Apricot and Caramelized Nuts ★★

Serves 6
Preparation time: 15 minutes
Chilling time: 6 hours
Cooking time: 15 minutes

For the cream
Place the cream of rice and sugar in a heavy-bottom saucepan over medium heat. Gradually pour in the milk, whisking constantly. Gently bring to a boil. Allow to simmer for 3 minutes or until the cream thickens, stirring constantly with a wooden spoon.

Remove from the heat and stir in the orange flower water. Divide between six glasses or bowls. Cover with plastic wrap and chill for 6 hours.

For the garnish
Soak the dried apricots in the hot tea for 30 minutes. Drain and slice.

Lightly oil a baking sheet: you will need it to cool the caramelized pistachios.

In a dry nonstick pan over high heat, toast the pistachios for 30 seconds, they should be lightly colored. Stir in the sugar and allow to caramelize, swirling the pan from time to time, without using a wooden spoon. It should take 2 to 3 minutes for the pistachios to be coated with a fine layer of caramel. Turn them onto the prepared baking sheet and leave to cool for 30 minutes, then chop roughly.

Just before serving, place the sliced dried apricots on top of the creams and sprinkle with chopped caramelized pistachios.

● Chef's notes
The traditional Lebanese recipe for this dessert is made with cow milk, but it is equally delicious with unflavored soy or rice milk. Cornstarch (cornflour) can be used to replace the cream of rice. If you have a little extra time, you can also use rice flour, allowing an additional 10 minutes or so for the cream to thicken over low heat. And, of course, it requires constant stirring.

● Good to know
Known in Lebanese cuisine as Muhallabieh, this flan is also found in the rest of the Middle East. In Algeria, it is known as mhalbi *and flavored with cinnamon. Other flavors that are used include rose water, cardamom, and honey syrup.*

⧍ Techniques
Caramelizing Nuts, p. 131
Soaking Dried Fruits, p. 143

Banana and Coconut Milk Cake ★

Serves 4 to 6
Preparation time: 20 minutes
Cooking time: 30 minutes, plus 10 minutes
Cooling time: 2 hours

Peel and slice the bananas.

To make the syrup, place the sugar in a heavy-bottom saucepan and pour in the water to dissolve it. Add the banana slices, set the saucepan over low heat, and cook for 10 minutes. Drain, reserving the syrup.

Combine the rice and tapioca flours with the sugar. Stir in the coconut milk and syrup; this should form a fluid batter.

Lightly oil the loaf pan. Arrange a row of banana slices at the bottom, reserving some for the next layer, and pour over half of the batter. Arrange the remaining banana slices over this, and cover with the remaining batter. Place the pan in the steamer and cook for 30 minutes, by which time the batter should be set and opaque. Leave to cool for at least 2 hours.

Just before serving, prepare the *nuoc dua* sauce. Combine the coconut milk, water, and salt in a heavy-bottom saucepan and bring to a boil. Pour in the tapioca. Reduce the heat to low and cook for 5 to 10 minutes, stirring frequently, until the liquid thickens.

Slice the cake, drizzle with sauce, and sprinkle with sesame seeds or peanuts.

● Chef's notes

This cake, a Vietnamese specialty known as Banh Chuoi Hap Nuoc Dua, *will keep for up to 3 days, well wrapped and refrigerated. Before serving, allow it to come to room temperature.*
It can also be made with tapioca starch—just ½ tablespoon is enough—potato starch, or cornstarch. The trick is to allow the preparation to gel slightly.

Ingredients

Syrup
¾ cup (200 ml) water
¼ cup (2 oz./50 g) light brown sugar

Cake
3 ripe bananas (10 oz./300 g when peeled)
⅓ cup (2 oz./50 g) rice flour
⅓ cup (2 oz./50 g) tapioca flour
¼ cup (2 oz./50 g) granulated sugar
1 cup (250 ml) coconut milk
1 teaspoon oil (peanut or sunflower),
   for the mold

Sauce (*nuoc dua*)
¾ cup (200 ml) coconut milk
1 tablespoon water
1 pinch salt
2 tablespoons tapioca
2 tablespoons toasted sesame seeds, or roasted,
   unsalted chopped peanuts

Equipment
8-inch (20-cm) loaf pan
Steamer

Wheat

David Toutain

David Toutain has his roots in the earth—his grandfather was a farmer. He became interested in cooking at an early age, training with several Michelin-starred chefs: he undertook an apprenticeship with Franck Quinont at the Manoir du Lys, then with Bernard Loiseau. By the time he was twenty, he was working at the famous Arpège, where he became Alain Passard's sous chef in just one year. His three-year stint there triggered a passion for the world of vegetables.

He continued his career with starred chefs Pierre Gagnaire and Bernard Pacaud before working as second-in-command to Marc Veyrat. After his experiences abroad (the Mugaritz in Spain and the Corton in New York), he returned to France in 2011 and became chef at the Agapé Substance.

At the end of 2013, Toutain opened his own restaurant, where he gives free rein to his passion for vegetables, translating the ingredients into a rigorous, flavorsome cuisine with original taste combinations and textures.

In the recipe he presents here, wheat is showcased in the roasted flour for the ice cream and the delicate streusel, while the creamed potato blurs the boundaries between sweet and savory to bring us an imaginative and utterly unexpected dessert.

Restaurant David Toutain
29 Rue Surcouf
75007 Paris
France
Website: davidtoutain.com

French Toast, Roasted Wheat Ice Cream, and Hay-Cooked Creamed Potato

For the creamed potatoes: Steam the potatoes for 20 minutes, puree finely, dry in an oven at 320°F (160°C/Gas Mark 3) for 30 minutes, and cool. Bring the milk and cream to a boil. Remove from the heat, incorporate the hay, cover, and allow to infuse for 30 minutes, then strain. Whisk the egg yolks with the sugar. Pour the strained milk into the mixture in a steady stream, whisking continuously, and return to the saucepan. Heat to 180°F (82°C), stirring constantly. When it thickens, remove from the heat and allow to cool. Stir it into the cooled potato flesh. Pour the mixture onto a baking sheet set over a bain-marie. Bake at 250°F (120°C/Gas Mark ½) for 20–25 minutes and allow to cool. Process the mixture until smooth, strain through a fine-mesh sieve, and reserve in the refrigerator.

For the vanilla streusel: Place the eggs in salted boiling water for 10 minutes, until hard-boiled. Dip them in cold water, shell, and take out the yolks. Place the yolks in the refrigerator. Spread the flour over a baking sheet and roast at 320°F (160°C/Gas Mark 3) for 25 minutes. Allow to cool. Sift and set aside 2 cups (9 oz./250 g). Soften the butter with the sugar, vanilla seeds, and fleur de sel. Mash the cooled egg yolks and sift to form a fine powder. Incorporate the 2 cups (250 g) of flour and egg yolks into the mixture. Do not overwork: the dough should remain sandy. Sprinkle the crumbly mixture over a baking sheet and bake at 335°F (170°C/Gas Mark 4) for 13 minutes to make a streusel.

For the meringue shards: Dissolve the powdered milk in 2 tablespoons of water. Prepare a syrup: combine the sugar with the 3 ⅓ tablespoons (50 ml) water and heat to 244°F (118°C). While the syrup is cooking, whisk the egg whites in a stand mixer until they hold soft peaks. Drizzle the syrup over the beaten eggs, whisking continuously, then whisk for an additional 4 minutes. Stir in the dissolved powdered milk and whisk until the meringue has cooled to lukewarm. Spread it very thinly over a silicone mat and bake at 175°F (80°C/Gas Mark ¼) for 8 hours. It should be very crisp.

For the French toast: Beat the eggs with the sugar, cream, and Calvados. Pour into a large dish and soak the 3 brioche slices for 1 hour, then drain. Melt the butter in a skillet and fry the slices until golden. Allow to cool and cut into ¼-inch (5 mm) cubes.

For the roasted wheat flour ice cream: Spread the flour on a baking sheet and roast at 400°F (200°C/Gas Mark 6) for 20 minutes. Sift and set aside ⅓ cup (2 ½ oz./45 g). Make a custard: heat the milk, cream, and honey together. Meanwhile, whisk the egg yolks with the sugar until the mixture becomes pale and reaches the ribbon stage. Drizzle in the hot milk mixture, continuing to whisk, and return to the saucepan. Heat to 180°F (82°C), stirring constantly. When it thickens, remove from the heat, allow to cool, and weigh out 1 ¾ lb. (800 g). Combine this quantity of custard with the flour. Process in an ice-cream maker according to instructions.

To serve: Place the brioche cubes under the broiler very briefly. Break the meringue into shards. Place small scoops of ice cream on the plates with the vanilla streusel. Drizzle with the creamed potato sauce, insert meringue shards, and scatter with warm brioche cubes.

Serves 8

Preparation time: 1 hour; Soaking time: 1 hour; Cooking time: 10 hours

Ingredients

Creamed potatoes
9 oz. (250 g) floury potato flesh
1 cup (250 ml) whole milk
1 cup (250 ml) whipping cream
1 handful organic hay
3 organic egg yolks
Scant ⅓ cup (2 oz./60 g) granulated sugar

Vanilla streusel
3 organic eggs
2 ½ cups (10 ½ oz./300 g) all-purpose flour
2 sticks (9 oz./250 g) lightly salted butter, room temperature
⅔ cup (4 oz./125 g) granulated sugar
½ teaspoon (3 g) fleur de sel
1 Madagascar vanilla bean, slit lengthwise, seeds scraped

Meringue shards
3 ½ oz. (100 g) powdered milk
1 cup (7 oz./200 g) granulated sugar
2 tablespoons, plus 3 ⅓ tablespoons (50 ml) water
Scant cup (7 oz./200 g) egg whites

French toast
3 organic eggs
¾ cup (5 oz./150 g) sugar
1 ¼ cups (300 ml) whipping cream, 35 percent butterfat
1 tablespoon (20 ml) Calvados
1 tablespoon plus 1 teaspoon (20 g) butter
3 slices brioche, each ⅜ inch (1 cm) thick

Ice cream
4 cups (1 liter) whole milk
1 cup (250 ml) whipping cream, 35 percent butterfat
2 tablespoons plus 1 teaspoon (2 oz./50 g) multi-floral honey
1 ½ cups (14 oz./400 g) organic egg yolks
½ cup (3 ½ oz./100 g) granulated sugar
½ cup (2 oz./60 g) all-purpose flour

Freekeh-Stuffed Eggplant ★

Serves 6

Preparation time: 20 minutes
Cooking time: 1 hour 20 minutes

Preheat the oven to 350°F (180°C/Gas Mark 4).

Wash and dry the eggplants. Cut them in two lengthwise, leaving the stem. With a sharp knife, score the flesh in a crisscross pattern. Brush the open halves with olive oil and season lightly with salt. Bake for 40 minutes and allow to cool to room temperature.

Rinse and dry the cilantro and parsley and pick off the leaves. Set aside a few cilantro leaves for garnish. Peel the garlic clove and remove the green shoot. Scoop out the pulp of the preserved lemon and remove the seeds. Reserve the peel.

With a knife or in a food processor, chop the cilantro, parsley, and garlic. Add the spices, lemon pulp, and remaining olive oil. Process or pulse just enough to make a rough paste. In a pot of salted boiling water, cook the *freekeh* for 30 minutes, then drain.

Rinse and dry the grapes. Cut each grape in half and remove the seeds. Finely slice the scallions and finely dice the lemon peel. Roughly chop the walnuts.

Combine the *freekeh*, paste, grapes, walnuts, and scallions. Garnish the eggplant halves with the mixture, and scatter with a few cilantro leaves. Serve at room temperature.

● Chef's notes
This freekeh salad can also be used to garnish other vegetables,
such as bell peppers and onions, cooked or raw.

❘ Techniques
Preparing Garlic, p. 29
Preparing Fresh Herbs, p. 38

Ingredients
3 long eggplants (aubergines)
5 tablespoons (75 ml) olive oil
1 bunch cilantro (coriander)
12 sprigs flat-leaf parsley
1 clove garlic
1 preserved lemon
½ teaspoon paprika
½ teaspoon cumin
2 pinches chili pepper,
as strong or mild as you like
¾ cup (7 oz./200 g) *freekeh*
(dried, smoked green wheat)
1 bunch purple grapes
3 scallions (spring onions)
1 handful walnuts
Fine sea salt and freshly ground pepper

Ingredients

Focaccia

1 ¼ cups (300 ml) lukewarm water
(approximately 85°F/30°C)

Scant ½ cup (100 ml) white wine

2 cups (500 ml) olive oil, plus extra for
the baking sheet

¾ oz. (20 g) fresh (compressed) yeast

1 tablespoon honey

4 ½ cups (1 ¼ lb./560 g) all-purpose flour,
or 4 ⅓ cups (1 ¼ lb./560 g) spelt

2 teaspoons (10 g) fine sea salt

For brushing

4 tablespoons water

2 tablespoons olive oil

½ tablespoon fleur de sel

Garnish

3 tablespoons (1 oz./30 g) raisins

1 bunch Swiss chard (approximately 1 lb./500 g)

1 onion

1 clove garlic

1 tablespoon olive oil

2 cups (500 ml) vegetable broth

8 oz. (250 g) vegetarian soft creamy goat cheese,
crumbled

1 teaspoon aniseed

1 teaspoon thyme flowers

2 pinches ground chili pepper, according to taste

Fine salt and freshly ground pepper

Equipment

Stand mixer or food processor with a dough hook

Techniques

Preparing Swiss Chard, p. 15

Making Yeast-Raised Dough, p. 63

Soaking Dried Fruits, p. 143

● Chef's notes

Before baking, you can combine some chopped rosemary leaves with olive oil and sprinkle the dough with the mixture.

Focaccia is also delicious served plain along with salad or cheese.

Keep in mind that it dries out quickly. If you want to reheat the focaccia, moisten the surface lightly before placing it briefly in the oven.

Swiss Chard and Goat Cheese Focaccia ★★

Serves 6

Preparation time: 40 minutes

Resting time: 3 hours 30 minutes

Cooking time: 45 minutes

For the focaccia

Combine the water, wine, olive oil, yeast, and honey. Leave to rest for 10 minutes, until the mixture becomes slightly foamy. In the bowl of the stand mixer fitted with a dough hook, mix the flour and salt. Make a well in the center and, working at low speed (1 or 2), gradually drizzle in the liquid. Knead for 5 minutes. Increase the speed to 4 and knead for 10 minutes; the dough should be very soft. Cover with a clean, slightly damp cloth, and leave to rise for 2 hours, until doubled in volume.

Brush a 12 × 16-inch (30 × 40-cm) rimmed baking sheet lightly with oil. Transfer the dough to the baking sheet and use your fingers to spread it evenly over the entire sheet. Cover with a clean, slightly damp cloth and leave to rise again for 1 hour 30 minutes, until well risen.

For the garnish

Soak the raisins in hot water. Prepare the chard: separate the green parts from the white. Finely slice the white parts. Roll up the green leaves and chop them. Peel and dice the onion. Peel and finely dice the garlic.

In a skillet over medium-high heat, heat the olive oil. Lightly brown the onion and garlic for 5 minutes and add the chopped white parts of the Swiss chard. Season lightly with salt and pour in the broth. Reduce the heat to low, simmer for 10 minutes, and add the chopped green parts. Cook for an additional 10 minutes: the chard should be tender and all the broth absorbed. Remove from the heat. Drain the raisins and stir them into the chard with the goat cheese, aniseed, thyme flowers, ground chili, and season with pepper.

To finish

Position a rimmed baking sheet at the lowest level of the oven. Preheat the oven to 450°F (230°C/Gas Mark 8). To remove the air from the dough, use your fingers to make indentations evenly over the surface. Combine the water and oil and brush the dough with the mixture, filling the hollows you have made. Sprinkle with the fleur de sel.

Pour 3 tablespoons (50 ml) of water into the baking sheet at the bottom of the oven. Place the focaccia in the oven for 15 to 20 minutes, until well risen and golden. Allow to cool to lukewarm on the baking sheet.

Gently reheat the garnish. Cut the focaccia into squares and cut the squares horizontally in two. Fill them generously with the Swiss chard garnish and serve at room temperature.

Pasta with Genovese Pesto ★

Serves 6
Preparation time: 15 minutes
Cooking time: 20 minutes

For the pesto
Peel the garlic cloves and remove the green shoots. Wash and dry the basil and pick off the leaves. If you are using a food processor, use the pulse function to combine the garlic, basil, and pine nuts: this avoids over-processing. Add the cheese. Switch to low-medium speed and pour in the olive oil in a steady stream, stopping when blended. Adjust the seasoning by adding salt and pepper.

For the pasta
Peel the potatoes and cut them into small cubes. Trim the green beans. Bring 6 ¼ quarts (6 liters) to a boil and add a generous amount of salt. Drop the potatoes into the water, reduce the heat, and simmer for 10 minutes.

Add the pasta to the pot, stir, and cook for an additional 5 minutes. Add the green beans and continue cooking for 4 to 5 minutes. Drain the pasta with the potatoes and beans, reserving a little of the cooking liquid.

To finish
Pour the pesto into a large skillet. Stir in 1 to 2 tablespoons of the cooking liquid to thin it. Stir in the pasta with the vegetables. Using two wooden spoons, mix until combined.

Serve immediately, accompanied by extra grated cheese for guests to add.

● Chef's notes
Traditionally, pesto was made using a mortar and pestle. Today, these implements are often replaced by a food processor, which—unfortunately—tends to heat the ingredients and alter their natural tastes. A juice extractor makes excellent pesto, so if you have one, give it a try.
This dish is usually made with Parmigiano Reggiano (Parmesan) or an equal mix of Parmesan and pecorino, both of which contain animal rennet. Non-vegetarians should feel free to substitute these cheeses. As for the choice of which to use, the argument among the Genovese goes back a long time. It comes down to a question of taste. If you use half of each, keep in mind that pecorino is less salty than Parmesan.
When fresh green beans are not in season, they can be replaced by frozen. To use frozen beans, add them to the pot 6 minutes before the pasta is done. Store any remaining pesto in a jar and pour in just enough olive oil to cover the surface. It will keep in the refrigerator for 10 days.

Techniques
Preparing Garlic, p. 29
Preparing Fresh Herbs, p. 38

Ingredients
3 potatoes (approximately 7 oz./200 g)
4 oz. (120 g) green beans
1 tablespoon kosher salt
1 lb. (500 g) *trenette* or linguine pasta

Pesto
2 cloves garlic
1 bunch basil
2 tablespoons (20 g) pine nuts
4 tablespoons (40 g) freshly grated vegetarian Parmesan-style hard cheese
⅓ cup (80 ml) olive oil
Fine salt and freshly grated pepper
Freshly grated vegetarian Parmesan-style hard cheese, or vegan "Parmesan" (see p. 124), to serve

Equipment
Food processor or mortar and pestle

Ingredients

4 oz. (120 g) vegetarian Parmesan-style hard
  cheese
4 cups (1 liter) cow milk
5 tablespoons (2 ½ oz./70 g) unsalted butter
1 cup plus 2 tablespoons (7 oz./200 g) fine grain
  wheat semolina
1 egg, lightly beaten
1 small pinch nutmeg
¼ teaspoon fine salt

Gnocchi *alla Romana* ★

Serves 4
Preparation time: 15 minutes
Resting time: 1 hour
Cooking time: 20 minutes

Grate the cheese. In a large saucepan over high heat, bring the milk to a boil with 3 tablespoons (50 g) of the butter and the salt. Pour the semolina into the milk, stirring constantly. Reduce the heat to low and simmer for 2 minutes, until the semolina mixture pulls away from the sides of the saucepan.

Remove from the heat and beat in the egg with half of the grated cheese and the nutmeg.

Spread the semolina mixture over a large rimmed pan or ovenproof dish to a thickness of approximately ¾ inch (1.5-2 cm). Smooth the surface. Allow to cool to room temperature for 1 to 2 hours.

Preheat the oven to 410°F (210°C/Gas Mark 6).

Using a glass or cookie cutter with a diameter of approximately 2 inches (5-6 cm), cut out rounds of gnocchi dough. Place them in an ovenproof dish and dot with small knobs of the remaining butter. Sprinkle with the remaining cheese.

Bake for 15 minutes, until the gnocchi are golden on top. If necessary, place them very briefly under the broiler. Serve hot.

● Chef's notes

This Italian starter is excellent served with sautéed spinach or a dish of ratatouille.
You can prepare it 2 to 3 days ahead of time. Store the rounds in the refrigerator and sprinkle with cheese just before baking. Serve hot.

❘ Techniques
Making Polenta Slices, p. 72

Berber-Style Mint and Vegetable Couscous ★

Serves 6
Preparation time: 30 minutes
Cooking time: 35 minutes

Pick the leaves off the mint and chop them finely. Using a fork, beat the chopped leaves into the butter and set aside. Peel the carrots, potatoes, and turnips. Cut them into very small dice, about ⅛ inch (3 mm). Cut the unpeeled zucchini and eggplant into dice of the same size. Drop the fava beans into a pot of salted boiling water and cook for 2 minutes. Transfer immediately into a bowl of ice water and then remove the skins.

Steam the potatoes for 5 minutes. Add the carrots, turnips, zucchini, and eggplant. Cook for about 15 minutes, until slightly firm. Leave the vegetables in a dish while you proceed with the recipe.

Pour the couscous into a large mixing bowl and use your hands to combine it with 1 tablespoon of the olive oil, the salt, and water. Continue working until it looks like wet sand. Place it in the basket of the couscous pot or steamer and steam for 5 minutes. Tip it back into the mixing bowl and add the remaining olive oil. Using a fork, stir the olive oil in, making sure to separate any lumps: the texture should be fine. Return it to the basket and steam again for 5 minutes.

Combine the couscous with the vegetables. Steam together for an additional 5 minutes. Transfer to a serving platter and serve with knobs of mint-flavored butter.

● **Good to know**
Mint-flavored butter is not a traditional accompaniment to this dish but makes it even tastier.
The method for making couscous given here is a simplified version of what is usually a time-consuming process.
The word couscous is derived from the Arabic kaskasa, meaning "to pound."

⚲ **Techniques**
Blanching, p. 41
Steaming, p. 41

Ingredients
4 sprigs mint, washed and dried
5 tablespoons (3 oz./80 g) unsalted butter, softened
2 carrots
2 potatoes
2 new turnips with their stems
2 zucchini (courgettes)
1 eggplant (aubergine)
2 handfuls shelled fresh fava (broad) beans
1 ½ cups (10 oz./300 g) fine grain couscous
2 tablespoons olive oil
½ teaspoon fine salt
4 tablespoons cold water

Equipment
Couscous pot or steamer

Ingredients

1 cauliflower (trimmed weight 1 ¼ lb./600 g)
Approximately 2 cups (9 oz./250 g)
　whole-wheat macaroni
2 cups (500 ml) vegetable broth
4 oz. (125 g) vegetarian hard cheese (cheddar,
　Emmental, etc.), grated
3 tablespoons (50 ml) heavy cream
　or crème fraîche
½ tablespoon Dijon mustard
¼ cup (½ oz./15 g) homemade bread crumbs
1 tablespoon kosher salt
Fine salt, freshly grated pepper, and freshly
　grated nutmeg
Butter to grease the dish

Equipment

10-inch (25-cm) long ovenproof dish

Cauliflower Mac and Cheese ★

Serves 6
Preparation time: 20 minutes
Cooking time: 40 minutes

Preheat the oven to 400°F (200°C/Gas Mark 6). Grease the ovenproof dish well with the butter.

Wash the cauliflower and separate it into florets. Steam for 15 minutes, until the tip of a knife slides in easily.

Bring a pot of water to a boil with the kosher salt. Cook the macaroni for 7 to 8 minutes, until only half cooked–well done on the outside but still firm inside, as it will finish cooking in the oven. Drain well.

Blend the cauliflower with the broth, two thirds of the grated cheese, and the cream. Stir in the mustard. Season with salt and pepper and add nutmeg to taste.

Combine the macaroni with the cauliflower-cheese sauce. In a mixing bowl, combine the bread crumbs with the remaining grated cheese. Spread the macaroni, coated with the sauce, evenly in the prepared dish. Sprinkle with the bread crumbs and cheese.

Bake for 20 minutes, until the top is a nice golden brown.

● Chef's notes

Instead of macaroni, you can use small pasta of your choice, such as ziti, coquillettes (small curved tubes), or penne. It is important to precook it only until half done, as it will finish cooking in the sauce when baked.
This dish can be prepared a day ahead: combine the pasta and sauce in the dish, cover with plastic wrap, and refrigerate. Simply sprinkle with the bread crumb and grated cheese mixture just before placing in the oven.

Techniques
Preparing Vegetable Broth, p. 31
Steaming, p. 41

Wheat

Seitan Kebabs with *Dengaku* Sauce ★

Serves 4
Soaking time (for the skewers): 30 minutes
Preparation time: 15 minutes
Cooking time: 10 minutes

Soak the wooden skewers in water for 30 minutes.

For the sauce
Combine the sugar with the *mirin* and sake. Allow 5 minutes for the sugar to dissolve. With a fork, stir in the miso paste and oil and mix thoroughly until an emulsion forms.

For the kebabs
Preheat the broiler. Cut the seitan into bite-sized cubes. Slice the green parts of the scallions into short lengths. Thread the seitan cubes onto the skewers, alternating them with the pieces of scallion.

Brush the seitan cubes with a little sauce. Turn the skewers over and brush the other side. Place the kebabs under the broiler for 3 minutes, keeping a careful eye on them. Turn them and broil on the other side.

Serve accompanied by a salad, rice, or crudités, with the remaining *dengaku* sauce on the side.

● Chef's notes
Any leftover dengaku *sauce can be stored in an airtight container in the refrigerator for up to 2 weeks. You can use it to prepare other traditional Japanese dishes, such as* nasu dengaku *(glazed eggplant) and grilled tofu slices.*

❘ Techniques
Preparing Seitan, p. 69

Ingredients
14 oz. (400 g) homemade seitan
  (see technique p. 69)
2 scallions (spring onions)

Sauce
2 teaspoons brown sugar
1 tablespoon *mirin*
1 tablespoon sake
2 tablespoons white miso
2 tablespoons toasted sesame oil

Equipment
8 wooden skewers

Glamorgan Sausages ★

Serves 4 (makes 12 sausages)
Preparation time: 40 minutes
Chilling time: 30 minutes
Cooking time: 20 minutes

In the bowl of the food processor, pulverize the bread to make bread crumbs. Set aside just under one quarter (2 ½ oz./75 g) to bread the sausages.

Wash the leeks and slice them finely. Melt the butter in a skillet over medium heat. Add the leeks, season lightly with salt, and soften for 10 minutes.

Finely grate the cheese and chop the parsley finely. Pick the leaves from the thyme sprigs.

In a mixing bowl, combine the larger quantity of bread crumbs, grated cheese, leeks, parsley, mustard, thyme, and nutmeg. Stir in 1 egg.

Separate the two remaining eggs, pouring the whites into a separate bowl and adding the yolks to the leek mixture. Pour the milk into the leek mixture and stir until it is malleable. Adjust the seasoning with salt and pepper and mix through.

Divide the preparation into 12 equal portions. On a work surface, roll them into sausage shapes about 4 inches (8-10 cm) long with a diameter of about 1 inch (2-3 cm). Chill for 30 minutes.

With a fork, lightly beat the egg whites, just enough to liquefy them. Pour the bread crumbs for breading into a soup plate. Dip the sausages first into the egg whites and then into the bread crumbs to coat them.

In a skillet over high heat, heat the oil and brown the sausages for 10 minutes, turning them regularly.

Serve three sausages per person, accompanied by a green salad or coleslaw, and chutney or other condiments.

Ingredients
12 oz. (325 g) day-old or dried bread
2 leeks, white and softer green parts
   (approximately 5 oz./150 g)
1 tablespoon (¾ oz./20 g) butter
7 oz. (200 g) vegetarian cheddar or Caerphilly
   cheese
10 sprigs flat-leaf parsley
5 sprigs thyme
2 teaspoons ground mustard seeds,
   or 1 teaspoon hot English mustard
Grated nutmeg to taste
3 eggs
Scant ½ cup (100 ml) milk
2 tablespoons oil for frying
Fine salt and freshly grated pepper

Equipment
Food processor

● Chef's notes
You might want to substitute scallions for the leeks.

● Good to know
This dish dates back to the nineteenth century. It originated in Wales, in the historic county of Glamorgan. Made with leeks, the symbol of Wales, and Glamorgan cheese, a traditional hard cheese that can no longer be found, it is a tasty way to use leftovers.

Techniques
Cleaning Leeks, p. 24
Breading, p. 77

Bulgur and Squash Kibbe ★★

Serves 6
Preparation time: 30 minutes
Soaking time: 15 minutes
Cooking time: 1 hour

Steam the squash for 20 minutes, until a knife slips in easily. Mash it, place in a fine-mesh sieve, and allow to drain while you proceed with the recipe.

Soak the bulgur in a large mixing bowl of cold water for 15 minutes. Drain through a fine-mesh sieve.

In a mixing bowl, combine the bulgur, mashed squash, olive oil, *ras el hanout*, and salt.

For the stuffing
Peel and finely chop the onions. Heat the olive oil in a skillet over high heat and lightly brown the onions for a few minutes. Season with salt, reduce the heat to low, and cover with the lid. Allow the onions to soften for 20 minutes; they should be very tender. Roughly chop the walnuts and combine them with the onions, pomegranate molasses, mint, thyme, and cumin.

To assemble
Preheat the oven to 350°F (180°C/Gas Mark 4). Lightly oil the ovenproof dish.

Spread half of the squash-bulgur mixture over the base of the dish, pressing it down with your hands to form an even layer. Spread an even layer of the stuffing over this. Cover the stuffing with a second even layer of the remaining squash-bulgur mixture. Using a pointed knife, draw a decorative pattern on the surface. Bake for 40 minutes, until golden.

Serve hot or warm.

● Chef's notes
If you prefer, you can replace the onions with chopped, softened eggplants.
Kibbe may be prepared a day ahead and reheated just before serving.
This is a vegetarian version of a Lebanese dish, traditionally made with ground meat and cracked wheat, layered and baked or shaped into ovals with a stuffing.

Techniques
Preparing Squash, p. 17
Dicing Onions, p. 39
Steaming, p. 41

Ingredients
1 lb. (500 g) peeled, seeded, and cubed red kuri
or butternut squash
1 ½ cups (7 oz./200 g) fine bulgur wheat
2 tablespoons olive oil
1 teaspoon *ras el hanout* spice mix
½ teaspoon fine salt

Stuffing
2 tablespoons olive oil
1 lb. (500 g) red onions
½ cup (2 oz./50 g) walnuts
2 tablespoons pomegranate molasses
1 teaspoon dried mint
1 teaspoon dried thyme
½ teaspoon cumin

Equipment
Food processor, potato ricer, or vegetable mill
6 × 10-inch (15 × 25-cm) ovenproof dish

Barley, Millet, and Other Grains

Thierry Marx

Thierry Marx was trained in pastry-making by the craftsmen's guild Les Compagnons de Devoir in 1978. He then enlisted in the army and it was several years before he turned his attentions back to cuisine. After working at French Michelin-starred restaurants Ledoyen, Taillevent, Robuchon, and Alain Chapel, he set off for Sydney, where he worked as the chef at the Regency Hotel, before moving to Asia and working in Singapore, Hong Kong, and Tokyo. A martial arts enthusiast, he acquired a deeper understanding of Asian culture during this time. Japan has become his second gastronomic homeland and continues to play a decisive role in his approach to both life and cuisine.

On his return to France, he was awarded a first Michelin star at the Roc-en-Val restaurant in Montlouis-sur-Loire, and then at the Cheval Blanc, in Nîmes, in 1991. For ten years, he was chef at the Château Cordeillan-Bages in Pauillac, where his innovative culinary techniques were rewarded with two Michelin stars in 1999. *Le Chef* magazine named him Chef of the Year in 2006, and in 2010 he was appointed executive chef at the Mandarin Oriental Paris. He is involved in training programs for young chefs and is committed to transmitting his knowledge to the upcoming generations.

By placing the spotlight on lesser-used grains in a recipe that is contemporary yet simple to make, Marx brings together three values that are dear to his heart: balance, tradition, and innovation.

Le Mandarin Oriental Paris
251 rue Saint-Honoré
75001 Paris
France

Serves 4

Preparation time: 10 minutes
Resting time: 1 hour
Cooking time: 3 minutes per blini

Ingredients

7 tablespoons (3 ½ oz./100 g) butter
1 cup (250 ml) soy milk
⅓ oz. (8 g) fresh (compressed) yeast
1 cup (4 oz./125 g) buckwheat flour
1 ¼ cups (4 oz./125 g) oats
1 teaspoon roasted soy flour (kinako)
2 egg yolks
6 egg whites
1 tablespoon plain strained or
   Greek-style yogurt

Souffléed Buckwheat and Oat Blinis

Clarify the butter: in a small saucepan over low heat, melt the butter. Pour it carefully into a cup, leaving the white solids at the bottom of the pan.

Warm the soy milk. Crumble the yeast into the soy milk and stir it in until dissolved.

Combine the buckwheat flour, oats, and roasted soy flour. Beat the egg yolks with a fork and incorporate them into the dry ingredients. Stir in the yogurt. Pour the soy milk mix into the mixture, stir to combine, and leave to rest at room temperature for 1 hour.

Stir the clarified butter into the batter. Beat the egg whites until they hold soft peaks and fold them into the batter, taking care not to deflate the mixture.

Heat a nonstick blini pan over low heat. Pour a little of the batter into the pan and cook for 3 minutes, until golden on both sides. Remove and continue with the remaining batter. Allow the blinis to rest for 3 minutes before serving.

Quinoa Soup ★

Serves 4
Preparation time: 20 minutes
Cooking time: 30 minutes

Rinse and drain the quinoa. Peel the potatoes, onion, and garlic. Remove the green shoot from the garlic cloves and chop them finely. Finely chop the onion. Roughly chop the tomatoes. Rinse, dry, and roughly chop the leafy vegetables.

In a large pot over high heat, heat the oil. Soften the onion and garlic for 2 minutes. Reduce the heat to medium and add the pieces of tomato and leafy vegetables. Reduce the heat to low and soften for 3 minutes. Add the quinoa and potatoes.

Pour in the boiling water and add ½ teaspoon of salt and freshly ground pepper to taste. Cover with the lid and cook for 20 to 25 minutes over medium heat, until the quinoa is done. Stir in the herbs and chili pepper, if using, and serve in bowls.

● Chef's notes

In Peru and Bolivia, the thickness of this soup varies with the seasons, with the regions, and with what is available. On the high plateaus, it is often thickened with grated cheese that is added two minutes before the quinoa is done. Sometimes an egg is cracked into the hot liquid to give it more consistency. The fresh herbs traditionally used in Peru and Bolivia for this recipe are hard to find, but if you use oregano, dried mint, or cilantro, the result will be true comfort food. The aji amarallo, a small yellow chili pepper from the Andes, is usually added. If you can't find it, any chili pepper of your choice will add pizzazz to your soup.

❙ Techniques
Preparing Garlic, p. 29
Cooking Quinoa, p. 75

Ingredients
1 scant cup (5 oz./150 g) quinoa
(white, black, red, or mixed)
4 medium potatoes (approximately 1 lb./500 g)
1 onion
2 cloves garlic
2 ripe tomatoes, or scant ½ cup (100 ml) *passata*
(strained tomatoes)
4 handfuls leafy vegetables (Swish chard, spinach,
kohlrabi leaves, or cabbage leaves)
2 tablespoons peanut or sunflower oil
2 cups plus scant ½ cup (600 ml) boiling water
(3 times the volume of quinoa, which should be
measured in the same cup)
Fresh herbs, according to taste and season
(cilantro [coriander], oregano, etc.)
Ground chili pepper, according to taste (optional)
Fine salt and freshly ground pepper

Ingredients

Amaranth patties

1 clove garlic

10 sprigs herbs, according to taste
(parsley, cilantro [coriander], or chives)

1 cup (7 oz./200 g) amaranth, cooked and cooled

5 oz. (150 g) grated vegetables (carrots, zucchini
[courgettes], etc.)

⅓ cup (1 ¾ oz./50 g) cornstarch or potato starch

1 egg

1 teaspoon crumbled dried thyme

2 tablespoons oil (sunflower, grape-seed,
or peanut)

Fine salt and freshly ground pepper

Avocado cream

2 ripe avocados

1 tomato

1 small scallion (spring onion), or ½ white onion

½ green Serrano chili pepper, or a few drops
Tabasco® sauce

Leaves from 5 sprigs cilantro (coriander)

Juice of ½ lime

½ teaspoon fine salt

Amaranth Patties
and Avocado Cream ★★

Serves 4 (makes 8 patties)
Preparation time: 15 minutes
Cooking time: 10 minutes

For the amaranth patties

Preheat the oven to 210°F (100°C/Gas Mark ¼). Peel and finely grate the garlic clove. Pick the leaves off the herbs and chop them finely.

In a mixing bowl, combine the amaranth, vegetables, garlic, chopped herbs, cornstarch, egg, and thyme. Season with salt and pepper.

In a large skillet, heat the oil over medium-high heat. Drop tablespoons of the amaranth mixture into the skillet and flatten them slightly with the back of the spoon. Cook for 2 ½ minutes, turn them with a wide spatula, and cook for 1 minute on the other side.

Transfer the patties to an ovenproof dish and place in the oven. Continue with the remaining amaranth mixture, placing them in the oven as soon as they are cooked to keep warm.

For the avocado cream

Remove the seeds of the tomato and cut into small cubes (there is no need to peel the tomato). Finely chop the scallion. Seed the chili pepper and chop it finely. Finely chop the cilantro leaves.

Cut the avocados in two, remove the pits, and scoop out the flesh. Drizzle over with the lime juice so that they do not brown and mash roughly with a fork. Stir in the tomato cubes, scallion, chili pepper, cilantro, and salt. Mix well and place in the refrigerator until you are ready to serve.

 Chef's notes

You can also make these patties using quinoa.
Amaranth naturally produces a viscous substance, which makes the patties fairly soft. Be sure to use starch to bind them rather than flour: that's the secret to making crispy patties.

Techniques
Preparing Chilies, p. 23
Dicing Onions, p. 39
Cooking Quinoa, p. 75

Barley, Millet, and Other Grains

Citrus Beet and Sprouted Buckwheat Salad ★

Serves 4
Preparation time: 15 minutes

For the salad
Peel the beets. Using the mandolin, slice them as finely as possible, transferring the slices to a bowl of cold water as you work. Peel the grapefruit, taking care to remove all the white pith. Cut out the segments from between the membranes. Carefully dry the beet slices. In a salad bowl, combine them with the sprouted buckwheat and grapefruit segments.

For the vinaigrette
Cut the preserved lemon in two lengthwise. Scoop out the flesh and the seeds. Finely chop the peel.

Cut the orange in half. Squeeze one half. Scoop out the flesh of the other half and stir carefully into the salad.

In a small mixing bowl, combine the orange juice, diced lemon peel, chopped dill, olive oil, a pinch of salt, and freshly ground pepper. Carefully toss the salad with the vinaigrette. Leave at room temperature for 30 minutes before serving.

● Chef's notes
This salad can be stored for 24 hours, chilled. The beets will make it progressively turn pink.
Sprouted buckwheat, once it is removed from the sprouting or jelly jar, can be kept in an airtight container in the refrigerator for up to 3 days. But do remember to rinse and dry it just before using.

Techniques
Using a Mandolin, p. 40
Sprouting Buckwheat, p. 74
Removing the Peel and Pith from Citrus Fruit, p. 140

Ingredients
Salad
14 oz. (400 g) assorted colored beets
(Chioggia, yellow, white, etc.)
2 pink grapefruit
1 ^{2}/$_3$ cups (7 oz./200 g) sprouted buckwheat

Vinaigrette
1 salt-preserved lemon
1 orange
4 tablespoons chopped dill
¼ cup (60 ml) olive oil
Fine salt and freshly ground pepper

Equipment
Mandolin

Ingredients

1 small bunch watercress (approximately
    3 ½ oz./100 g)
1 head broccoli (approximately 1 lb./450 g)
1 tablespoon kosher salt
8 oz. (250 g) soba noodles
1 piece daikon (Japanese white radish),
    weighing 2 ½ oz. (75 g), grated

Seasoning

1 teaspoon white miso paste
1 tablespoon rice vinegar
4 tablespoons (60 ml) sesame oil
3 tablespoons soy sauce
1 teaspoon grated ginger
1 tablespoon sesame seeds
4 *umeboshi* (Japanese fermented plums),
    to garnish (optional)

Soba Noodles with Broccoli and Watercress ★

Serves 4
Preparation time: 10 minutes
Cooking time: 15 minutes

Carefully wash and dry the watercress. Wash the broccoli and separate it into florets, reserving the thick stem to use for a soup or broth.

Steam the broccoli florets for 7 to 8 minutes, depending on the texture you prefer, but they should remain firm. Dip them briefly into a large bowl of cold water with ice cubes to refresh and drain well.

Bring a large pot of water to a boil with the kosher salt. Drop the soba noodles in, stir, and wait until the water comes to a boil again. Immediately pour in 1 ⅔ cups (400 ml) of cold water. Again, wait for the water to come to a boil, then remove from the heat and drain the noodles.

For the seasoning
In a salad bowl, whisk the white miso with the rice vinegar, sesame oil, soy sauce, and ginger. Stir in the sesame seeds.

To serve
Place the drained soba noodles, broccoli florets, and watercress in the salad bowl, and mix to coat the ingredients in the seasoning sauce. Divide among four plates or bowls, sprinkle with grated daikon, and garnish with an *umeboshi*.

● Chef's notes
Instead of rice vinegar, why not try ume su, *vinegar made from* umeboshi?
One of the many benefits of these very sour, fermented plums is that they aid digestion.
Soba noodles, made from buckwheat, usually contain a little wheat flour to hold them together. If you are intolerant or sensitive to gluten, check the ingredients on the package.

❙ Techniques
Peeling Fresh Ginger, p. 29
Blanching, p. 41
Steaming, p. 41

Barley, Millet, and Other Grains

Barley and Mushroom Risotto ★

Serves 4
Preparation time: 30 minutes
Cooking time: 45 minutes

Peel the carrots and onion and cut into small dice. Pull off the outer fibers of the celery and cut it into sticks. Clean the button mushrooms with a damp cloth and slice them.

In a skillet over high heat, sauté the mushrooms with 2 pinches of salt so that they render all their water (there is no need to add any oil). Bring the broth to a boil with the bay leaf, thyme, and garlic clove.

Pour 2 tablespoons of the olive oil into a large skillet over high heat. Soften the onion, carrots, and celery for 2 minutes. Pour in the barley, stir, and sauté for 2 to 3 minutes until lightly colored. Add half of the broth, stir, and cook until all the liquid has been absorbed, stirring from time to time. Discard the bay leaf and thyme and reserve the garlic clove. Pour the remaining broth over the barley and vegetables. Allow to cook until the liquid has been completely absorbed.

With a knife, slit the garlic clove and scrape out the flesh. Crush it with the remaining olive oil, season with pepper, and add the mixture to the risotto. Stir briskly to incorporate and serve on heated plates.

● Chef's notes
If you use hulled barley, increase the cooking time by 15 to 30 minutes. Instead of barley, you might want to try the equivalent amount of spelt or einkorn wheat. Both require a slightly longer cooking time: taste regularly to check for doneness. And as with most risotto dishes, serve with a generous helping of grated vegetarian Parmesan-style hard cheese or vegan "Parmesan" (see p. 124).

❘ Techniques
Preparing Vegetable Broth, p. 31
Making Risotto, p. 52
Sautéing Mushrooms, p. 98

Ingredients
1 cup (7 oz./200 g) pearl barley
2 large carrots (approximately 5 oz./150 g)
1 large yellow onion (approximately 3 oz./80 g)
1 medium stalk celery (approximately 1 ½ oz./40 g)
14 oz. (400 g) button mushrooms
2 ½–3 cups (600–700 ml) vegetable or mushroom broth
1 bay leaf
2 sprigs thyme
1 clove garlic, unpeeled
3 tablespoons olive oil
Fine salt and freshly ground pepper

Ingredients

Topping

1 unwaxed orange
2 shallots
10 oz. (300 g) butternut squash
1 lb. (500 g) Brussels sprouts
1 clove garlic, unpeeled
2 tablespoons olive oil, plus extra
   for the dish or pan
2 sprigs thyme
½ cup (2 oz./50 g) pecans
Fine salt and freshly ground pepper

Millet torte

Scant ½ cup (3 oz./80 g) millet flakes
1 ¼ cups (300 ml) milk
3 tablespoons walnut oil
3 eggs
1 small pinch grated nutmeg
Fine salt and freshly ground pepper

Equipment

10-inch (24-cm) diameter ovenproof dish
   or cake pan

Nut and Vegetable Millet Torte ★ ★

Serves 4 as a main dish (6 as a starter)
Preparation time: 30 minutes
Cooking time: 50 minutes

For the topping
Preheat the oven to 350°F (180°C/Gas Mark 4). Lightly oil the dish or pan.

Finely grate the zest of the orange, taking care not to include the bitter white pith, and squeeze the juice. Peel and dice the shallots. With a vegetable peeler, peel the butternut and cut it into small cubes. Remove the outer leaves of the Brussels sprouts and cut them into two or four pieces, depending on their size.

Spread the Brussels sprouts, butternut squash, shallots, and garlic clove on a baking sheet. In a small bowl, combine the olive oil, orange zest, and orange juice, and drizzle the mixture over the vegetables. Season with salt and pepper and crumble the thyme leaves over. Turn the vegetables over using your hands to ensure that they are evenly coated.

Bake for 30 minutes, stirring two or three times, until the vegetables are tender and nicely colored. With a sharp knife, open the garlic clove, scoop out the flesh, and mix it into the other ingredients.

For the torte
In a heavy-bottom saucepan, bring the milk to a boil with the oil, salt, and freshly ground pepper. Pour in the millet flakes, stir to combine, and cover with the lid. Remove from the heat and allow the millet flakes to swell for 10 minutes.

Separate the eggs. Beat the egg yolks and nutmeg into the swollen millet flakes. In a clean, dry mixing bowl, whisk the egg whites with a pinch of salt until they hold soft peaks. Carefully fold them into the millet mixture, taking care not to deflate it–it should remain light. Pour the batter into the prepared dish and bake for 20 minutes, until nicely golden on top. It will rise but flop slightly when removed from the oven. Do not turn out of the dish.

To serve
In a dry skillet over medium heat, lightly toast the pecans. Transfer to a bowl and reheat the vegetables in the same skillet. Spoon the topping with the pecans over the millet torte and serve in the baking dish.

● Chef's notes
This dish was inspired by a recipe created by Michel Bras, a three Michelin star chef. It is an unusually light and tasty grain cake that you can vary over the seasons with the vegetables of your choice. You can also substitute buckwheat or oats for the millet.

❙ Techniques
Preparing Squash, p. 17

Plum and Cinnamon Oat Slices ★

Serves 6
Preparation time: 25 minutes
Cooking time: 30 minutes

Preheat the oven to 400°F (200°C/Gas Mark 6). Butter the pan and then line it with parchment or waxed paper, ensuring that it is higher than the sides. This will make it easier to remove the cake from the pan.

In a mixing bowl, combine the sugar with the cinnamon. Melt the butter in a small saucepan over low heat. Cut the plums into halves, remove the pits, and slice finely. Sprinkle with 1 tablespoon of the sugar-cinnamon mixture and set aside at room temperature.

In a large mixing bowl, combine the flour, oats, remaining sugar-cinnamon mixture, and salt. Pour in the melted butter and stir with a wooden spoon until combined. Then, use your hands to mix the ingredients thoroughly: the batter should be soft. If it seems too dry, add 1 or 2 tablespoons of cold water.

Divide the batter into two equal parts. With your hands, spread half of the batter over the base of the prepared pan, pressing it down firmly. Cover with the sliced plums, pressing them into an even layer.

Cover the layer of plums with the remaining oat batter, working with your hands again. Bake for 30 to 40 minutes, until the dough is lightly colored and the plums are caramelized.

Leave to cool for 15 minutes. Carefully pull on the parchment paper to unmold the cake without turning it upside down. Allow to cool to luke-warm and cut into 12 squares. Serve warm or cool.

● Chef's notes
Stored in an airtight metal container, these slices keep well for up to 3 days.

Ingredients
1 lb. (500 g) purple plums
Generous ½ cup (4 oz./120 g) light brown sugar
½ teaspoon cinnamon
2 sticks (8 oz./220 g) butter, plus a little extra for the pan
2 cups plus scant ½ cup (10 oz./275 g) whole-wheat flour
1 ½ cups (5 oz./150 g) oats
1 good pinch fine salt

Equipment
Nonstick 8-inch (20-cm) square pan, or rectangular 6 × 10-inch (15 × 25-cm) pan

Peach and Red Currant Cobbler ★★

Serves 6 to 8
Preparation time: 25 minutes
Cooking time: 30 minutes

Preheat the oven to 400°F (200°C/Gas Mark 6). Butter the cake pan. Finely grate the zest of the half lemon. Peel and pit the peaches and cut them into slices.

Arrange them evenly over the base of the dish with the red currants and sprinkle with the rice flour, sugar, and lemon zest. Stir carefully to combine and reserve at room temperature.

For the cobbler dough
In a mixing bowl, combine the cornmeal, all-purpose flour, baking powder, and salt. Add the butter and work it in lightly with your fingertips until it reaches the consistency of coarse sand.

Beat the eggs with the syrup, buttermilk, and vanilla seeds or extract. Pour the egg mixture into the dry ingredients. Using a wooden spoon, stir until just combined and smooth. Drop the batter in spoonfuls over the fruit and bake for 20 to 30 minutes, until the top is golden. Serve warm with vanilla ice cream or whipped cream.

● Chef's notes

The starch used in this recipe absorbs the excess juices from the fruit. In addition to the three types of starch given in the list of ingredients, arrowroot can also be used. You'll need to adjust the quantity depending on how ripe the fruits are, the quantity of juice they exude, and the desired texture—more or less moist.
You can make delicious cobblers with apricots, rhubarb, berries, and even pears. Adjust the quantity of sugar according to the acidity of the fruit.

❙ Techniques
Peeling Soft Fruit, p. 139

Ingredients

6 ripe yellow peaches (approximately
  1 ½ lb./700 g when peeled and pitted)
4 oz. (125 g) red currants
½ organic or unwaxed lemon
1-2 tablespoons rice flour, cornstarch, or potato
  starch, depending on the ripeness of the peaches
¼ cup (2 oz./50 g) light brown sugar
A little butter for the cake pan

Cobbler dough
1 scant cup (4 oz./120 g) finely ground cornmeal
  (maize flour)
¾ cup plus 2 tablespoons (3 ½ oz./100 g)
  all-purpose flour
2 teaspoons baking powder
1 good pinch salt
5 tablespoons (3 oz./80 g) butter, chilled and diced
2 jumbo (UK extra-large) eggs
⅓ cup (80 ml) corn syrup, maple syrup,
  or agave syrup
¾ cup (200 ml) buttermilk or plain yogurt
Seeds of ½ vanilla bean or 1 teaspoon vanilla
  extract

Equipment

7-inch (18-cm) diameter or 8-inch (20-cm) square
  cake pan or ovenproof dish

Citrus-Flavored Barley Water ★

Serves 6
Preparation time: 5 minutes
Cooking time: 30 minutes
Chilling time: 3 hours minimum

Bring the water to a boil and pour in the pearl barley. Cook for 30 minutes, until the pearl barley is well cooked and the liquid reduced by half. Drain, reserving all the liquid; you should have between 1 ½ and 2 ¼ cups (600-800 ml).

Strain the liquid through a fine-mesh sieve while it is still hot and stir in the citrus juice and sugar. Mix until the sugar has dissolved.

Pour into a clean bottle, allow to cool, place in the refrigerator for at least 3 hours, and serve with ice. Stored in the refrigerator, this drink keeps for no longer than 2 days.

● Chef's notes
The cooked pearl barley should be retained. Sauté it and serve with vegetables; season it and add to a salad; or eat it, porridge-style, with fruit for breakfast.

● Good to know
Barley-based drinks have been consumed since ancient times, particularly in Greece. Roasted barley drinks continue to be drunk in India (sattu), Japan (mujicha), Italy, and elsewhere. In Asia, they are enjoyed hot or cold.

Ingredients
8 ½ cups (2 liters) water
1 generous cup (8 oz./220 g) pearl barley
1 cup (250 ml) squeezed citrus juice of your choice (lemon, lime, orange, grapefruit, etc.)
½ cup–½ cup plus 2 tablespoons (3 ½–4 oz./ 100-125 g) granulated sugar, depending on the sourness of the citrus juice selected

Barley, Millet, and Other Grains

Pulses

Mauro Colagreco

Mauro Colagreco, born in Argentina to a family of Italian origin, trained in Buenos Aires and arrived in France in 2001. He worked for Bernard Loiseau in Saulieu, and in 2003 joined the staff at Alain Passard's Arpège, before going on to work with Alain Ducasse at the Plaza Athénée and then Guy Martin at the Grand Véfour. These masters of their craft are all distinguished by their predilection for vegetables and their great creativity, which allowed Colagreco to broaden his horizons and strengthen his confidence in his personal style—one that is open-minded, generous, and inclusive.

In 2006, he settled in at the Mirazur in Menton, near the Italian border, and there his inventiveness took full flight. "The bounty offered by the earth here has influenced my cuisine and led me to create my own vegetable garden. When one sees vegetables growing, quite naturally, next to one another, it's a sign that they are meant to be together on the plate."

Gault et Millau named him Chef of the Year in 2008. He has two Michelin stars and the World's 50 Best Restaurants listing has ranked his restaurant at number eleven. Colagreco weaves his magic into Mediterranean cuisine, bringing a global dimension to it.

Peas—those fragile pulses that symbolize spring—are given pride of place here, with whipped cream tinted with parsley, spinach, and scallions on a background of herbs, fruit, and vegetables orchestrated in a symphony of greens.

Le Mirazur
30 Avenue Aristide Briand
06500 Menton
France
Website: mirazur.fr

Serves 4
Preparation time: 40 minutes

Ingredients
1 lb. (500 g) small, sweet peas in their pods

Chlorophyll-green cream
2 oz. (50 g) parsley
2 oz. (50 g) spinach
2 oz. (50 g) scallions (spring onions),
    green part only
Scant ½ cup (100 ml) crème fraîche
    or heavy cream, 34 percent butterfat

Vinaigrette
5 tablespoons (75 ml) lime juice
²/₃ cup (150 ml) finest quality olive oil
Fleur de sel to taste

Garnish
3 ½ oz. (100 g) sugar snap peas
3 ½ oz. (100 g) baby fennel stalks
2 medium kiwi fruit
1 round white turnip
4 shoots wall pennywort
    (*Umbelicus rupestris*)
8 chickweed leaves (*Stellaria media*)
1 lime

All-Green

For the peas
Shell the peas and select the sweetest and most tender. Place them in the refrigerator.

For the chlorophyll-green cream
Using a juicer, make a juice with the parsley, spinach, and scallions. Strain through a fine-mesh sieve and refrigerate. In a bowl, whisk the cream, adding the chlorophyll juice, and continue whisking until the mixture holds soft peaks and reaches a light green color.

For the vinaigrette
Pour the lime juice into a mixing bowl with a little fleur de sel. Pour the olive oil in a steady stream, whisking constantly, until the mixture emulsifies. Place in the refrigerator.

For the garnish
Open the sugar snap peas and immerse them briefly in a bowl of ice water. Remove them from the water and cut them into triangles with sides measuring about ¾ inch (1.5 cm). Cut the fennel stalks into fine slices. Peel the kiwis and cut them into rounds measuring ¼ inch (5 mm) in diameter. Cut each round into two pieces. Using a mandolin, cut the white turnip into very fine slices; use a 1-inch (2.5-cm) pastry cutter to cut them into rounds. Place in a bowl of ice water to firm up until they are crisp. Clean the herbs well and store in an airtight plastic container. Cut out the segments of the lime from between the membranes and dice the flesh finely to make a *brunoise*.

To serve
Place two scoops of green whipped cream on each plate. Arrange the other ingredients on the plates so as to create as much volume as possible. Serve well chilled.

Three Sisters Soup with Squash, Corn, and Beans ★

Serves 4
Preparation time: 30 minutes
Cooking time: 45 minutes

Peel and chop the onion. Remove the outer fibers from the celery stalks and chop them finely. Crush the garlic cloves. Cut the squash into small dice.

Drizzle the peanut oil into a large pot over high heat. Add the onion, celery, and squash. Soften for 5 minutes. Pour in the vegetable broth, season with salt, and add two of the oregano sprigs and the chili pepper. Cover with the lid, reduce the heat to low, and simmer for 25 minutes.

Add the corn kernels and cook for an additional 10 minutes without the lid. Add the kidney beans and continue simmering, uncovered, for 5 minutes. Adjust the seasoning, adding salt, pepper, and chili pepper if necessary. Crumble the remaining oregano leaves into the soup and serve hot.

● Chef's notes

This soup is particularly good when made with all fresh ingredients, but if you're in a hurry, use canned red kidney beans (be sure to rinse them well) and frozen or canned corn, for which you will need approximately 6 oz. (180 g). If you're using prepared ingredients, add the corn and kidney beans when the squash is extremely soft and about to fall apart; they will only require 5 minutes in the hot soup to warm up.

● Good to know

The "Three Sisters" is an Amerindian reference to the side-by-side cultivation of squash, climbing beans, and corn. The corn functions as both a climbing pole and meshing for the beans, which capture the nitrogen that favors the growth of the corn and squash. The squash leaves retain the moisture in the earth and prevent weeds from growing. This mutually beneficial farming trio is also of high nutritional value, with the beans providing two amino acids, lysine and tryptophan, which are lacking in corn. Together, the three provide nutritious vegetable protein.

❙ Techniques

Preparing Squash, p. 17
Preparing Corn, p. 18
Preparing Garlic, p. 29
Cooking Pulses, p. 82

Ingredients
1 onion
2 stalks celery, weighing about 3 oz. (80 g)
2 cloves garlic
1 lb. (500 g) trimmed squash of your choice
(butternut, acorn, buttercup, or red kuri)
2 tablespoons peanut oil
3 ¼ cups (800 ml) vegetable broth
3 sprigs fresh oregano
½ teaspoon ground chili pepper,
mild or strong, according to taste
Kernels of 2 ears corn
1 ½ cups (8 oz./250 g) cooked kidney beans
Fine salt and freshly ground pepper

Ingredients

Dosa pancakes

1 ⅓ cups (4 oz./120 g) chickpea flour

⅓ cup (2 oz./50 g) rice flour

½ cup minus 1 tablespoon (2 oz./50 g)
  all-purpose flour

½ teaspoon fine salt

1 teaspoon baking soda

2 tablespoons whole milk plain yogurt

2 ¾ cups (700 ml) lukewarm water

2 tablespoons ghee or clarified butter,
  to cook the pancakes

Filling

2 lb. (900 g) firm, waxy potatoes

1 onion

1 small fresh green chili pepper

3 stalks fresh curry leaves

1 small piece fresh ginger, ¾–1 ½ inches
  (2–4 cm), according to taste

2 tablespoons ghee for cooking

2 tablespoons *urud dhal* (split black
  gram beans), optional

2 teaspoons yellow or brown mustard seeds

2 teaspoons cumin seeds

1 ½ teaspoons ground coriander

1 teaspoon turmeric

½ teaspoon garam masala

Equipment

Pancake maker

Techniques

Preparing Chilies, p. 23

Peeling Fresh Ginger, p. 29

Making Clarified Butter and Ghee, p. 113

Spicy Potato *Dosas* ★ ★

Makes 6 pancakes

Preparation time: 30 minutes

Cooking time: 30 minutes

For the *dosa* pancakes

Combine the chickpea flour, rice flour, all-purpose flour, salt, and baking soda. Stir in the yogurt. Pour in the water in a steady stream, whisking until the batter is smooth. If you wish, you can make the batter in a blender. Set aside at room temperature while you make the filling.

For the filling

Preheat the oven to 300°F (150°C/Gas Mark 2).

Peel the potatoes and cut them into 1-inch (2.5-cm) cubes. Parboil them in salted boiling water for 10 minutes and drain. Peel and dice the onion. Remove the seeds of the chili pepper and dice it finely. Pick the curry leaves from the stalks. Peel and grate the ginger.

Heat the ghee or clarified butter in a skillet over high heat. Pour in the *urud dhal*, mustard seeds, and cumin, and heat for 30 seconds, until they just begin to pop. Stir in the onion, ginger, and chili pepper and brown lightly for 2 minutes. Add the remaining spices, season with salt, and sauté for 1 minute. Coat the potato cubes in the spice mix and sauté for 5 to 10 minutes, until nicely colored and cooked through. Stir in the curry leaves and transfer the contents of the skillet to an ovenproof dish. Place in the oven and lower the temperature to 210°F (100°C/Gas Mark ¼) to keep the garnish warm while you prepare the *dosa* pancakes.

To finish

Melt the ghee in the pancake maker, ensuring it is well coated. Stir the batter and pour a ladleful into the pancake maker, tilting it for an even thickness. Allow to cook for 2 to 3 minutes, until the edges are a nice golden color and crinkle a little. Spoon one sixth of the potato filling over the *dosa* and roll it up. Remove from the pancake maker and repeat with the remaining batter and filling to make six *dosas* altogether. Serve with mango and pomegranate raita (see recipe p. 303).

● Chef's notes

In India, a spice mix is known as a masala, while "curry" is the name of a plant with small, round leaves often used as a masala ingredient.

Authentic masala dosas—thin, crispy pancakes—are made using two fermented pastes: one of rice and one of hulled urud dhal. They are tricky to get right. This simplified version is an everyday recipe made in many Indian homes.

Southern Black-Eyed Peas with Greens and Cornbread ★

Serves 4
Soaking time: 8 hours
Preparation time: 40 minutes
Cooking time: 1 hour

For the black-eyed peas with greens
Soak the black-eyed peas for 8 hours. Cook them in a pot of boiling water for 45 minutes to 1 hour, until tender. Drain well.

Wash and dry the collard greens and chop roughly, setting aside a few for garnish. Peel and dice the onion and garlic cloves. In a skillet, soften them in the oil. Add the collard greens, bay leaf, vegetable broth, vinegar, and salt. Reduce the heat to low and simmer for 30 minutes, until the leaves are tender. Stir in the black-eyed peas. Adjust the seasoning, adding salt and vinegar to taste.

For the cornbread
Preheat the oven to 400°F (200°C/Gas Mark 6). Butter the pan. In a small heavy-bottom saucepan over low heat, melt the butter. In a large mixing bowl, combine the all-purpose flour, cornmeal, baking powder, baking soda, and salt. In a medium mixing bowl, whisk the buttermilk with the eggs.

Pour the melted butter into the buttermilk-egg mixture. Pour the liquid into the dry ingredients, whisking constantly until the batter is smooth. Do not overmix; this will ensure that the baked cornbread is soft and moist.

Pour the batter into the prepared pan and bake for 20 to 25 minutes, until a knife tip inserted into the center comes out dry and the surface is golden. Allow to cool in the pan for 10 minutes, turn out, and cut into squares. Serve warm with the black-eyed peas and leafy greens.

● Chef's notes
Buttermilk is the residual liquid that remains after cream has been churned into butter. It is rich in lactic ferments, low in fat, and has a good tang. It is used to make light, well-risen doughs. If you don't have buttermilk, simply stir the juice of one quarter of a lemon into the same volume of milk given here and allow to rest for 5 minutes until it curdles slightly. If you prefer, you can do the same with soy milk.

● Good to know
In Texas and other southern states, this symbolic dish is traditionally eaten on New Year's Eve. With the black-eyed peas representing coins, the leafy greens standing for dollars, and the cornbread as yellow as gold, it ensures that money will not be lacking in the year to come. Similar symbols are found in many other countries, with lentils having the same significance in Italy, for example. Further proof, if it were needed, that pulses are a real treasure!

Ingredients
Black-eyed peas with greens
1 generous cup (6 oz./180 g) black-eyed peas
1 ¼ lb. (600 g) collard greens, or a mixture of greens (leaves from kohlrabi, broccoli, turnips, spinach, and kale)
1 large onion, weighing approximately 3 ½ oz. (100 g)
2 cloves garlic
2 tablespoons oil (sunflower or olive)
1 bay leaf
Scant ½ cup (100 ml) vegetable broth
1 tablespoon red wine vinegar
1 teaspoon fine salt
Freshly ground pepper

Cornbread
5 tablespoons (2 ½ oz./70 g) butter, plus a little extra for the pan
⅔ cup (3 oz./80 g) all-purpose flour
Generous ½ cup (3 ½ oz./100 g) cornmeal (maize flour)
1 ½ teaspoons baking powder
½ teaspoon baking soda
½ teaspoon fine salt
1 cup minus 2 tablespoons (220 ml) buttermilk
2 eggs

Equipment
8-inch (20-cm) square pan

Techniques
Dicing Onions, p. 39
Cooking Pulses, p. 82

Ingredients
1 ⅓ cups (7 oz./200 g) dried fava (broad) beans
2 lemons
2 cloves garlic
10 sprigs parsley
3 tablespoons olive oil
1 teaspoon cumin
1 small pinch cayenne pepper
½ teaspoon fine salt
4 eggs
2 tomatoes
1 onion
A dozen green olives

Ful Medames ★

Egyptian Stewed Fava Beans

Serves 4
Soaking time: 8 hours
Preparation time: 30 minutes
Cooking time: 3 hours 30 minutes

Soak the dried beans in a large bowl of cold water for 8 hours. Simmer them for about 3 hours, until very tender and some are beginning to fall apart. If you prefer, cook them in a pressure cooker for 1 hour. Drain, reserving a ladleful of the cooking liquid.

Squeeze the lemons and peel and crush the garlic cloves. Finely chop the parsley. Using a fork, roughly mash the fava beans. Season with olive oil, garlic, lemon juice, chopped parsley, cumin, cayenne pepper, and salt. If you wish to adjust the texture, incorporate as much of the reserved cooking liquid as you need.

Hard-boil the eggs and shell them. Cut the tomatoes into quarters. Finely dice the onion.

Serve the *ful medames* hot with the eggs, tomatoes, and green olives on the side. Pickled green chili peppers and pita can be served as accompaniments.

● Chef's notes
Since the fava beans take so long to cook, you'll save time if you have a pressure cooker. Or use canned beans, on sale at Middle Eastern grocery stores.

● Good to know
This dish, whose main ingredient is dried fava beans, is a traditional Egyptian breakfast food. It is served with a few vegetables—tomatoes and cucumber— and a hard-boiled egg, either on a plate or in pita bread. In Egypt, the beans are simmered gently overnight and seasoned in the morning.
Ful medames is a dish found throughout the Middle East, with local variations. In Syria, it is drizzled with tahini, and chili peppers are also widely used.

┃ Techniques
Preparing Garlic, p. 29
Cooking Pulses, p. 82
Hard-Boiling Eggs, p. 104

Middle Eastern Lentils, Rice, and Fried Onions ★

Serves 4
Preparation time: 20 minutes
Cooking time: 45 minutes

Peel the onions and slice them finely with a mandolin. Heat the olive oil in a skillet over medium-high heat and fry the onions for 20 minutes, stirring frequently, until they are nicely caramelized. Season with salt and remove from the skillet, leaving the oil.

Precook the lentils in salted boiling water for 15 minutes and drain. Rinse the rice well.

In the skillet used for the onions, lightly color the rice and spices. Add the cooked lentils, half the caramelized onions, and cover with hot water. Season with salt and simmer over low heat for approximately 20 minutes, until all the liquid has been absorbed.

Transfer to a serving dish and cover with the remaining caramelized onions. Serve, drizzled lightly with lemon juice, adding a spoonful of Greek yogurt to each plate.

● **Chef's notes**

Cooking times for lentils vary. Precooking in water softens them, and after this step they should be slightly firm but no longer have any crunch—taste to test. To reduce their cooking time, you can also soak them overnight.

● **Good to know**

This "poor man's dish," as this hearty rice, lentil, and fried onion meal is popularly known, is found in different versions and under different names (mjaddara, majadra, and variations) throughout the Middle East and in Syria, Egypt, and Lebanon. It was originally prepared with bulgur wheat. Spices change from one country to another; cinnamon may be added, as well as cayenne pepper and others.

❚ **Techniques**
Using a Mandolin, p. 40

Ingredients

8 oz. (250 g) white or yellow onions
5 tablespoons (75 ml) olive oil
⅔ cup (4 oz./125 g) brown lentils
1 generous cup (7 oz./200 g) long grain rice
½ teaspoon cumin
½ teaspoon allspice (Jamaican pepper)
Fine salt and freshly ground pepper

To serve
Lemon juice
Greek yogurt or sheep milk yogurt

Ingredients

Dhal

1 cup (7 oz./200 g) hulled, split black gram beans
  (white *urad dhal*)
1 onion
1 clove garlic
¾–1 ¼-inch (2–4-cm) piece of ginger, to taste
2 tablespoons ghee or coconut oil
1 teaspoon turmeric
1 cup (250 ml) coconut milk
1 cup (250 ml) *passata* (strained tomatoes)
1 teaspoon garam masala
1 small pinch ground red chili pepper
Juice of ½ lime

Raita sauce

¼ red onion
1 small green chili pepper (or more or less,
  according to taste)
½ firm but ripe mango, weighing 5 oz. (150 g)
Seeds of ¼ pomegranate
6 sprigs cilantro (coriander)
½ teaspoon cumin seeds
½ teaspoon fine salt
½ teaspoon garam masala
1 cup (250 ml) whole milk plain yogurt
  or Greek yogurt

Techniques

Preparing Chilies, p. 23
Preparing Garlic, p. 29
Peeling Fresh Ginger, p. 29
Dicing Onions, p. 39
Making Clarified Butter and Ghee, p. 113
Preparing Pomegranates, p. 134
Preparing Mangoes, p. 136

Urad Dhal with Mango and Pomegranate Raita ★

Serves 4
Preparation time: 20 minutes
Cooking time: 40 minutes

For the *dhal*

It is best to measure the *dhal* in a cup or measuring beaker. Prepare twice its volume of hot water. Peel and dice the onion. Peel and grate the garlic and ginger.

Melt the ghee in a skillet over medium heat and soften the garlic, onion, ginger, and ground turmeric for 3 minutes. Add the split black gram beans and pour in twice the volume of hot water. Cover with the lid, reduce the heat to low, and simmer for 25 minutes.

Pour in the coconut milk and tomato *passata*. Add the garam masala and chili pepper. Cover with the lid and simmer over low heat for an additional 15 minutes. Season with salt, remove from the heat, and stir in the lime juice.

For the raita sauce

Peel and finely dice the onion. Remove the seeds from the chili pepper and dice it finely. Peel the mango and cut it into small cubes. Remove the seeds of the pomegranate and chop the cilantro leaves.

With a mortar and pestle, coarsely grind the cumin seeds with the salt. Combine the onion, mango, pomegranate seeds, cilantro, garam masala, cumin, chili, and yogurt. Serve the raita with the *dhal*, accompanied by basmati rice.

● Chef's notes

The cooking time required for pulses varies according to the hardness of the water used. It is best to use filtered water, and it is important to taste regularly to check that it reaches the consistency you prefer.

● Good to know

In India, "dhal" is a generic term that designates various pulses like lentils or split peas. By extension, the same term is used for this dish. Its consistency varies across the regions of the country, and depends, too, on the taste of the cook. Toor dhal is made with yellow lentils, chana dhal with dark-skinned chickpeas, mung dhal with mung bean, urad dhal with black gram beans, improperly known as "black soy beans," which also go by the name of "white lentils" when they are hulled and split. Massoor dhal is made with red lentils.

Falafel and Tabbouleh ★ ★

Serves 4
Soaking time: 8 hours
Preparation time: 40 minutes
Chilling time: 4 hours, including 1 hour for the tabbouleh
Cooking time: 15 minutes

For the falafel

Soak the chickpeas in a large bowl of water for 8 hours. Drain and dry very carefully. Peel the garlic cloves and remove the green shoots. Peel the onion and chop it roughly.

In the food processor fitted with a blade knife, or in a blender, briefly process the chickpeas with the onion and garlic. The mixture should retain some coarseness. Add the herbs and spices, salt, pepper, baking soda, and sesame seeds, and process until smooth. Transfer to a dish or bowl, cover with plastic wrap, and place in the refrigerator for 4 hours.

For the tabbouleh

Rinse the bulgur. Soak it for 15 minutes in 1 cup (250 ml) of boiling water, then drain well, pressing down firmly to extract as much liquid as possible. Peel and dice the onion. Remove the seeds of the tomatoes and dice the flesh finely. Place in a fine-mesh strainer over a bowl to catch the juice from the pieces. Pick the leaves of the parsley and mint and chop finely.

In a salad bowl, combine the bulgur, onion, drained tomato dice, parsley, mint, lemon juice, and olive oil. Season with salt and pepper and place in the refrigerator for 1 hour.

To cook the falafel

Preheat the oven to 210°F (100°C/Gas Mark ¼).

Using a teaspoon, scoop out portions of the chickpea preparation and roll them into small balls between your hands. You should have 20 to 25 balls. Heat the oil in a large skillet. Fry the falafel, browning them lightly all over, which should take about 4 minutes in all. Place on sheets of paper towel to drain, then place in the oven to keep warm while you continue cooking the remaining balls.

Serve hot, accompanied by the tabbouleh and *tarator* sauce.

● Chef's notes

Once the falafel have been fried, you can cool and store them for 2 days in the refrigerator or 2 months in the freezer. They are often served in a pita sandwich with shredded red and white cabbage, cucumber slices, tomatoes, and fermented turnip pickles.
To make a gluten-free version of this dish, substitute 3 ½ oz. (100 g) of cauliflower "couscous" (see technique p. 20) for the bulgur.

Ingredients
Falafel
1 generous cup (7 oz./200 g) dried chickpeas
2 cloves garlic
1 small onion (2-3 oz./60-80 g)
1 tablespoon chopped cilantro (coriander)
1 tablespoon ground cumin
1 tablespoon ground coriander
1 teaspoon dried mint
½ teaspoon salt
½ teaspoon freshly ground pepper
½ teaspoon baking soda
1 teaspoon white sesame seeds
Scant ½ cup (100 ml) oil for frying
(corn or sunflower)

Tabbouleh
¼ cup (1 oz./30 g) fine bulgur wheat
1 onion
2-3 tomatoes (14 oz./400 g)
2 or 3 bunches flat-leaf parsley (4 oz./120 g)
10 sprigs mint
Juice of 1 large lemon
Scant ⅓ cup (70 ml) olive oil
Fine salt and freshly ground pepper

Equipment
Blender or food processor

Techniques
Preparing Fresh Herbs, p. 38
Dicing Onions, p. 39
Making *Tarator* Sauce, p. 125

Ingredients

Generous ¾ cup (5 oz./150 g)
  dried red kidney beans
¾ cup (5 oz./150 g) dried lima (butter) beans
  or pink beans
2 large onions (7 oz./200 g)
2 carrots (7 oz./200 g)
2 to 3 stalks celery (7 oz./200 g)
2 cloves garlic
1 small fresh red chili pepper (or more or less,
  according to taste)
1 red bell pepper
2 tablespoons olive oil
1 teaspoon mild paprika
½ teaspoon ground coriander
1 teaspoon ground cumin
2 cups plus scant ½ cup (600 ml) *passata*
  (strained tomatoes)
⅔ cup (150 ml) vegetable broth
1 bay leaf
2 cloves
1 teaspoon dried oregano
1 generous pinch sugar
1 small pinch ground chili pepper (cayenne
  or ancho chili)
Fine salt and freshly ground pepper

To serve

1 bunch cilantro (coriander)
⅔ cup heavy cream, crème fraîche, or vegan
  (cashew nut) heavy cream (see p. 120)
4 oz. (125 g) vegetarian hard cheese (cheddar,
  Emmental, etc.), freshly grated

Techniques

Preparing Bell Peppers, p. 22
Preparing Chilies, p. 23
Preparing Garlic, p. 29
Preparing Vegetable Broth, p. 31
Dicing Onions, p. 39
Cooking Pulses, p. 82
Making Uncooked Vegan Heavy Cream, p. 120

Two-Bean Chili Sin Carne ★

Serves 4 to 6
Soaking time: 8 hours
Preparation time: 25 minutes
Cooking time: 2 hours 30 minutes

Soak the beans together for 8 hours. Rinse and cook in boiling water for 1 hour 30 minutes, or in a pressure cooker for 30 minutes. Taste to test for doneness: they should retain some firmness. Drain well.

Peel and dice the onions. Peel the carrots and chop them into chunks. Remove the tough fibers from the celery stalks and cut them into slices. Peel the garlic cloves and remove the green shoots. Seed the fresh chili pepper and chop it finely. Peel the bell pepper and dice it.

Heat the oil in a skillet over medium-high heat. Soften the onion, garlic, and chili pepper for 2 minutes. Add the celery, carrots, and bell pepper. Sauté for 5 minutes. Stir in the paprika, coriander, and cumin. Continue to sauté for 1 minute, then pour in the tomato *passata* and the vegetable broth. Add the bay leaf, cloves, oregano, and sugar, and season with the ground chili pepper, salt, and pepper.

Bring to a boil. Reduce the heat to low and add the beans. Cook for 30 to 45 minutes, depending on the firmness of the beans. Some of them will disintegrate and thicken the sauce.

Pick the leaves off the cilantro and chop. Remove the chili from the heat and stir in half of the chopped cilantro leaves. Place the remainder in a bowl.

Serve the chili in soup plates, accompanied by tortillas, chopped cilantro, cream, and grated cheese.

● Chef's notes

To give the illusion of a chili con carne, add 8 oz. (250 g) chopped seitan (see technique p. 69), or 1 oz. (30 g) textured soy protein (weight before rehydrating), rehydrated in vegetable broth (see technique p. 91). Brown lightly with the onions and proceed with the recipe.
To gain time, you can also use 3 ½ cups (1 ¼ lb./600 g) canned beans, well rinsed and drained.

● Good to know

It is a popular misconception that chili, whether con carne or sin carne, is Mexican. In fact, it originated in Texas. As its name indicates, chili is one of its most important ingredients, both fresh (habanero, serrano, or jalapeño) and dried (ancho chili, chipotle, and others). Make this dish your own by adding spices to your taste.

Chicago Navy Bean Pie ★★

Serves 6
Preparation time: 20 minutes
Chilling time: 1 hour
Cooking time: 55 minutes

For the pastry dough
In a mixing bowl, combine the flour and salt. Make a well in the center and add the butter. Working with your fingertips, rub the ingredients together until the texture resembles coarse sand. Pour in the vinegar and then the water and knead lightly until the dough forms a ball. Cover with plastic wrap and place in the refrigerator for 1 hour.

For the filling
In the blender or food processor, puree the cooked navy beans. Add the eggs, evaporated milk, sugar, butter, flour, vanilla extract, cinnamon, and nutmeg. Process until smooth.

To assemble and bake
Preheat the oven to 350°F (180°C/Gas Mark 4). Butter the tart pan.

On a lightly floured surface, roll the dough to a thickness of ¼ inch (6 mm). Line the prepared tart pan and trim the edges. Place a sheet of waxed or parchment paper over it and fill with pie weights. Bake for 15 minutes, until barely colored. Carefully remove the pie weights and waxed paper and pour the bean filling into the tart crust. Bake for 40 minutes, until the filling is set and a light golden color.

● Chef's notes
For best results when making the dough, it's important to use well-chilled butter. If the weather is hot, place the diced butter in the freezer for 30 minutes before incorporating it.
The dough can also be made in the bowl of a food processor fitted with the blade knife. In this case, combine the dry ingredients, incorporate the butter using the pulse function, and finally incorporate the liquid ingredients. Stop the food processor as soon as the dough forms a ball.
This dough can be prepared up to 2 days ahead, and frozen for up to 2 months.

● Good to know
Bean pie was created in the 1930s in Chicago using the nutritional principles of Elijah Muhammad, the founder of the Nation of Islam, which forbade the consumption of the sweet potato, a vegetable often used to make desserts. The pie is still eaten from Detroit to Washington.

❘ Techniques
Making Shortcrust Pastry Dough, p. 65
Rolling Out Pastry Dough, p. 66
Lining a Tart Pan, p. 67
Baking Blind, p. 76
Cooking Pulses, p. 82

Ingredients
Pastry dough
1 ½ cups (6 ½ oz./180 g) all-purpose flour, plus a little extra for rolling
¼ teaspoon fine salt
7 tablespoons (4 oz./110 g) butter, chilled and diced, plus a little extra for the pan
1 teaspoon cider vinegar
3 tablespoons ice water

Filling
1 cup (6 oz./180 g) cooked, rinsed, and dried navy (haricot) beans
2 eggs
½ cup (120 ml) evaporated milk (unsweetened)
1 cup minus 2 ½ tablespoons (6 ½ oz./170 g) light brown sugar
4 tablespoons (60 g) melted butter
1 tablespoon (20 g) all-purpose flour
2 teaspoons vanilla extract
1 teaspoon cinnamon
½ teaspoon grated nutmeg

Equipment
10-inch (24-cm) diameter tart pan
Blender or food processor

Soybeans

Christophe Moret

Christophe Moret trained with Bruno Cirino at the Grand Hôtel de Saint-Jean-de-Luz and continued at Château Ezra, before joining Jacques Maximin at Théâtre in Nice in 1989. His encounter with Alain Ducasse in 1990 marked the start of their collaboration at the famed Louis XV and then at 59 Poincaré and Spoon. In 2003, Moret became chef at the three Michelin star Plaza Athénée, and seven years later took the reins at the gourmet Lasserre restaurant, where he created a vegetarian menu that showcased tofu, einkorn wheat, and the vegetables of which he is so fond. In 2015, he became executive chef of the three restaurants of the luxury Shangri La in Paris, where he brings together French and Asian gastronomy. The menus include many vegetarian and vegan dishes, and Moret works with a number of local producers in the greater Paris region.

Moret—a tofu enthusiast ever since he discovered it in Asia—makes his own in his kitchens, guaranteeing a product of the finest quality that reveals the true taste of this often overlooked ingredient in the West. Here, combined with herbs in the style of a royale—a molded custard that is generally cut when set—tofu moves into another taste dimension.

Shangri-La Paris
10 Avenue d'Iéna
75116 Paris
France

Serves 4

Preparation time: 45 minutes; Chilling time:
1 hour; Marinating time: 1 hour

Ingredients

Tofu

⅓ oz. (10 g) *nigari*

1 ⅔ cups (325 ml) soy
milk

1 tablespoon each
chopped chervil,
lemon balm, cilantro
(coriander), parsley,
and mint

Vegetables

1 yellow beet

1 Chioggia beet

1 Red Meat radish

2 scallions (spring
onions), outer layer
removed

2 yellow carrots

2 purple carrots

2 orange carrots

Olive oil

Vegetable broth

1 white Belgian endive

1 red Belgian endive

1 romaine lettuce
heart

1 pear, preferably
Conference

1 Thai green mango

4 radishes with their
greens

2 fennel bulbs

1 wood-stove cooked
Crapaudine beet

1 Granny Smith apple

Marinade

Scant ½ cup (100 ml)
mineral water

¼ cup (60 ml) white
vinegar

3 tablespoons (2 oz./
60 g) acacia honey

Herb sauce

1 shallot

1 tablespoon (15 ml)
olive oil

Scant ½ cup (100 ml)
white wine

1 tablespoon white
vinegar

⅔ cup (150 ml) soy milk

1 handful each
chervil, lemon balm,
cilantro (coriander),
parsley, and mint

Herb-Infused Tofu, Marinated Vegetables, and Herb Sauce

For the herb-infused silken tofu

Dilute the *nigari* in a scant ½ cup (100 ml) water. Heat the soy milk to 113°F (45°C). Pour the diluted *nigari* into the soy milk, stirring with a flexible spatula, and add the herbs. Divide between four soup plates, pouring to a depth of ¾ inch (2 cm). Place in the refrigerator for at least 1 hour.

For the marinated vegetables

Using a mandolin, slice the beets, Red Meat radish, and prepared scallions into 1/16-inch (2-mm) slices. Combine all the ingredients for the marinade and bring to a boil. Pour it, still hot, over the sliced vegetables and marinate for 1 hour at room temperature.

For the other vegetables

Peel the remaining vegetables and any fruit that may require peeling. Slice the carrots with a mandolin and sweat them, without allowing them to color, in a skillet with olive oil and enough vegetable broth to cover them. Remove from the heat and set aside. Cut the Belgian endives and romaine leaves into feather shapes. Slice the pear and mango with a mandolin. Using a ¾-inch (2-cm) pastry cutter, cut the pear slices into rounds. Cut the mango into triangles with 1-inch (2.5-cm) sides. Using a mandolin, cut the four radishes and fennel bulbs as finely as possible. Reserve them in ice water so that they remain crisp. Cut the beet with a mandolin and roll the slices into ½-inch (1-cm) diameter tubes.

For the herb sauce

Peel and dice the shallot. Sweat it in olive oil, deglaze with white wine, and reduce until dry. Add the vinegar and reduce until dry again. Heat the soy milk to 113°F (45°C) and stir in the herbs and shallot. Process in a powerful blender to make a smooth green sauce.

To serve

Drain the marinated vegetables. Carefully pat dry the vegetables that have been in ice water. Arrange the vegetables over the tofu, pour over the warm herb sauce, and serve immediately.

Ingredients

7 oz. (200 g) tempeh
4 oz. (125 g) uncooked soy vermicelli
¼ cup (1 oz./30 g) cashew nuts
4 handfuls mixed herbs of your choice (mint,
   cilantro [coriander], watercress, chives, etc.)
12 radishes
4 handfuls baby spinach leaves
Juice of ½ lemon
12 rice-paper wrappers

Sesame sauce
2 tablespoons mayonnaise
2 tablespoons rice vinegar
1 ½ tablespoons tamari (soy) sauce
2 teaspoons tahini (pureed sesame seeds)
1 teaspoon toasted sesame oil
1 teaspoon *mirin*
1 teaspoon granulated sugar

Herby Spring Rolls with Sesame Sauce ★ ★

Serves 4 to 6 (makes 12 spring rolls)
Preparation time: 30 minutes

Steam the tempeh for 10 minutes. When it has cooled enough to handle it, crumble with your hands and allow to cool completely. Soak the soy vermicelli in boiling water for 5 minutes. Rinse under cold water and, with a pair of scissors, cut roughly into pieces.

Roast the cashew nuts in a small skillet and chop them roughly. Pick the leaves of the herbs and chop them roughly. Wash the radishes and slice them finely with a mandolin. Rinse and dry the baby spinach leaves.

To make the filling, use your hands to combine the baby spinach leaves, herbs, radishes, soy vermicelli, cashew nuts, tempeh, and lemon juice.

Moisten a rice-paper wrapper and place it flat on your work surface. At the nearest end, place a small handful of the filling. Fold the sides inward and then fold over the base of the sheet to enclose the filling. Roll up firmly. Continue with the other wrappers until all of the remaining filling is used up.

For the sesame sauce
In a mixing bowl, combine all the ingredients. Use a fork to mix them until they form an emulsion.

● Chef's notes

Depending on the season, and on your taste, you may want to replace the radishes with some finely sliced cucumber, white radish (daikon), black radish, or raw carrots. And instead of the tahini-flavored sauce made here, why not try a vegan tofu mayonnaise (see technique p. 89) or a dengaku sauce (see recipe p. 266).
If you don't have soy vermicelli, you could use rice vermicelli.
The filling will keep in an airtight container for up to 12 hours ahead of time, well chilled. However, it is important to prepare the spring rolls at the last minute so that they remain fresh and do not dry out.

❘ Techniques

Using a Mandolin, p. 40
Using Rice-Paper Wrappers, p. 54
Cooking Tempeh, p. 93

Chinese Tofu and Black Mushroom Dumplings ★ ★ ★

Makes about 40 dumplings
Preparation time: 50 minutes
Resting time: 30 minutes
Cooking time: 15 minutes

For the dumpling dough
Bring the water to a boil. Place the flour in a mixing bowl. Gradually pour the water over the flour, using a pair of chopsticks to incorporate it. (Alternatively, use a wooden spoon.) Mix until just combined. Leave the dough to cool for 15 minutes. When it is cool enough to handle, knead it until smooth. Cover with plastic wrap and allow to rest while you prepare the stuffing.

For the stuffing
Press the tofu. Soak the dried black mushrooms in hot water for 10 minutes. Drain and chop finely. Carefully clean the leek and slice it. Sauté the leeks in a nonstick pan for 5 minutes until softened. Peel and grate the ginger. Chop the chives very finely. Crumble the tofu. Combine all the ingredients and allow to rest while you fold the dumplings.

For the dumplings
Divide the dough into four parts. On a work surface dusted with starch, roll each one into a long log. Cut the logs into pieces about 1 ¼-1 ½ inches (3-4 cm) long and use your hands to flatten them into rounds. Roll them into disks on the work surface, ensuring that they do not overlap. With your finger or a pastry brush, moisten the rim of each disk with a little water. Place 1 to 2 teaspoons of stuffing in the center. Fold over, pressing firmly to remove any air bubbles. Continue until all the ingredients are used up.

Heat half of the oil in a skillet over medium-high heat. Working in batches, place the dumplings in the skillet, making sure they do not touch, and fry for 2 to 3 minutes, until lightly golden. Pour in 3 tablespoons (50 ml) water, immediately cover with a lid, and cook for 5 minutes, until all the water has been absorbed. Continue with the remaining dumplings.

To prepare the sauce, combine all the ingredients in a mixing bowl. Serve it with the hot dumplings.

● Chef's notes
If you are pressed for time, use store-bought Chinese dumpling dough. It is much finer and contains egg, but it can be folded and cooked exactly like homemade dough.
These dumplings can be frozen raw. Arrange them on a baking sheet and freeze them overnight, then transfer them to freezer bags or airtight containers, in which they will keep for 2 months. There is no need to defrost them before cooking; simply cook them in the skillet for 2 to 3 minutes longer.

Ingredients
Dumpling dough
Generous ¾-1 cup (200-220 ml) water
2 ½ cups (10 ½ oz./300 g) all-purpose flour
Potato starch or cornstarch, for rolling the dough

Stuffing
10 oz. (300 g) firm tofu
1 handful (⅔ oz./20 g) Chinese dried black mushrooms
1 leek, white part only (3 ½ oz./100 g)
1-inch (2.5-cm) piece ginger
12 sprigs chives
2 tablespoons soy sauce
1 tablespoon potato starch or cornstarch
1 pinch sugar
Fine salt to taste

To cook
¼ cup (60 ml) sunflower oil
⅔ cup (150 ml) water

Sauce
3 tablespoons dark rice vinegar
2 tablespoons light soy sauce
1 tablespoon sesame oil
Chili paste or fresh chili to taste (optional)

Equipment
A pair of chopsticks (optional)

Techniques
Cleaning Leeks, p. 24
Peeling Fresh Ginger, p. 29
Shaping Chinese Dumplings, p. 70
Pressing Tofu, p. 88
Rehydrating Dried Mushrooms, p. 99

Ingredients

½ red cabbage (about 1 lb./500 g)

2 shallots

8 oz. (250 g) smoked tofu

2 cooking apples

1 sprig rosemary

2 tablespoons sunflower or canola oil

2 tablespoons cider vinegar

1 clove

8 oz. (250 g) prepared chestnuts,
    vacuum-packed or frozen

Tabasco® to taste

Fine salt and freshly ground pepper

Sautéed Red Cabbage with Smoked Tofu and Chestnuts ★

Serves 6

Preparation time: 20 minutes
Cooking time: 30 minutes

Remove the hard core of the cabbage and shred the leaves finely. Peel the shallots and cut them into slices lengthwise. Cut the smoked tofu into dice. Cut the apples into halves, remove the cores, and dice them. Pick the leaves off the rosemary, gather them together on a chopping board, and cut them as finely as possible with a large knife.

In a skillet over medium-high heat, heat 1 tablespoon of the oil. Lightly brown the tofu on all sides and transfer to a plate. Lightly brown the diced apple and transfer to a plate.

Drizzle in the remaining oil, increase the heat to high, and add the cabbage to the skillet. Season with salt and sauté for 5 minutes, until wilted.

Add the vinegar and clove, reduce the heat to low, cover with the lid, and simmer for 10 minutes. Stir in the apples, chestnuts, and shallots. Cover with the lid and simmer for an additional 10 minutes, stirring frequently, until the cabbage has softened.

Remove from the heat and discard the clove. Stir in the tofu, rosemary, and Tabasco®, and serve immediately.

● Chef's notes

Chestnuts are delicious when prepared from scratch but it's a time-consuming process. Vacuum-packed chestnuts, which are very tasty, or frozen chestnuts can also be used. Canned chestnuts are best avoided, however, as they are too floury.

Techniques
Pressing Tofu, p. 88

Soybeans

Sautéed Spinach and Chanterelle Mushrooms with Tofu ★

Serves 4
Preparation time: 15 minutes
Marinating time: 30 minutes
Cooking time: 15 minutes

For the tofu
Peel and grate the ginger. To make the marinade, combine the soy sauce, sugar, sesame seed oil, and sesame seeds in a deep dish. Pat the tofu dry, cut it into large dice, and combine with the marinade. Allow to marinate for 30 minutes, or at least while you continue preparing the rest of the dish.

For the vegetables
Carefully wash the spinach leaves and chop them roughly if they are large. Using a clean, dry cloth, clean the chanterelle mushrooms and slice them if they are large; if not, leave them whole. Peel the garlic clove and remove the green shoot. Chop the garlic clove and slice the scallion.

Drain the marinated tofu, reserving the marinade. In the wok over high heat, heat 1 tablespoon of the oil. Lightly brown the tofu and transfer it to a dish.

Heat the remaining oil and add the mushrooms, garlic, and scallion. Season lightly with salt so that they render their water and sauté for 5 to 8 minutes, until the water has evaporated and the mushrooms are golden. Transfer to a bowl.

Place the spinach in the same wok, season lightly with salt, and cook for 1 to 2 minutes, until wilted. Stir in the chanterelle mushrooms, tofu, and half of the reserved marinade. Still working over high heat, sauté for 2 to 3 minutes. Adjust the seasoning, adding some or all of the remaining marinade, to taste. Sprinkle with sesame seeds, stir, and sauté for an additional minute.

● Chef's notes
You can sauté the chanterelle mushrooms and spinach and marinate the tofu up to 24 hours ahead of time. That way, all you'll have to do is lightly brown the tofu in the wok before combining with the other ingredients for a dish that's quick to put together.

Techniques
Preparing Garlic, p. 29
Peeling Fresh Ginger, p. 29
Sautéing Mushrooms, p. 98

Ingredients
Tofu
1-inch (2.5-cm) piece ginger
¼ cup (60 ml) soy sauce
2 teaspoons brown sugar or agave or maple syrup
1 teaspoon toasted sesame seed oil
2 tablespoons sesame seeds,
plus extra to garnish
8 oz. (250 g) firm tofu

Vegetables
1 ¼ lb. (600 g) fresh spinach
10 oz. (300 g) chanterelle mushrooms
1 clove garlic
1 scallion (spring onion)
2 tablespoons olive oil
Fine salt and freshly ground pepper

Equipment
Wok or large skillet

Ingredients

Sauce
¾ cup (4 oz./120 g) unsalted peanuts
1 clove garlic
½ fresh chili pepper, (or more or less, to taste)
1 oz. (30 g) palm sugar
2 limes
1 teaspoon tamarind paste
⅓-scant ½ cup (80–100 ml) coconut milk

Salad
1 lb. (500 g) baby potatoes
2 chayotes
4 eggs
8 oz. (250 g) tempeh
1 tablespoon oil of your choice
  (coconut, sesame, etc.)
2 small cucumbers
½ green cabbage, such as Napa (Chinese) cabbage
4 handfuls mung bean sprouts

Equipment
Blender or powerful food processor

Techniques
Preparing Chilies, p. 23
Steaming, p. 41
Cooking Tempeh, p. 93
Hard-Boiling Eggs, p. 104
Making a Nut Paste, p. 118

Gado-Gado with Tempeh ★

Serves 4
Preparation time: 30 minutes
Cooking time: 20 minutes

For the sauce
In a small skillet over medium heat, lightly roast the peanuts, stirring regularly. Alternatively, place them in a 350°F (180°C/Gas Mark 4) oven for about 8 minutes, keeping a careful eye on them, until they turn a golden color. Peel the garlic. Remove the seeds of the chili pepper and cut a piece the size of your choice, depending on how hot you want the dish. Squeeze the limes.

Roughly chop the palm sugar. Process it until reduced to a coarse powder and add the garlic, chili pepper, and peanuts. Process until reduced to a fine powder. Add the lime juice and tamarind paste and, with the processor running, pour in the coconut milk in a steady stream until the mixture reaches the desired texture–thick or runny, as you prefer. You may not need to use all the coconut milk.

For the salad
Scrub the potatoes. Peel the chayotes and cut them into halves. Steam the chayote pieces for 5 minutes, add the potatoes, and cook for an additional 15 minutes, until a knife inserted into one of them slides in easily. Hard-boil the eggs for 10 minutes in simmering water. Cut the tempeh into rectangles. In a skillet with the oil, lightly brown them for 2 minutes on each side.

Wash, dry, and slice the cucumber and cabbage. Rinse and dry the mung bean sprouts. Divide the potatoes, chayotes, cabbage, cucumber, egg, and tempeh among the plates. Garnish with the sauce and serve.

● Chef's notes
Chayotes originated in the Americas but are now grown in many countries. Technically a fruit but often used as a vegetable, they are known as pear squash (they are light green and pear-shaped) or Buddha's hand melon, and lend themselves to a variety of uses.
This dish, known as gado-gado in Indonesia, can be varied according to the season and the vegetables available. Radishes, tomatoes, and any type of lettuce all work well. You can also use firm tofu cut into strips, as they do in Indonesia. What's important is to present a varied assortment: gado-gado literally means "mix-mix," so mix to your heart's content!
Stored in an airtight container in the refrigerator, the sauce will keep for up to 5 days.
If you're in a hurry, use unsweetened store-bought peanut butter instead of peanuts for the sauce.

Chow Mein with Tofu ★

Serves 4
Preparation time: 30 minutes
Soaking time: 15 minutes
Cooking time: 20 minutes

Pat the tofu dry and cut it into cubes. In a mixing bowl, combine the oyster sauce, 1 tablespoon of soy sauce, the five-spice powder, and the sriracha. Pour it over the tofu, stir to combine, and leave to marinate while you prepare the rest of the dish.

Rehydrate the black mushrooms in a bowl of hot water for 15 minutes. Rinse and slice them finely. Peel the carrots and cut them into julienne sticks. Shred the cabbage and slice the celery stalk and onion. Peel the garlic clove, remove the green shoot, and crush.

Cook the noodles in a pot of salted boiling water according to the instructions on the package and drain them.

Drain the tofu, reserving the marinade. Drizzle half of the oil into the wok over high heat and lightly brown the tofu cubes for 2 minutes, then remove from the wok. Drizzle the rest of the oil into the wok and add the onion and garlic; sauté for 2 minutes, then add the cabbage. Sauté for 2 to 3 minutes, stirring continuously, then stir in the black mushrooms, carrots, and celery. Continue cooking, stirring all the while, for an additional 2 to 3 minutes, then add the noodles, reserved marinade, and remaining soy sauce. Add the tofu back into the wok and cook for 1 to 2 minutes; the noodles should be coated with sauce and the tofu must be heated through.

● Good to know

The name "chow mein" is an Anglicized version of the Chinese term for stir-fried noodles. Chinese communities have made it part of American-Chinese cuisine. There are many variations of this dish, as in this recipe where celery replaces the traditional water chestnuts. It can also be made with beef or chicken, as well as tofu, as here, and you'll find it served differently in each restaurant you try.

❙ Techniques
Preparing Garlic, p. 29
Rehydrating Dried Mushrooms, p. 99

Ingredients
5 oz. (150 g) lacto-fermented tofu
1 tablespoon vegetarian oyster sauce
3 tablespoons mushroom-flavored soy sauce
1 teaspoon five-spice powder
1 teaspoon sriracha (chili sauce), or more to taste
5 dried Chinese black mushrooms
2 carrots
½ Napa (Chinese) cabbage
1 stalk celery
1 onion
1-2 cloves garlic
7 oz. (200 g) Chinese wheat noodles
2 teaspoons toasted sesame oil

Equipment
Wok

Ingredients

6 dried shiitake mushrooms
⅓ oz. (10 g) black mushrooms
1 ½ oz. (40 g) soy vermicelli
1 sheet dried tofu skin (soybean milk skin)
2 oz. (50 g) canned bamboo shoots (net weight)
3 ½ oz. (100 g) seitan
8 pieces fried tofu
½ Napa (Chinese) cabbage
   (approximately 10 oz./300 g)
2 stalks celery
2 carrots
2 cloves garlic
1 onion
1 ¼-inch (4-cm) piece ginger
2 tablespoons peanut or sesame oil
2 oz. (50 g) soy or mung bean sprouts
2 tablespoons soy sauce
2 tablespoons Shaoxing wine
1 teaspoon sugar

Buddha's Delight: *Lo Han Chai* ★★

Braised Vegetables with Soy Vermicelli

Serves 4
Preparation time: 20 minutes
Cooking time: 10 minutes

In two separate bowls, soak the shiitake and black mushrooms in hot water until rehydrated. Immerse the soy vermicelli in boiling water and leave to swell for 5 minutes. Soak the tofu skin in hot water for 10 minutes.

Drain and rinse the black mushrooms and cut them into slices. Drain the soy vermicelli and tofu skin. Shred the tofu skin. Drain the shiitakes, reserving the soaking liquid, and slice them finely. Drain and rinse the bamboo shoots.

Cut the seitan into bite-sized pieces and cut the pieces of fried tofu in two. Shred the cabbage and finely slice the celery stalks. Peel the carrots and slice them thinly. Peel the garlic cloves, remove the green shoots, and chop finely. Peel and dice the onion. Peel and grate the ginger.

Drizzle the oil into a skillet over high heat and sauté the onion, garlic, and ginger for 1 minute. Add the cabbage and carrots and fry for 3 to 4 minutes.

Stir in the vermicelli, seitan, fried tofu, tofu skin, bamboo shoots, and soy sprouts. Sauté for 2 to 3 minutes, then add the soy sauce, Shaoxing wine, sugar, and 2 tablespoons of the shiitake soaking liquid. Reduce the heat to low, simmer briefly to heat through, and serve immediately.

● Good to know

Buddha's Delight, also known as Lo Han Chai, is the traditional dish served on the first day of the Chinese New Year. It has undergone many transformations among the communities of the Chinese diaspora, with variations between regions and even families. It is always vegetarian as, according to Buddhists, no creatures should be killed on the first day of the lunar year. Water chestnuts, gingko nuts, and lotus seeds may be added. Traditionally, it comprises at least ten different ingredients, but there may be as many as thirty-five.

Techniques

Preparing Garlic, p. 29
Peeling Fresh Ginger, p. 29
Preparing Seitan, p. 69
Rehydrating Dried Mushrooms, p. 99

Orange and Pistachio Loaf ★

Serves 6
Preparation time: 20 minutes
Cooking time: 45 minutes
Cooling time: 2 hours

Preheat the oven to 350°F (180°C/Gas Mark 4). Lightly oil the loaf pans.

Finely grate the orange and lemon zests. Squeeze the oranges and half of the lemon; you should have approximately ¾ cup (200 ml) of juice. In a small skillet over medium heat, lightly roast the pistachios. Allow to cool and chop roughly.

Whisk the eggs with the sugar until the mixture has become pale and doubled in volume. Whisk in the tofu, and then fold in the flour, baking powder, and salt. Do not overmix. Stir in the grated citrus zests and pistachios until evenly distributed.

Pour the batter into the prepared pans and bake for 25 to 30 minutes, until nicely golden on the top.

When you remove the loaves from the oven, lightly prick them with a toothpick or knife tip. Drizzle the orange and lemon juice over. You may not need all of it, depending on how moist you would like the loaves to be. Allow to cool in the pans for 2 hours. Turn out of the pans and slice finely to serve.

● Chef's notes

You can replace the pistachios with other nuts or seeds of your choice—try hazelnuts, almonds, or pumpkin seeds.
This loaf cake will keep for up to 2 days, well protected in plastic wrap.
This recipe uses silken tofu, which gives a moist texture without adding any fat. It was inspired by a recipe by French cook, author, and journalist Elisabeth Scotto, one of the first in France to introduce tofu into the recipes published in her columns in the early 1980s.

Ingredients

2 organic or unwaxed oranges
1 organic or unwaxed lemon
⅓ cup (2 oz./50 g) shelled unsalted pistachios
3 eggs
⅔ cup (4 ½ oz./130 g) brown sugar,
plus 1 tablespoon (20 g) for the syrup
5 ½ oz. (160 g) silken tofu
¾ cup plus 2 tablespoons (3 ½ oz./100 g)
all-purpose flour
1 teaspoon baking powder
1 good pinch salt

Equipment

Two 3 × 5 ¾-inch (6 × 15-cm) loaf pans

Mushrooms and Seaweed

Emmanuel Renaut

Emmanuel Renaut began his career at the Hôtel de Crillon with Christian Constant, working side by side with Yves Camdeborde and Eric Fréchon. He went on to work with Yves Thuriès and Marc Veyrat and then took the helm of the famed Claridge's hotel in London. In 1997, this mountain lover opened his restaurant in Megève in the Alps. As a Compagnon du Tour de France, he was trained by this centuries-old craftsmen's guild, and he also holds the prestigious title of Meilleur Ouvrier de France, which he was awarded in 2004. His restaurant, Flocons de Sel, gained its three Michelin stars in 2012.

"Sweet fir buds, mushrooms, meadowsweet, gentian—I have no need to seek inspiration far away, because I have all that I need at hand. Everything that grows around me is part of my garden. Technique makes way for emotion: dishes must appear natural and no one should have an inkling of how much work goes into making them. Morel mushrooms, amaretto sabayon, peas, and elderflower: it seems as if they were just made to go together," he declares.

Vegetarian dishes feature on his menu all year round. In this recipe, Renaut presents a foraged mushroom, served raw, with one of his favorite condiments, coffee—a real surprise—used as a spice to heighten the flavors.

Flocons de Sel
1775 Route du Leutaz
74120 Megève
France
Website: floconsdesel.com

Serves 4

Maceration time: 12 hours
Preparation time: 30 minutes
Cooking time: 1 hour

Ingredients

50 coffee beans
¾ cup (200 ml) grape-seed oil
2 medium eggplants (aubergines)
1 small pinch ground coffee
2 large, firm porcini
20 leaves sheep sorrel (*Rumex acetosella*)
Traditional balsamic vinegar
  (Aceto Balsamico Tradizionale)
Maldon salt
Fine salt and freshly ground pepper

Porcini, Eggplant Caviar, and Coffee

Coffee-flavored oil
A day ahead, roast the coffee beans under the broiler. Place them, still hot, in a jar with the grape-seed oil. Leave to macerate.

Coffee-flavored eggplant caviar
Preheat the oven to 265°F (130°C/Gas Mark ½).

Wash the eggplants and cut them in two. Drizzle a few drops of coffee-flavored oil over each half and wrap in aluminum foil with 5 coffee beans. Place in the oven and cook for approximately 1 hour. When soft, scoop out the flesh with a spoon, process in a blender, and strain through a fine-mesh sieve if necessary. Season with fine salt and pepper and keep warm.

To serve
Slice the porcini finely. In four bowls, place some warm eggplant caviar with the sheep sorrel and sliced porcini on top. Drizzle over a few drops of coffee-flavored oil and bal-samic vinegar and sprinkle with a few grains of Maldon salt and a little ground coffee.

Serve immediately so that the porcini retain their crunch.

Ingredients

⅔ oz. (20 g) dried sea spaghetti,
  or 3 oz. (80 g) fresh

⅔ oz. (20 g) enoki mushrooms (you will
  not need them all)

1 ½ cups (10 oz./300 g) cooked, unseasoned
  Japanese round grain rice

3 ¼ cups (800 ml) seaweed dashi

2 leaves nori

1 teaspoon roasted green tea (*hojicha*)

2 teaspoons sesame seeds

Soy sauce, to serve

Japanese Tea and Rice with Sea Spaghetti and Enoki Mushrooms ★

Serves 4

Preparation time: 10 minutes

Soaking time: 30 to 60 minutes

Cooking time: 2 minutes

Soak the sea spaghetti in a large bowl of water for 30 to 60 minutes. Drain and set aside. Trim the bases of the enoki mushrooms.

Divide the rice, seaweed, and mushrooms between four large bowls. Roast the nori seaweed. Heat the dashi to 175°F (80°C) and infuse the tea in it for 2 minutes, then strain.

Pour the liquid into the bowls and sprinkle with pieces of roasted nori and sesame seeds.

Serve with soy sauce on the side.

● Good to know

Ochazuke, as this is known in Japan, is a traditional dish served at the end of a meal. The custom of pouring tea over the last bowl of rice has become a dish in its own right, often with the addition of slices of fish or chicken and various condiments. This combination of mushrooms and seaweed may not be traditional, but ochazuke lends itself well to the pairing: warming them up with hot liquid brings out the best of their flavors.

❚ Techniques

Making Sushi Rice, p. 55

Making Seaweed Broth (Dashi), p. 97

Rehydrating Dried Seaweed, p. 99

Roasting Nori Seaweed, p. 100

Seaweed Tartare ★

Serves 4
Preparation time: 15 minutes
Soaking time: 30 minutes (if using dried seaweed)

Soak the dried seaweed to rehydrate it; if you are using fresh seaweed, desalt it. Rinse the capers under running water long enough to remove as much salt as possible. Peel the shallot. Carefully drain the seaweed, pressing it between your hands to remove as much water as possible.

Place all the ingredients, with the exception of the olive oil and mustard, in the bowl of the food processor fitted with the blade knife. Pulse only enough to ensure that the texture retains some roughness.

Add the mustard and drizzle in the olive oil, processing until the mixture is completely emulsified. Taste and adjust the seasoning if necessary.

● Chef's notes
This tartare will keep for up to 5 days, stored in an airtight jar in the refrigerator.
It's important to rinse salt-packed capers well.
You may have to add a note of acidity to your tartare: use a little lemon juice or vinegar, as you prefer.
Most seaweed works well in tartares; kombu, however, with its somewhat thick texture, is one to avoid.
This tartare is delicious on bread for pre-dinner drinks, but can also be served as an accompaniment to steamed vegetables, mixed with leaf vegetables and used to fill a tart, or as a dip for crudités.

Techniques
Desalting Seaweed, p. 97
Rehydrating Dried Seaweed, p. 99

Ingredients
⅓ oz. (10 g) dried sea lettuce, or 2-2 ½ oz. (30-40 g) fresh
⅓ oz. (10 g) dried wakame, or 2-2 ½ oz. (30-40 g) fresh
⅙ oz. (5 g) dried dulse, or 1 oz. (25-30 g) fresh
1 tablespoon salt-packed capers
½ shallot
4 gherkins brined in vinegar
¼ teaspoon French mustard
¼ cup (60 ml) olive oil
Freshly ground pepper

Equipment
Food processor

Vegetable *Maki* with Miso Soup ★ ★ ★

Serves 4
Preparation time: 45 minutes
Resting time: 30 minutes, plus 1 hour drying time
Cooking time: 30 minutes

For the rice

Rinse the sushi rice under running water until the water runs clear from the bottom of the strainer. Allow the rice to dry at room temperature for at least 1 hour. Transfer the rice to a heavy-bottom skillet or cast-iron pot and pour in the cold water. Cover with the lid and bring to a boil. Reduce the heat to low and cook for 10 to 13 minutes, until all the water has been absorbed. Leave the lid on and let rest for 10 to 15 minutes.

Meanwhile, prepare the seasoning. In a saucepan, combine the vinegar, sugar, and salt. Place over low heat and heat until the sugar and salt have dissolved.

Transfer the cooked rice to a large dish, if possible a dish with a flat bottom. Traditionally, a wooden receptacle is used, but glass or plastic are fine. *Do not use metal.* Pour the seasoning over the entire surface of the rice and use a wooden spoon to incorporate it, lifting the rice up and turning it. Be careful not to break the grains. Allow to cool to room temperature before using.

For the *maki*

Cut the cucumber into sticks. Peel the avocado and slice it. Squeeze lemon juice over the slices to prevent them from browning. Peel the carrots and, using a mandolin, cut them into fine julienne sticks. Roll the *maki* according to the technique explained on p. 56, placing a little wasabi on the rice before making the rolls.

For the miso soup

Soak the wakame for 15 minutes. Drain and slice it. Cut the tofu into dice. Finely slice the scallion stalks. In a pot, bring the dashi to a simmer with the sliced ginger and sake and remove from the heat. Dilute the miso paste with a ladleful of the dashi, then return it all to the pot. Stir until the miso paste has dissolved. Return the pot to the burner and add the wakame and tofu. Use just enough heat to bring the soup back to a simmer. Add the scallions and remove immediately from the heat: miso soup should never boil. Serve immediately with the *maki*.

● Chef's notes

These maki *can hold a wide variety of fillings, such as:*
– oven-roasted, cooled vegetables (see recipe p. 226)
– steamed, diced tofu, or pieces of tempeh (see technique p. 93)
– pickled vegetables (see technique p. 35)
– fried mushrooms, especially shiitake, at room temperature
– a finely rolled omelet
– herbs and small salad greens, such as arugula and lambs' lettuce
– pieces of fruit, such as strawberries and mangoes.

Ingredients

Sushi rice and seasoning
2 ¾ cups (8 oz./500 g) round grain sushi rice
3 cups (750 ml) cold water
¼ cup (60 ml) rice vinegar
3 ½ tablespoons (40 g) sugar
2 teaspoons fine salt

Filling
1 cucumber
2 ripe avocados
2 carrots
Juice of 1 lemon
10 to 12 sheets nori

Soup
1/6 oz. (5 g) dried wakame
8 oz. (250 g) tofu
3 scallion (spring onion) stalks (green part only)
3 ¼ cups dashi (seaweed broth)
6 thin slices fresh, peeled ginger
2 tablespoons sake
2 oz. (60 g) white miso paste

To finish
Slices of pickled ginger (*gari*)
Wasabi
Soy sauce

Equipment
Maki mat (*makisu*)
Large, flat-bottomed dish for the cooked rice; it must be non-metallic

Techniques
Using a Mandolin, p. 40
Making Sushi Rice, p. 55
Making *Maki*, p. 56
Making Seaweed Broth (Dashi), p. 97
Rehydrating Dried Seaweed, p. 99

Ingredients

Mushroom and apricot topping
6 dried apricots
Scant ½ cup (100 ml) hot water
2 scallions (spring onions) with stalks
1 lb. (500 g) chanterelle mushrooms
A drizzle of olive oil
2 sprigs fresh rosemary
⅔ cup (150 ml) vegetable or mushroom broth
Fine salt and freshly ground pepper

Polenta
3 ¼ cups (800 ml) vegetable broth
¾ cup (200 ml) whole milk
½ bay leaf
½ teaspoon salt
Generous ¾ cup (5 oz./150 g) precooked polenta
2 tablespoons (1 oz./30 g) butter
1 tablespoon mascarpone or heavy cream

Mushroom and Apricot Polenta ★

Serves 4
Preparation time: 25 minutes
Cooking time: 25 minutes

For the mushroom and apricot topping
Soak the dried apricots in hot water. Drain and cut them into strips. Chop the bulbs of the scallions, reserving the stalks. Clean the chanterelle mushrooms and trim the stems. Immerse them for 1 minute in a pot of salted boiling water and drain carefully.

Heat the olive oil in a skillet over high heat. Sauté the scallions for 2 minutes, until very lightly colored. Add the chanterelles and cook briefly, then add the apricots, rosemary sprigs, and broth. Reduce the heat to low, cover with the lid, and simmer for 15 minutes.

For the polenta
Meanwhile, to prepare the polenta, bring the vegetable broth to a boil with the milk, bay leaf, and salt. Pour in the polenta and cook according to the instructions on the package (this usually takes approximately 5 minutes), stirring constantly. Remove the bay leaf and stir in the butter and mascarpone. Whisk briskly until incorporated and adjust the seasoning.

To finish
Carefully remove the rosemary from the mushroom and apricot mixture. Slice the scallion stalks and stir in. Season with salt and pepper.

Spoon the creamy polenta onto the plates and arrange the mushroom topping over it. Serve immediately.

● **Good to know**
This delicious association of dried apricots and chanterelle mushrooms is an original idea by Régis Marcon, who uses the flavor pairing, with variations, in several of his dishes.

Techniques
Preparing Vegetable Broth, p. 31
Preparing Polenta, p. 71
Making Mushroom Broth, p. 96
Sautéing Mushrooms, p. 98
Soaking Dried Fruits, p. 143

Indian Mushroom Hotpot ★

Serves 4
Preparation time: 20 minutes
Cooking time: 30 minutes

In a small skillet over medium heat, lightly color all the spices for a few seconds, until fragrant. Immediately transfer them to a plate to cool. Grind in a coffee grinder or spice mill.

Remove the stems of the button mushrooms, clean if necessary, and cut them into thick slices. Remove the bases of the tomatoes and chop them roughly. Remove the stem of the pepper and peel and dice it. Peel the garlic cloves and onion. Remove the green shoots from the garlic cloves. Dice the onion and grate the garlic cloves. Peel and grate the ginger. Remove the seeds of the chili peppers and dice them finely. In a skillet over high heat, melt the ghee. Sauté the mushrooms: they should render their water and color very lightly when the water evaporates. Transfer the mushrooms to a dish.

In the same skillet, lightly brown the onion for 1 minute, then add the ginger and garlic and cook for an additional 1 minute. Reduce the heat to medium and add the bell pepper, chili peppers, and tomatoes. Sauté for 5 minutes. Stir in the spices and mushrooms. Pour in ¼–⅓ cup (50-80 ml) water, cover with the lid, and simmer for 10 minutes.

Taste for doneness. If necessary, cook for a few minutes longer without the lid to reduce the sauce. Serve with rice or chapatis.

● Chef's notes
This recipe can also be made with paneer *(see technique p. 110).*

● Good to know
There are many versions of kadai, *as this dish is known in India, both vegetarian and containing meat. It takes its name from the cooking utensil used to prepare it—a* kadai, *also called a* karahi, *resembles a flat-bottomed wok with looped handles.*

❘ Techniques
Preparing Chilies, p. 23
Preparing Garlic, p. 29
Peeling Fresh Ginger, p. 29
Dicing Onions, p. 39
Sautéing Mushrooms, p. 98
Making Clarified Butter and Ghee, p. 113

Ingredients
1 ¼ lb. (600 g) button mushrooms
4 tomatoes or ⅔ cup (150 ml) *passata*
(strained tomatoes)
½ red bell pepper
2 cloves garlic
1 onion
1-inch (2–3-cm) piece ginger
1 small red chili pepper (more or less, to taste)
1 small green chili pepper (more or less, to taste)
2 tablespoons ghee

Spice mix
1 teaspoon coriander seeds
½ teaspoon cumin seeds
1 cinnamon stick
1 green cardamom pod
2 cloves
2 black peppercorns
½ teaspoon salt

Ingredients

Croquettes
1 lb. (500 g) floury potatoes
½ tablespoon kosher salt
Scant ½ cup (100 ml) milk
1 tablespoon (²/₃ oz./20 g) butter,
  chilled and diced
½ oz. (15 g) dried dulse
2 egg whites
½ cup (2 oz./60 g) all-purpose flour
3 oz. (80 g) homemade bread crumbs
Scant ½ cup (100 ml) oil for frying

Asparagus salad
8 green asparagus spears
Juice of ½ lemon
1 teaspoon hazelnut oil
1 teaspoon *gomasio*
1 tablespoon sesame seeds
Freshly ground pepper

Techniques
Peeling Asparagus, p. 36
Breading, p. 77
Rehydrating Dried Seaweed, p. 99
Making *Gomasio*, p. 119

Dulse Croquettes with Asparagus Salad ★★

Serves 4
Preparation time: 30 minutes
Freezing time: 30 minutes
Cooking time: 35 minutes

For the croquettes
Peel the potatoes, cut them into evenly sized pieces, and rinse well under running water. Place in a pot, cover with cold water, and add the kosher salt. Bring to a boil and cook for 20 to 25 minutes, until a knife tip slides in easily. Drain immediately (they should not absorb any more water). Return to the pot and mash with a potato ricer. Over low heat, gently dry out the mashed potatoes, stirring constantly with a wooden spoon.

Bring the milk to a boil. Remove the mashed potatoes from the heat and pour in the milk in a steady stream. Stir it in and incorporate the butter and a little freshly ground pepper. Mix briskly so that the butter melts into the mashed potatoes and forms an emulsion, and adjust the seasoning.

While the mashed potatoes are cooling, soak the dulse. Drain, chop roughly, and stir into the mashed potatoes. Using two spoons, shape mashed potato/dulse croquettes. Place in the freezer for 30 minutes: freezing allows them to be handled more easily.

Place the egg whites in a soup plate and whisk lightly with a fork, just enough to liquefy them. Place the flour and bread crumbs in two other soup plates. Remove the croquettes from the freezer and roll them in the flour, then in the egg white, and then coat them in the bread crumbs. In a large skillet, heat the oil over medium-high heat. Fry the croquettes for 3 to 4 minutes on each side, until golden, and drain on sheets of paper towel.

For the asparagus salad
Trim the hard base of the asparagus stems and peel with a vegetable peeler. As soon as the tender flesh is visible, use the vegetable peeler (or a shaver) to make fine shavings. Season with the lemon juice, hazelnut oil, *gomasio*, sesame seeds, and pepper. Serve with the croquettes.

● Chef's notes
These croquettes can also be served with seaweed tartare (see recipe p. 335).
If you have leftover mashed potatoes from another dish, use them to make this recipe.
The croquettes may be frozen once you have shaped them and will keep for up to 3 months. Bread them without defrosting according to the instructions in the recipe, but fry over medium heat for 5 minutes on each side to heat them through thoroughly.

Japanese-Style Soy Balls with Wakame-Cucumber Salad ★★

Serves 4
Preparation time: 30 minutes
Chilling time: 30 minutes
Cooking time: 10 minutes

For the salad
If you are using fresh, salted wakame, desalt it (see technique p. 97). If you are using dried wakame, soak it (see technique p. 99). Wash and dry the cucumber. Using a mandolin, slice it finely. Place the slices in a colander, sprinkle with fine salt, and leave to drain for 5 minutes. Rinse, pressing with your hands, and dry carefully. Drain and slice the wakame, depending on the size of the pieces once they have swelled.

In a mixing bowl, combine the rice vinegar, sesame oil, tamari (soy) sauce, sugar, and sesame seeds. Add the cucumber and wakame, combine well, and place in the refrigerator for at least 30 minutes while you prepare the soy balls.

For the soy balls
Press the tofu between two boards to drain it of some of its water. Cut the carrots into very small dice and finely slice the green beans, or chop finely the vegetables of your choice. Immerse them in salted boiling water for 1 minute, refresh, and dry carefully. Wash, dry, and finely snip the chives.

In the food processor, process the tofu with the sake, soy sauce, egg, and ginger. Stir in the vegetables and chives. Lightly oil your hands. Take 2 tablespoons of the tofu mixture and roll it into a ball between your palms. Continue, using up the remaining mixture. Pour the oil into a skillet to a depth of just under 1 inch (2 cm) and place over medium-high heat. Carefully place the balls in it and fry for 2 to 3 minutes on each side, until lightly golden. Serve with the salad.

● Chef's notes
The tofu mixture can be made ahead of time and shaped and fried at the last minute.
If it seems a little too soft to be shaped into balls, stir in 1 tablespoon of a gluten-free starch of your choice.

Techniques
Using a Mandolin, p. 40
Blanching, p. 41
Pressing Tofu, p. 88
Desalting Seaweed, p. 97
Rehydrating Dried Seaweed, p. 99

Ingredients
Salad
2 oz. (50 g) fresh, salted wakame, or ⅓ oz. (10 g) dried wakame
1 cucumber
1 tablespoon rice vinegar
1 teaspoon sesame oil
1 teaspoon tamari (soy) sauce
1 teaspoon sugar
2 tablespoons sesame seeds
Fine salt

Soy balls
8 oz. (250 g) firm tofu
1 ½ oz. (40 g) vegetables (peeled carrots, trimmed green beans, etc.)
A few sprigs chives
1 tablespoon sake
1 teaspoon soy sauce
1 egg
1 teaspoon grated ginger
Oil for frying

Equipment
Food processor

Ingredients

Kale chips
6 large leaves kale
2 tablespoons olive oil
1 teaspoon spice of your choice (curry, mild
   paprika, smoked paprika, or garam masala)

Tofu mayonnaise
3 ½ oz. (100 g) silken tofu
½ clove garlic
½ teaspoon turmeric
1 teaspoon French mustard
1 tablespoon olive oil
½ teaspoon cider vinegar
Fine salt and freshly ground pepper

Garnish
1 radish
2 sprigs cilantro (coriander)

Burgers
2 tablespoons linseeds
3 tablespoons water
½ clove garlic
¼ red onion
Leaves from 8 sprigs cilantro (coriander)
1 scant cup (5 ½ oz./160 g) cooked navy
   (haricot) beans
½ cup (3 ½ oz./100 g) cooked quinoa
2 teaspoons olive oil
1 tablespoon tomato paste
2 good pinches cumin
2 good pinches dried chili powder, to taste
   (Jamaican pepper, *piment d'Espelette*, etc.)
Fine salt and freshly ground pepper

Mushrooms and marinade
4 Portobello mushrooms
1 tablespoon tamari (soy) sauce
1 tablespoon balsamic vinegar
1 tablespoon olive oil
Juice of ½ lemon
1 pinch fine salt

Equipment
Food processor or blender

Portobello Burgers and Kale Chips ★★

Serves 2
Preparation time: 40 minutes
Marinating time: 30 minutes
Cooking time: 45 minutes

For the kale chips
Prepare the kale chips using the technique on p. 33.

For the tofu mayonnaise
Prepare the mayonnaise using the technique on p. 89.

For the garnish
Peel the radish, slice it finely, and place in a bowl of ice water so that it retains its crunch.

For the burgers
Preheat the oven to 350°F (180°C/Gas Mark 4). Process the linseeds in the blender or food processor. Stir in the water and leave to rest for 10 minutes, until gelled. Process the garlic, onion, and cilantro leaves together. Add the cooked navy beans and pulse briefly: the mixture should not be smooth. Stir in the cooked quinoa (no processing is required at this stage), olive oil, spices, tomato paste, and gelled linseeds. Season with salt and pepper. Using a pastry or tartlet ring, shape two burgers. Place them on a baking sheet and cook for 15 minutes.

For the mushrooms
Remove the stem of the Portobello mushrooms, reserving them to make a broth (see technique p. 96). Score the surface of the cap with a sharp knife. Combine all the ingredients for the marinade in a dish just big enough to hold the caps. Place them, scored side downward, in the marinade and marinate for 15 minutes. Turn and marinate for an additional 15 minutes. Preheat the oven to 320°F (160°C/Gas Mark 3). Drain the Portobello caps, place in an ovenproof dish, and cook for 10 minutes. Turn, brush with the marinade, and cook for an additional 10 minutes.

To serve
Place 1 mushroom cap on each plate, round side downward. Spoon in 2 teaspoons of the tofu mayonnaise. Place a burger over that with a few slices of radish and a sprig of cilantro. If you wish, add a little more tofu mayonnaise and then top with another mushroom cap. Serve accompanied by the kale chips.

Techniques
Preparing Kale Chips, p. 33
Using a Mandolin, p. 40
Cooking Quinoa, p. 75
Cooking Pulses, p. 82
Making Vegan Tofu Mayonnaise, p. 89
Making Linseed Gel, p. 124

Vanilla Flans with Peach Coulis ★

Serves 4
Preparation time: 10 minutes
Cooking time: 3 minutes
Chilling time: 3 hours

For the flans
Slit the vanilla bean in half lengthwise. Scrape out the seeds with a sharp knife. In a heavy-bottom saucepan, combine the milk of your choice, the sugar or syrup, and the vanilla seeds. Sprinkle the agar-agar over, whisk it in, and bring the mixture to a boil. Simmer for 2 minutes then pour into small molds or ramekins. Allow to cool, and place in the refrigerator for at least 3 hours to allow the flans to set.

For the coulis
Immerse the peaches for 10 seconds in boiling water. Peel them and remove the pits. Cut them into pieces and process in the blender or food processor with the liqueur and lemon juice.

Turn the flans out of their molds, drizzle with peach coulis, and serve.

● Chef's notes
Adapt your coulis according to the season: use strawberries, apricots, nectarines, or raspberries in summer, and mango, passion fruit, or pineapple in winter.
Instead of the coulis, you can drizzle the flans with a little syrup or honey, sprinkle them with brown sugar, or serve with fruit salad.
Food made with agar-agar can become watery, so serve the flans within 24 hours and do not freeze.
Egg- and gelatin-free, these 100 percent vegan flans are light and easy to digest. Use the recipe as a base to experiment with for other dessert ideas.

❙ Techniques
Gelling with Agar-Agar, p. 101
Peeling Soft Fruit, p. 139

Ingredients
Flans
1 vanilla bean
2 cups (500 ml) almond, soy, or rice milk
Scant ⅓ cup (2 oz./60 g) sugar, or 2 tablespoons plus 2 teaspoons (2 oz./60 g) rice syrup or agave syrup
1 teaspoon (2 g) agar-agar

Coulis
2–3 yellow peaches
(approximately 10 oz./300 g net)
3 tablespoons (50 ml) peach liqueur
A few drops lemon juice

Equipment
Food processor or blender

Eggs and Dairy Products

Edouard Loubet

Born in the Savoie region, Edouard Loubet was elected Meilleur Apprenti de France (best apprentice of France) before crossing the Atlantic, where he worked in Chicago and Quebec City. On his return to France, he trained with Alain Chapel and Marc Veyret. In 1992, he took the helm of the Moulin de Lourmarin in the Lubéron region of the south of France. There, at the age of twenty-four, he became France's youngest Michelin-starred chef. In 2007, he transferred his gastronomic restaurant and its two stars to La Bastide de Capelongue in Bonnieux nearby, where he cultivates his vegetable garden, giving herbs, plants, and vegetables of all sorts pride of place in his cuisine. "Staying in tune with nature means constant spontaneity and true harmony," says the chef, who, in 2012, was awarded five *toques* by the prestigious gastronomic guide *Gault et Millau*—its highest rating.

Loubet is attached to his adopted region and stays in close contact with local producers, drawing up his menu as the seasons there change; seasons that, according to him, comprise one winter and one summer, but two springs and two falls.

The *crespeou*—a Provençal layered omelet cake that uses ingredients that are both foraged and farmed—can be adapted over the seasons to take advantage of nature's changing bounty.

La Bastide de Capelongue
Les Claparèdes
Chemin des Cabanes
84480 Bonnieux
France
Website: capelongue.com

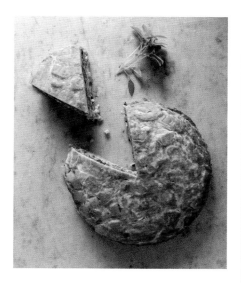

Serves 4
Preparation time: 15 minutes
Cooking time: 10 minutes

Ingredients
Crespeou

1 bunch parsley
1 bunch chives
1 onion
1 large potato
1 red bell pepper
1 yellow bell pepper
1 zucchini (courgette)
12 eggs
1 pinch salt
1 pinch white pepper

Tomato gazpacho

10 oz. (300 g) bright red, ripe tomatoes,
   peeled and diced
50 leaves basil
2 tablespoons (25 ml) olive oil
1 teaspoon tomato paste
1 teaspoon salt
A few celeriac leaves

Provençal Layered Omelet

A layered omelet cake with herbs and vegetables, the *crespeou* takes on different colors and flavors depending on the region of Provence in which it is made. In Nice, green Swiss chard is traditional, while in the Comtat Venaissin, emblematic olives and bell peppers bring touches of black and red.

Crespeou may be eaten hot or cold, and is delicious accompanied by a green salad. If you prefer, you can leave the omelets slightly runny.

For the *crespeou*
Chop the herbs. Separately, cut the vegetables into fine dice. Cook each vegetable separately. In each of four round-bottomed mixing bowls, whisk 3 eggs seasoned with salt and freshly ground pepper. Prepare four omelets: the first with the parsley and chives, another with the onion and potato, a third with the bell peppers, and the last one with the zucchini. Layer the omelet in this order to form a cake and place in the refrigerator.

For the tomato gazpacho
Place the tomatoes, basil, oil, tomato paste, salt, and celeriac leaves in a pot and bring to a boil. Simmer for 5 minutes and drain through a conical metal sieve. Adjust the seasoning and place in the refrigerator. Serve chilled. Just before serving, drizzle a little olive oil over the surface and add a large basil leaf.

To serve
On each plate, place a slice of *crespeou* and a generous spoonful of tomato gazpacho. Decorate with a basil leaf.

Ingredients

1 large onion
2 cloves garlic
2 tablespoons (1 oz./30 g) butter
2 teaspoons dried mint
1 pomegranate
10 sprigs cilantro (coriander)
10 sprigs dill
1 tablespoon cornstarch
2 cups (1 lb./500 g) whole milk yogurt
  (cow or sheep milk)
2 ½ cups (600 ml) vegetable broth
1 teaspoon fine salt
1 large egg, lightly beaten
1 ¾ cups (7 oz./220 g) cooked chickpeas
½ cup (3 ½ oz./100 g) cooked brown rice
Fine salt and freshly ground pepper

Iranian Herby Yogurt Soup ★★

Serves 4
Preparation time: 10 minutes
Cooking time: 10 minutes

Peel and finely dice the onion and garlic. Melt the butter in a skillet and sauté the onion and garlic for 10 minutes, until lightly browned. Stir in the dried mint, remove from the heat, and transfer to a bowl. Set aside.

Peel the pomegranate and take out half of the seeds (reserve the other half for a fruit salad or other dish). Pick the leaves of the herbs and chop them.

Combine the cornstarch with 2 tablespoons of the yogurt. Pour the remaining yogurt into a pot with the vegetable broth, salt, yogurt-cornstarch mixture, and the lightly beaten egg. Stirring constantly, heat over medium-low heat; do not allow to boil. When the mixture is smooth, stir in the chickpeas and rice.

Heat the soup, stirring constantly, over low heat, until it is warmed through and slightly thickened. Season with pepper, remove from the heat, and stir in the herbs.

Pour into soup plates, scatter with pomegranate seeds, and add the buttery garlic-onion-mint mixture.

● Chef's notes
This is a very adaptable recipe that allows you to use leftover grains and pulses. If you wish, replace the rice with barley or spelt, and the chickpeas with lentils or beans.
For the soup to remain smooth and creamy, it is important not to boil it. Heat it over low heat and stir continuously.

● Good to know
The traditional Iranian recipe, known as asheh mast, *is made with meatballs, but this vegetarian version is just as delicious.*

❙ Techniques
Preparing Fresh Herbs, p. 38
Dicing Onions, p. 39
Making Creole Rice, 50
Making Slow-Cooked (Pilaf) Rice, 51
Cooking Rice in a Rice Cooker, p. 59
Cooking Pulses, p. 82
Preparing Pomegranates, p. 134

Pan-Fried Cheese and Greek Salad ★

Serves 4
Preparation time: 15 minutes
Cooking time: 20 minutes

For the salad

Peel the cucumber and dice it. Rinse and dry the tomatoes. Cut them into quarters. Peel the onion and slice it into fine rounds. In a salad bowl, combine the vinegar, olive oil, oregano, salt, and pepper. Place the vegetables and olives in the bowl and mix carefully. Place the feta on the top so that each guest can take as much as they want. Place in the refrigerator while you prepare the cheese slices (*saganaki*).

For the cheese slices (*saganaki*)

Cut each slice of cheese into two. Coat the slices on all sides in the flour and shake lightly to remove any excess. In a nonstick pan, heat the olive oil over medium-high heat. Fry the cheese for 1 ½ minutes, until golden. Turn with a wide spatula and fry for 1 minute on the other side. The cheese should be hot but not melted. Drain any excess oil with sheets of paper towel.

Cut the lemon into quarters.

Serve the *saganaki* piping hot, with the lemon wedges for the guests to squeeze, accompanied by the Greek salad.

● Chef's notes

Saganaki is traditionally made with kefalotyri, *which usually contains animal rennet; vegetarian versions of* halloumi, *another Greek cheese, are more readily available.*

● Good to know

Saganaki is the name of the small pan with two handles in which the cheese is fried. It has given its name to many other dishes.

Ingredients

Greek salad

1 spiny cucumber
1 lb. (500 g) ripe tomatoes
1 small red onion
1 tablespoon red wine vinegar
2 tablespoons olive oil
1 teaspoon dried oregano
12 black Kalamata olives
3 ½ oz. (100 g) feta, in pieces
Fine salt and freshly ground pepper

Cheese slices

7 oz. (200 g) vegetarian *halloumi* cheese, in two 1-inch (2.5-cm) slices
Scant ⅓ cup (2 oz./50 g) all-purpose flour
Scant ½ cup (100 ml) olive oil
1 lemon

Chinese Egg and Scallion Pancakes ★

Makes 6 pancakes
Preparation time: 15 minutes
Resting time: 10 minutes
Cooking time: 15 minutes

In a mixing bowl, combine the flour, cornstarch, salt, and water together to form a smooth batter. You can also make it in a blender or using an immersion blender. Leave to rest for 10 minutes at room temperature.

Finely chop the scallions, both the white and green parts. Whisk the eggs with the toasted sesame seed oil and water.

Lightly oil the pancake pan and place over high heat. Drop in a small ladleful of batter and tilt the pan to spread it evenly. Cook for 1 minute and turn.

Carefully pour one sixth of the egg-onion mixture over the pancake, ensuring that it stops spreading a little short of the edge of the pancake. Allow to cook briefly, until the surface of the mixture is opaque. Remove the pancake from the pan and repeat with the remaining batter and egg-onion mixture to make six pancakes altogether.

Combine all the ingredients for the sauce in a mixing bowl. Warm a serving dish.

Roll the pancakes and cut them into thick slices. Place them in the warmed dish and drizzle with the sauce. Serve with pre-dinner drinks or as a light main dish, accompanied by a bowl of rice.

● Chef's notes
*Vegetarian oyster sauce, as its name indicates, is a suitable substitute
for traditional oyster sauce and is available in Asian grocery stores.
If you do not have toasted sesame seed oil, use peanut oil and add 1 teaspoon
of sesame seeds to the whisked eggs.
If you do not have scallions, use a generous quantity of chives.*

● Good to know
*These pancakes originated in China and are eaten in Taiwan at breakfast,
or at other times of the day as a snack.*

Techniques
Preparing Fresh Herbs, p. 38

Ingredients
1 cup plus 1 tablespoon (5 oz./140 g)
all-purpose flour
$1/3$ cup (2 oz./60 g) cornstarch or potato starch
1 pinch salt
1 $1/3$ cups (330 ml) water
3 scallions (spring onions) with their stalks
6 eggs
1 tablespoon toasted sesame seed oil
2 tablespoons water
Neutral oil (sunflower or grape-seed), for frying

Sauce
1 tablespoon vegetarian oyster sauce
2 tablespoons soy sauce
2 teaspoons black rice vinegar
1 tablespoon honey
1 teaspoon toasted sesame seed oil
1 drop chili sauce

Equipment
8-inch (20-cm) nonstick pancake pan

Ingredients

1 onion (5-7 oz./150-200 g)
1 clove garlic
3 red bell peppers (about 1 lb./500 g)
3 green bell peppers (about 1 lb./500 g)
6 ripe tomatoes (about 1 ¾ lb./800 g)
1 ½ teaspoons cumin seeds
¼ cup (60 ml) olive oil
2 teaspoons brown sugar
1 bay leaf
2 sprigs thyme
1 teaspoon paprika
½ teaspoon *harissa* pepper paste
4-8 organic eggs
8-10 sprigs flat-leaf parsley

Shakshuka ★

Serves 4
Preparation time: 30 minutes
Cooking time: 40 minutes

Peel and finely dice the onion. Peel and crush the garlic clove. Remove the seeds from the bell peppers and cut them into slices. Cut each slice into three pieces. Remove the bases of the tomatoes and cut them into chunks.

In a large skillet over medium-high heat, roast the cumin seeds briefly until fragrant. Pour in the olive oil, increase the heat to high, and lightly brown the garlic and onion for 2 minutes.

Add the bell peppers, sugar, bay leaf, and thyme and season lightly with salt. Sauté for 5 minutes, then add the tomatoes, paprika, and *harissa*. Cover with the lid, reduce the heat to low, and simmer for 30 minutes. If the tomatoes render very little liquid, add a little water to prevent the *shakshuka* from sticking to the skillet.

With the back of a spoon, make four small hollows evenly over the *shakshuka*. Depending on the guests' appetite, break 1 or 2 eggs into each hollow. Allow to cook gently for about 8 minutes, until the white has set but the yolk is still runny.

Season with salt and pepper, garnish with a few leaves of parsley, and serve with fresh bread.

● **Chef's notes**
If you do not have harissa, *simply use cayenne pepper to taste.*
When tomatoes are not in season, it is preferable to use chopped, preserved tomatoes.
Some cooks like to add a pinch of cinnamon to the spices; others prefer cilantro to parsley—it's all a question of taste and what is available at the market.
Individual shakshukas can also be made in a small skillet (see photo).

● **Good to know**
This dish rich in bell peppers and spices, which comes to us from Tunisia, is very similar to the menemen *found in Turkey, where the eggs are scrambled, and Mexican* huevos rancheros, *traditionally eaten for breakfast.*

❘ **Techniques**
Preparing Bell Peppers, p. 22
Preparing Garlic, p. 29
Dicing Onions, p. 39

Paneer and Spinach Curry ★

Serves 4
Preparation time: 10 minutes
Cooking time: 10 minutes

In a large pot of salted boiling water, blanch the spinach for 10 seconds. Drain well, pressing down hard with your hands to remove as much water as possible. Chop the leaves and reserve at room temperature.

Peel and finely dice the onion. Remove the seeds of the chili pepper and dice finely. Peel the garlic cloves and remove the green shoots. Peel the ginger and turmeric. Grate the garlic, ginger, and turmeric. Cut the *paneer* into cubes.

In a skillet over medium-high heat, melt the ghee. Fry the *paneer* cubes for 2 to 3 minutes, until slightly crisp. Season lightly with salt and reserve at room temperature.

Place the onion, garlic, ginger, turmeric, and chili pepper in the skillet over medium-high heat. Add the garam masala and cook for 2 to 3 minutes, stirring frequently, until lightly colored.

Add the spinach to the skillet, stir, and sauté for 1 minute. Carefully stir in the *paneer* cubes and cook for an additional 2 minutes.

Serve with plain rice, chapatis, or naan bread.

● **Chef's notes**
If you do not have fresh turmeric, simply use ½ teaspoon of ground turmeric.

● **Good to know**
This dish is known in India as palak paneer. It can also be made with other leafy vegetables instead of spinach, such as turnip leaves, cabbage, mustard leaves, etc.

Techniques
Preparing Chilies, p. 23
Preparing Garlic, p. 29
Peeling Fresh Ginger, p. 29
Blanching, p. 41
Making Fresh Curds and *Paneer*, p. 110
Making Clarified Butter and Ghee, p. 113

Ingredients
1 ¾ lb. (800 g) fresh spinach
½ teaspoon salt
1 large onion
1 small green chili pepper
3 cloves garlic
1 ½-inch (4-cm) piece ginger
¾-inch (2-cm) piece turmeric root
10 oz. (300 g) *paneer* cheese
3 tablespoons ghee
2-3 teaspoons garam masala, to taste

Ingredients

1 leek
1 large yellow onion
2 cloves garlic
3 large ripe tomatoes, or ¾ cup (200 ml)
  passata (strained tomatoes)
1 organic or unwaxed orange
2 lb. (1 kg) waxy potatoes
2 tablespoons olive oil
Scant ½ cup (100 ml) white wine
1 dried bay leaf
3 stalks dried fennel
A few threads saffron
4 eggs
4 slices country bread
Salt and freshly ground pepper

Equipment

Cast-iron pot

One-Eyed Bouillabaisse ★★

Serves 4
Preparation time: 30 minutes
Cooking time: 35 minutes

Carefully clean the leek and slice it finely. Peel the onion and cut it into slices. Peel and chop the garlic cloves. Remove the bases of the tomatoes and chop them roughly. Zest the orange. Peel the potatoes and slice them.

Over high heat, heat the olive oil in the cast-iron pot and lightly color the leek and onion. Add the tomatoes, garlic, white wine, bay leaf, fennel stalks, and orange zest. Season with salt and pepper. Add the potatoes and pour in 4-6 cups (1-1.5 liters) hot water–enough to cover the potatoes. Simmer for 20 to 25 minutes, until the potatoes are tender.

Stir the saffron into the broth. Break the eggs, one by one, into a cup, and carefully tip them into the broth to poach at the surface. It should take 2 to 3 minutes for them to cook; the yolk should remain runny.

Place a slice of bread at the bottom of each of four soup plates. Pour 1 to 2 ladlefuls of the broth (without the potatoes and egg) over the bread to serve as an appetizer.

Then serve the potatoes with the poached eggs and remaining broth, seasoning them directly on the plates with a little olive oil and salt.

Alternatively, you can serve the whole broth together, for a substantial main course.

● Chef's notes
To poach the eggs easily, it is best to put very little salt in the soup—salt interferes with the coagulation of the egg white.

● Good to know
This Provençal recipe is inspired by fish bouillabaisse, retaining the traditional seasoning of saffron, fennel stalks, and orange zest.

▮ Techniques
Cleaning Leeks, p. 24
Poaching Eggs, p. 108

Eggs and Dairy Products

Fennel Tortilla ★

Serves 4 to 6
Preparation time: 20 minutes
Cooking time: 20 minutes, plus 40 minutes

Preheat the oven to 350°F (180°C/Gas Mark 4). Grease the cake pan well with oil.

Peel the potatoes and dice them. Precook them in salted boiling water for 20 minutes and drain. Peel the onion and, using the mandolin, slice it very finely. Peel and dice the garlic.

Drizzle half of the olive oil into a skillet over high heat. Fry the onion until lightly colored and remove from the skillet. Remove the outer leaves of the fennel bulb (use them in a soup or to add to a juice) and slice them finely with the mandolin. Remove the stalk and seeds of the bell peppers and slice them finely with the mandolin.

Whisk the eggs with the yogurt, paprika, salt, and pepper. Stir in the potatoes, onion, and garlic, along with the bell pepper and fennel slices.

Pour the preparation into the prepared pan. Bake for 30 to 40 minutes, until the tortilla is a lovely golden color. Serve warm or cool.

● Chef's notes

Traditionally, a tortilla is made with sautéed potatoes. This lighter version of the recipe requires precooking, which ensures that the potatoes are soft.
The type of potatoes you use determines the texture of the tortilla. If you use floury potatoes, the tortilla will be moister. If you use firm potatoes, the pieces will stay whole and the texture of the tortilla will be denser.
It is easier to keep an eye on the tortilla if it cooks in the oven rather than on the stove—and it's a guarantee of success!

Techniques
Preparing Fennel, p. 16
Preparing Bell Peppers, p. 22
Dicing Onions, p. 39
Using a Mandolin, p. 40

Ingredients
1 ½ lb. (700 g) potatoes (see Chef's notes)
1 yellow onion
1 clove garlic
2 tablespoons olive oil
1 bulb fennel
1 small red bell pepper
1 small green bell pepper
8 eggs
1 tablespoon Greek-style yogurt
(sheep or goat milk)
1 teaspoon mild or smoked paprika, to taste
Fine salt and freshly ground pepper
Oil to grease the pan

Equipment
10-inch (24-cm) diameter cake pan
Mandolin

Ingredients

Popovers
2 eggs
1 cup (4 oz./120 g) all-purpose flour
2/3 cup plus 1 tablespoon (160 ml) milk
  (cow, soy, rice)
2 pinches salt

Herb cream cheese
10 sprigs flat-leaf parsley
10 sprigs cilantro (coriander)
¼ red onion
8 oz. (250 g) vegetarian ricotta
  or creamy goat cheese
2 teaspoons olive oil
Zest of ¼ unwaxed lemon
Fine salt and freshly ground pepper

Equipment
Muffin pan
Immersion blender or blender

Popovers with Herb Cream Cheese ★

Serves 6
Preparation time: 20 minutes
Cooking time: 40 minutes

Grease the muffin pan with oil using a pastry brush. Place them in the oven and preheat to 425°F (220°C/Gas Mark 7).

For the popovers
With an immersion blender, process all the ingredients in a jug with a spout (or use a blender). Carefully take the hot muffin pan out of the oven and pour in the batter, filling them to three quarters. Bake for 20 minutes. Resist all temptation to open the door! If you do, they will flop. After 20 minutes, reduce the temperature to 350°F (175°C/Gas Mark 4) and bake for an additional 15 to 20 minutes, until the popovers are a lovely golden color.

For the herb cream cheese
Wash the herbs, dry them well, and chop finely. Peel and dice the onion. Combine the cream cheese, herbs, onion, olive oil, and lemon zest. Taste and adjust the seasoning if necessary by adding salt and pepper.

Spread the warm popovers with the herb cream cheese and serve.

● Good to know
These popovers are the American cousins of British Yorkshire pudding, and also have similarities with the French gougère.
Although traditionally served as an accompaniment to roasted meat dishes, they are excellent with cheese or a large salad.

❘ Techniques
Preparing Fresh Herbs, p. 38

Eggs and Dairy Products

Nuts and Seeds

Amandine Chaignot

Although she initially began studying to be a pharmacist, Amandine Chaignot decided to change course in 1998 and pursue her passion for cooking.

After graduating from the prestigious Paris cooking school Ferrandi, she worked with Bernard Leprince at Maison Prunier, Jean-Francois Piège at Plaza Athénée, Éric Frechon at Le Bristol, Yannick Alléno at Le Meurice, and Christopher Hache at Hôtel de Crillon, before becoming head chef at Raphaël in 2012. There, she developed her elegant, refined cuisine, revisiting the classics. Then she set off for London, where, since 2015, she has been executive chef at the Rosewood Hotel. Every Sunday, the hotel courtyard hosts a Slow Food market with local products that are a source of inspiration for the chef. Chaignot's cuisine reflects the cosmopolitan city where she is based and integrates influences from all over the world. The vegetarian options on her menu are many and varied.

In the dish Chaignot shares with us here, the culinary melting pot of London and pronounced Middle Eastern influences come together with tahini, pomegranate, and preserved lemon providing an unexpected backdrop to hearty slices of roasted cauliflower.

Rosewood London
252 High Holborn
London WC1V 7EN
United Kingdom
Website: rosewoodhotels.com/en/london

Serves 4

Preparation time: 30 minutes
Resting time: 24 hours
Cooking time: 5 hours, plus
  2 hours 15 minutes

Ingredients
Preserved lemon

1 organic lemon
1 ¼ cups (10 oz./300 g) fine salt
4 cups (1 liter) water
1 cup (7 oz./200 g) sugar

Red tahini

2 tomatoes
3 tablespoons (40 ml) olive oil
Thyme leaves to taste
4 oz. (120 g) tahini
Fine salt

Cauliflower and garnish

1 large cauliflower
4 tablespoons (60 ml) olive oil
1 clove garlic
Thyme leaves
1 pomegranate
1 bunch green grapes
1 red onion
1 handful arugula (rocket)

Roasted Cauliflower, Red Tahini, and Preserved Lemon

For the preserved lemon
Carefully wash the lemon. With a toothpick or needle, prick it all over at ½-inch (1-cm) intervals. Cover completely with salt and leave to rest for 24 hours at room temperature.

Bring the water and sugar to a boil to make a syrup. Plunge the lemon in the syrup, placing a rack or plate over it so that it remains submerged. Bring back to a boil, then reduce the heat as much as possible so that it simmers without boiling. Allow to cook for 5 hours, until the lemon is translucent. If the syrup evaporates, add a little water while it cooks. Allow to cool in the liquid, drain, and cut in half. Carefully remove the seeds, reserving the flesh and liquid to use as a base for a sauce. Cut the peel into small dice and reserve.

For the red tahini
To peel the tomatoes, immerse them in boiling water for 10 seconds. Refresh in ice water. Peel, cut into quarters, remove the seeds, and place the pieces in an ovenproof dish. Drizzle with the olive oil and sprinkle with thyme leaves and fine salt. Cook them in a 210°F (100°C/Gas Mark ¼) oven for 2 hours. Blend with the tahini and set aside.

For the cauliflower
Preheat the oven to 340°F (170°C/Gas Mark 3). Remove the green leaves from the cauliflower and cut it into four thick slices, ensuring that they remain whole. Place them on a baking sheet and season with the olive oil and salt. Place the whole garlic clove on the sheet and sprinkle the cauliflower slices with thyme. Roast for 15 minutes, then set aside but keep warm.

For the garnish
Remove the seeds of the pomegranate. Cut the grapes into quarters and remove the seeds. Peel and slice the red onion. Wash and dry the arugula.

To serve
On each plate, place a slice of warm cauliflower. Add three scoops of red tahini and scatter with diced preserved lemon peel, grape quarters, pomegranate seeds, and red onion slices. Add the arugula leaves and season lightly with olive oil.

Ajo Blanco ★

Chilled Almond Soup

Serves 4
Preparation time: 15 minutes
Chilling time: 12 hours, plus 1 hour

Peel the garlic clove and remove the green shoot. On a chopping board with a large knife, roughly chop the almonds and garlic. Transfer to a mixing bowl. Crumble the bread over the almonds and garlic, pour in the vinegar, and add a scant ½ cup (100 ml) of the water. Season with the salt and pepper. Cover the bowl and place in the refrigerator for 12 hours.

Transfer the contents of the mixing bowl to the blender. Pour in 1 ⅔ cups (400 ml) water and the olive oil. Blend and adjust the seasoning, adding salt and pepper if necessary. If the soup is too thick for your liking, stir in a little more water.

Place in the refrigerator for 1 hour, before serving with the green grapes.

● Chef's notes
If you have a juicer, juice the grapes to make fresh green grape juice that you can add directly to the soup to replace some of the water.

● Good to know
Ajo blanco is a cold soup that originated in Andalusia and is very popular there. The traditional Andalusian version is much richer in garlic. If you are a garlic fan, use up to two cloves.

❘ Techniques
Preparing Garlic, p. 29
Peeling Almonds, p. 117

Ingredients
1 clove garlic (or more, to taste)
1 scant cup (4 oz./120 g) peeled or blanched almonds
1 ½ oz. (40 g) day-old or dried bread (equivalent of one thick slice)
¼ cup (60 ml) sherry vinegar
2–2 ½ cups (500–600 ml) water
2 tablespoons olive oil
¾ teaspoon salt
Freshly ground pepper
1 bunch green grapes

Equipment
Blender

Ingredients

Tart shells

¾ cup plus 2 tablespoons (3 ½ oz./100 g) all-purpose flour

1 cup (3oz./80 g) ground blanched almonds

1 ½ oz. (40 g) vegetarian Parmesan-style hard cheese, freshly grated

½ teaspoon salt

1 stick plus 3 tablespoons (5 ½ oz./160 g) butter, room temperature, diced

2 egg yolks

Topping

1 organic or unwaxed lemon

6 baby artichokes

1 yellow summer squash (yellow courgette)

1 green zucchini (courgette)

2 scallions (spring onions)

1-2 tablespoons olive oil

½ cup (3 ½ oz./100 g) olive puree (see technique p. 125)

Generous ½ cup (4 oz./120 g) vegetarian ricotta or creamy sheep cheese

2 sprigs fresh thyme

Fleur de sel and freshly ground pepper

Techniques

Preparing Baby Artichokes, p. 14

Using a Mandolin, p. 40

Rolling Out Pastry Dough, p. 66

Making Olive Puree, p. 125

Mediterranean Vegetable Tartlets ★ ★ ★

Serves 6

Preparation time: 40 minutes

Chilling time: 1 hour

Cooking time: 15 minutes

For the tart shells

In a mixing bowl, combine the flour, ground almonds, cheese, and salt, and grind in a little pepper. Using your fingertips, rub in the butter until the mixture reaches a sandy texture. Alternatively, you can use a stand mixer with the paddle beater. Add the egg yolks and knead lightly until the dough forms a ball. Cover with plastic wrap and place in the refrigerator for 1 hour.

Preheat the oven to 325°F (160°C/Gas Mark 3).

Roll the dough between two sheets of parchment or waxed paper to a thickness of ¼ inch (5-6 mm) and cut it into six 4-inch (10-cm) squares. Prick them with the tines of a fork. Transfer the sheet of parchment paper directly onto a baking sheet and bake for 15 minutes, until lightly colored. Allow to cool on a rack.

For the topping

Fill a mixing bowl with water and squeeze in the juice of half of the lemon. Remove the outer leaves of the artichokes, remove the choke if necessary, and cut the heart into slices. As you cut them, drop them into the bowl of water so that they do not brown. Trim the tips of the summer squash and zucchini. Slice them finely, with a mandolin if possible. Peel the scallions and slice finely.

In a bowl, combine the zest and juice of the remaining lemon half. Stir in the olive oil. Pick off the leaves of the thyme and set aside.

Spread the olive puree over the pastry squares. Arrange the summer squash and zucchini rounds and artichoke and scallion slices over it. Crumble the ricotta on the top and drizzle with the lemon-flavored olive oil. Sprinkle with thyme and fleur de sel and serve immediately.

● Chef's notes

If you have any leftover dough, sprinkle it with sesame seeds, cut into small shapes, and bake, to make a delicious savory snack.

You can experiment with this recipe in many ways. Spread the tart crust with herb-flavored cream cheese (see recipe p. 367) or hummus (see technique p. 81) and use any vegetables you're fond of, cooked or raw: roasted bell peppers, marinated artichokes, blanched snow peas, etc.

Chickpea Fritters with Hemp and Pumpkin Seed Pesto ★ ★

Serves 4
Preparation time: 20 minutes
Chilling time: 12 hours
Cooking time: 20 minutes

For the fritters
Grease the loaf pan with oil. In a large mixing bowl, combine the chickpea flour, fine salt, and baking soda. Stir in the water, just as if you were making a pancake batter. If the batter is lumpy, process it with an immersion blender or in a blender until smooth. Transfer the batter to a saucepan over medium heat and bring to a boil, stirring constantly with a flexible spatula. Cook for 5 to 8 minutes, stirring constantly, until the batter is as thick as choux pastry. Pour it into the prepared loaf pan, smooth the surface, cover with plastic wrap, and place in the refrigerator for 12 hours.

When you are ready to proceed, preheat the oven to 210°F (100°C/Gas Mark ¼). Turn the dough out of the pan and cut it into ¾-inch (1.5-cm) slices. Cut the slices into sticks about the size of French fries. Pat them dry with sheets of paper towel. In a frying pan, heat half of the oil and fry half of the fritters for 4 to 5 minutes on each side, until golden. The fritters may well leave small bits in the oil, so change it and pour in the remaining oil. Fry the remaining fritters as for the previous batch.

Sprinkle with fleur de sel and place in the preheated oven to keep warm while you make the pesto.

For the pesto
Peel the garlic, remove the green shoot, and chop finely. Pick the leaves of the chervil, cilantro, and basil. Briefly process the garlic, herbs, and pumpkin seeds in the food processor or blender. Add the yogurt, hemp seeds, olive oil, and lemon juice, using the pulse function to ensure that the texture does not become too smooth. Season with salt and pepper, and, if necessary, add a little yogurt for a creamier texture. Serve with the fritters.

● Chef's notes
The unbaked fritter dough will keep for 2 days in the loaf pan, covered with plastic wrap, in the refrigerator.
The pesto can also be stored in an airtight jar in the refrigerator for 2 days. It makes a good filling for sandwiches and can also be served as a dip for crudités.

● Good to know
In the Marseille neighborhood of Estaque, there are still stands that sell these fritters, known as panisses. They are molded in cylinders and cut into rounds. If you want to reproduce the traditional shape of this street food, use cleaned, dried cans to mold them, or shape the lukewarm dough into large logs using plastic wrap.

Ingredients
Fritters
1 ⅔ cups (5 oz./150 g) chickpea flour
½ teaspoon fine salt
1 teaspoon (5 g) baking soda
1 ¼ cups (300 ml) water
¾ cup (200 ml) oil for frying
Fleur de sel

Pesto
1 small clove garlic
10 sprigs chervil
10 sprigs cilantro (coriander)
5 sprigs basil
3 tablespoons pumpkin seeds
3–4 tablespoons soy yogurt
3 tablespoons hemp seeds
1 tablespoon olive oil
A few drops lemon juice
Fine salt and freshly ground pepper

Equipment
8 ½-inch (22-24-cm) loaf pan
Food processor or blender

Techniques
Preparing Garlic, p. 29

Ingredients

Pita chips

4 pitas, preferably day-old or slightly dried
2 tablespoons olive oil
3 pinches fleur de sel
2 teaspoons dried oregano
½ teaspoon chili pepper flakes of your choice
   (*piment d'Espelette*, smoked paprika, etc.)

Pepper dip

3 red bell peppers
1 teaspoon cumin seeds
1 clove garlic
1 ¼ cups (4 oz./125 g) walnuts
2 tablespoons homemade bread crumbs
2 tablespoons pomegranate molasses
Juice of ½ lemon
3 tablespoons olive oil
1 teaspoon paprika, or other mild chili pepper
½ teaspoon smoked *pimentón*, or other smoked
   chili pepper
Fine salt and freshly ground pepper

Equipment

Blender or food processor

Techniques

Preparing Garlic, p. 29
Peeling Bell Peppers, p. 45

Hot Pepper and Walnut Dip with Pita Chips ★

Serves 4
Preparation time: 30 minutes
Chilling time: 1 hour

For the pita chips

Preheat the oven to 400°F (200°C/Gas Mark 6).

With a pair of scissors, cut the pita bread into triangles. Spread them in a single layer over a large baking sheet. In a mixing bowl, combine the olive oil, fleur de sel, oregano, and chili pepper flakes. Drizzle the mixture over the pita triangles and work it in with your fingers. Bake for 5 to 8 minutes, turning them once and keeping a careful eye on their color. They should be a light brown and become very crisp. Leave to cool on a rack and transfer to a serving bowl.

For the pepper dip

Set the oven to broil. Wash the bell peppers and char them under the broiler–the skin should blacken and the flesh should be very tender. Place in a mixing bowl and cover with plastic wrap. Leave for 15 minutes to cool. Peel and remove the seeds.

In a small dry skillet over medium heat, toast the cumin seeds until fragrant. Peel the garlic clove and remove the green shoot. Process the bell peppers in the food processor or blender with the garlic, walnuts, bread crumbs, pomegranate molasses, lemon juice, olive oil, salt, and spices. Taste and adjust the seasoning, adding salt and pepper if necessary. If the texture is too thick for your liking, add a little lemon juice or olive oil. Place in the refrigerator for 1 hour, before serving with the pita chips.

● Chef's notes

This pepper dip is even more delicious if the bell peppers are grilled on the barbecue, so if you have one, take advantage of it. If you don't, you can add to the smokiness by using smoked salt, such as smoked Anglesey or Maldon salt, or Spanish pimentòn de la Vera.
You can freeze this dip for up to 2 months.

● Good to know

Originally from Syria, this dip, known as muhammara, is made throughout the Middle East. It is found, with variations, in Lebanon and Turkey, where it is known as acuka.

Indonesian Bean Salad ★★

Serves 4
Preparation time: 20 minutes
Cooking time: 20 minutes

For the spicy coconut paste (*sambal*)
Peel the garlic. Squeeze the lime. Remove the stem and seeds of the chili pepper. Cut the coconut flesh into pieces. Peel the galangal. Chop the palm sugar roughly.

In the bowl of the food processor or blender, chop the garlic, chili pepper, and palm sugar. Add the galangal and kaffir lime leaves and process until the ingredients form a paste. Next, add the coconut, using the pulse function rather than processing continuously, until the paste reaches the texture of bread crumbs. Season with salt and pepper.

For the salad
Trim the snake beans and cook them in salted boiling water for 5 minutes, then refresh in ice water. Cut them into slices about 1/8-1/4 inch (3-5 mm) long. Finely slice the cucumber. Wash the soy sprouts and dry them carefully. Rinse and dry the Thai basil and pick off the leaves. Combine all the ingredients with the Thai basil.

Heat a small skillet over high heat and cook the coconut paste for 1 to 2 minutes. Pour it over the salad, mix through, and place in the refrigerator to chill. Serve well chilled.

● Chef's notes
Coconut sambal *is traditionally prepared with red curry paste rather than the fresh chili pepper indicated here. Curry paste usually contains dried shrimps, so check the list of ingredients if you wish to use it.*

● Good to know
This refreshing salad, typical of the center of the island of Java, is known locally as trancam. *It may also include shredded cabbage or banana. It's the sambal seasoning—a spicy coconut paste—that gives it its distinctive taste.*

❙ Techniques
Preparing Chilies, p. 23
Peeling Fresh Ginger, p. 29
Blanching, p. 41
Opening a Coconut, p. 129

Ingredients
Spicy coconut paste (*sambal*)
1 clove garlic
1 lime
1 small fresh red chili pepper
3 ½ oz. (100 g) fresh coconut
2/3-oz. (20-g) piece galangal
2/3 oz. (20 g) palm sugar
2 kaffir lime leaves
Fine salt

Salad
8 oz. (250 g) fresh snake beans,
or fresh green beans
1 small cucumber (about 5 oz./150 g)
4 handfuls mung bean sprouts
1 bunch Thai basil
1 lime

Equipment
Food processor or blender

Ingredients

Pudding

12 strawberries

1 kiwi fruit

4-6 tablespoons chia seeds, depending
on the texture desired

1 ¾ cups (450 ml) nondairy milk of your choice
(soy, almond, rice, or coconut)

1 tablespoon dried fruit of your choice
(raisins, goji berries, cranberries, etc.)

Green smoothie

1 ripe pear

½ banana

1 ⅓ cups (330 ml) almond milk

1 handful (about ⅔ oz./20 g) lettuce leaves
of your choice (romaine, lamb's lettuce, etc.)

1 handful (about ⅔ oz./20 g) shredded cabbage
of your choice (kale, green cabbage, Chinese
cabbage, etc.)

1 handful (about ⅔ oz./20 g) fresh spinach leaves

4 ice cubes

1 small piece fresh ginger, peeled

Equipment

Blender

Chia Pudding with a Green Smoothie ★

Serves 2

Preparation time: 15 minutes

Chilling time: 20 minutes to 12 hours

For the pudding

Hull the strawberries and slice them. Peel the kiwi fruit and cut it into rounds. Pour the chia seeds into a jar and cover with the milk. Close tightly with the lid and shake well to mix thoroughly.

Leave to rest for 20 minutes if you prefer a crunchy texture, or up to 12 hours in the refrigerator if you prefer the texture to be as creamy as tapioca. Just before serving, divide the pudding between two bowls and top with the strawberry and kiwi slices and dried fruit.

For the smoothie

Peel the pear and banana half and cut them into chunks. Pour the almond milk into the blender and add the lettuce, cabbage, and spinach leaves. Blend until perfectly smooth. Add the ice cubes, pear, banana, and ginger and blend until foamy.

● Chef's notes

This pudding is sweetened naturally by the fresh and dried fruit. If you would like additional sweetness, add a little rice or maple syrup.

Stored in an airtight container, the pudding will keep for up to 3 days in the refrigerator.

Experiment with the fruit for the smoothie: try mango or pineapple, or any of your favorite fruit.

If you use frozen fruit, there's no need to add the ice cubes.

● Good to know

Chia seeds are high in fiber and omega-3 fatty acids, which explains their status as a superfood. When they are immersed in a liquid, they become viscous and their texture softens enough for them to be eaten like porridge. They are filling and high in protein.

Techniques

Peeling Fresh Ginger, p. 29

Making Almond Milk, p. 122

Nuts and Seeds

Nut and Maple Syrup Tart ★ ★

Serves 6
Preparation time: 40 minutes
Chilling time: 1 hour
Cooking time: 45 minutes
Resting time 1 to 2 hours

For the tart shell(s)

In the bowl of the food processor fitted with the knife blade, combine the flour, sugar, chocolate, and salt. Process briefly, until the chocolate is cut into small pieces. Add the diced butter and process until the mixture reaches a sandy texture. Switch to the pulse function and pour in the ice water, pulsing to incorporate. Stop as soon as the dough pulls away from the sides of the bowl. Cover in plastic wrap and place in the refrigerator for 1 hour.

Preheat the oven to 320°F (160°C/Gas Mark 3). Butter the tart pan or tartlet pans. Roll out the dough between two sheets of parchment or waxed paper. Transfer to the prepared pan, or cut out rounds to fit the tartlet pans and line them with the rounds. Bake blind for 30 to 35 minutes, until an even golden color. If you are making tartlets, reduce the baking time to 20 to 25 minutes. You will need the oven at the same temperature to roast the nuts, so remove the tart shell(s) without turning the oven off. Leave the tart shell(s) to cool.

For the filling

Spread the nuts on a baking sheet and roast them in the oven for 10 minutes, keeping a careful eye on them and turning them regularly. Leave to cool, then chop roughly.

In a large saucepan over low heat, melt the butter. Pour in the flour, combine, and stir in the maple syrup and water. Increase the heat and bring to a boil, then reduce the heat to low and simmer for 10 to 15 minutes, stirring regularly, until the liquid has thickened but is still fluid.

Transfer the tart shell(s) to a serving dish. Pour in the maple syrup cream and scatter the chopped roasted nuts evenly over the top. Leave to rest at room temperature for 1 to 2 hours before serving, so that the maple syrup cream can set. Sprinkle with fleur de sel just before serving.

● Chef's notes

This tart shell, made with rye flour and chocolate, has a fairly intense taste. If you prefer milder flavors, simply replace it with a traditional shortcrust pastry (see technique p. 65).
If you do not have salted butter to hand, add a generous pinch of fine salt to the maple syrup cream.
Well covered in plastic wrap, the dough keeps for 3 days in the refrigerator, and for up to 2 months in the freezer.

Ingredients

Tart shell
2 ¼ cups (8 oz./220 g) rye flour
1 tablespoon plus 2 teaspoons (20 g) sugar
2 oz. (60 g) bittersweet baking chocolate, 70 percent cocoa
1 pinch salt
7 tablespoons (4 oz./110 g) butter, well chilled and diced, plus extra for the pan
Scant ½ cup (100 ml) ice water

Filling
3 ½ oz. (100 g) nuts of your choice (hazelnuts, almonds, macadamias, cashews, etc.)
5 tablespoons (2 ½ oz./75 g) salted butter, diced
⅔ cup (2 ½ oz./75 g) all-purpose flour
¾ cup (7 oz./220 g) maple syrup
1 ¼ cups (300 ml) water
Generous pinch fleur de sel

Equipment

9 ½-inch (24-cm) tart pan or six 4-inch (10-cm) tartlet pans
Food processor

Techniques

Making Shortcrust Pastry Dough, p. 65
Rolling Out Pastry Dough p. 66
Lining a Tart Pan, p. 67
Baking Blind, p. 76

Tahini and Sesame Seed Cookies ★

Makes about 2 dozen small cookies
Preparation time: 15 minutes
Chilling time: 2 hours
Cooking time: 12 to 15 minutes per batch

With an electric beater, whisk the butter, sugar, and vanilla extract together until creamy. Add the tahini and whisk until smooth.

In a mixing bowl, combine the flour, baking powder, and salt. Add to the butter-tahini mixture in stages, folding in the dry ingredients using a flexible spatula until incorporated. Do not overmix. Shape the dough into a ball, flatten to make a disk, and cover in plastic wrap. Place in the refrigerator for at least 2 hours. You can also make this dough a day in advance.

Preheat the oven to 350°F (180°C/Gas Mark 4). Line two baking sheets with parchment or waxed paper.

Pour the sesame seeds into a bowl. Take spoonfuls of the dough and roll them into balls with your hands. One by one, coat them completely in the sesame seeds, pressing them in lightly so that they adhere well.

Place them on the prepared baking sheet, allowing space for them to spread. Bake for 12 to 15 minutes, until they begin to crack lightly on the surface. Leave to cool for 30 minutes on the baking sheet: they are very crumbly while they are still hot, so wait until they have cooled before moving them.

● Chef's notes
Serve these cookies with a sorbet, or simply with a cup of tea.
Stored in an airtight container, the cookies keep for up to 1 week.
The raw dough can be frozen for up to 2 months. Either freeze the disk in its plastic wrap and defrost to shape, or shape the balls beforehand and coat them in the sesame seeds: simply increase the baking time by 5 to 7 minutes in the latter case.

Ingredients
7 tablespoons (4 oz./110 g) butter,
  room temperature
½ cup (3 ½ oz./100 g) light brown sugar
1 teaspoon vanilla extract
¾ cup (4 oz./110 g) tahini
1 ⅔ cups (5 ½ oz./160 g) whole-wheat flour
½ teaspoon baking powder
¼ teaspoon fine salt
¼ cup (1 oz./30 g) whole sesame seeds

Poppy Seed Cakes ★

Serves 6
Preparation time: 20 minutes
Cooking time: 20 minutes

Preheat the oven to 350°F (180°C/Gas Mark 4). Butter the muffin cups.

Separate the eggs. Grate the lemon zest and squeeze the juice. In a food processor or grinder, grind the poppy seeds; be careful not to allow them to heat up or they will form a paste. They should be crushed and form small clumps.

Over low heat, melt the butter. Whisk the egg yolks with the sugar until the mixture doubles in volume and becomes pale and thick; this should take up to 10 minutes. Pour in the melted butter in a steady stream, whisking continuously, then incorporate the potato starch. Stir the lemon zest and juice into the mixture.

Whisk the egg whites until they hold firm peaks. Stir one third of the egg whites briskly into the mixture. Then use a flexible spatula to carefully fold in the remaining two thirds, taking care not to deflate the mixture. Fill the muffin cups to two thirds with the batter.

Bake for 20 minutes, until well risen and a cake tester inserted into the center comes out dry. Serve warm or cooled.

Ingredients
4 eggs
1 organic or unwaxed lemon
1 cup plus scant ½ cup (7 oz./200 g) poppy seeds
7 tablespoons (3 ½ oz./100 g) butter, plus a little
  extra for the muffin cups
½ cup (3 ½ oz./100 g) light brown sugar
2 tablespoons (20 g) potato starch or rice starch

Equipment
6 muffin cups or ramekins

● Chef's notes
It is easier to maintain the moist texture of these cakes by making them in individual muffin cups or ramekins, rather than in a larger cake or loaf pan.
Once baked, they can be frozen for up to 2 months.

● Good to know
Poppy seed cake is a specialty of Germany and is also made in many other countries in eastern Europe. Poppy seeds, rich in oil, make a very moist, soft-textured cake that keeps well—and is flour-free!

Fruits

Claire Heitzler

Born in the Alsace region in eastern France, Claire Heitzler worked as an apprentice with renowned pastry chef Thierry Mulhaupt in Strasbourg, where she was named Best Apprentice in Alsace. After the solid grounding at the legendary Maison Troisgros in Roanne under Sébastien Dégardin, she traveled to Tokyo, working at Alain Ducasse's Beige restaurant for three years. From 2007 to 2010, Heitzler worked at the Park Hyatt in Dubai and then returned to France to work at Lasserre in Paris.

Voted pastry chef of the year in 2012 and 2013 by *Le Chef* magazine and the *Gault et Millau* gastronomic guide, Heitzler created a menu dedicated to her pastry creations in 2014, the same year she received the prize for excellence awarded by Relais Desserts, an organization that promotes fine French pastry-making.

With a predilection for desserts containing little added sugar, and particularly inspired by fruity flavors, Heitzler uses her ingredients as a foundation, working with them to vary their textures and then building up a simple, elegant balance of flavors. Her menu continually changes according to the seasons and her whims.

In this recipe, avocado and tangy grapefruit offset the smoothness of coconut, making for a surprising dessert with fruits that are often used in savory courses—here, they make a perfect ending to a meal.

Fluffy Coconut with Grapefruit and Creamed Avocado

Makes 20 portions

Preparation time: 1 hour 30 minutes; Freezing time: 3 hours; Cooking time: 15 minutes

Equipment

Two differently sized hemispherical silicone molds, ¼-filled with silicone combined with a hardener, dried until firm

Ingredients

Avocado puree

1 lb. (500 g) ripe avocado flesh
2 tbsp (30 ml) lemon juice
1 drizzle olive oil

Grapefruit marmalade

1 lb. (500 g) ruby grapefruit
1 cup (7 oz./200 g) sugar
1 vanilla bean

Coconut mousse

²/₃ cup (5 oz./150 g) egg whites
1 ½ cups (10 oz./300 g) sugar
Scant ½ cup (100 ml) water
1 ¼ cups (300 ml) crème fraîche, 35 percent butterfat
1 ¼ oz. (35 g) vegan gelatin powder (not agar-agar)

1 lb. (500 g) coconut puree
2 oz. (60 g) meringue
Ground coconut to coat

Grapefruit

3 ½ oz./100 g candied grapefruit peel
7 ruby grapefruit
1 heaping tbsp (½ oz./ 15 g) sugar

Orange zest

2 oranges
½ cup (3 ½ oz./100 g) sugar
¾ cup (200 ml) water

Coconut shavings

1 fresh coconut

Coconut sorbet

1 cup (250 ml) coconut milk
1 ½ oz. (40 g) trimoline
3 ½ tbsp (1 ½ oz./40 g) sugar
¹/₆ oz. (4 g) super neutrose
¼ oz. (7 g) dextrose
1 lb. (500 g) pureed coconut

Grapefruit caviar

¼ grapefruit

For the avocado puree: Scoop out the flesh of the avocados and strain through a fine-mesh sieve. Add the lemon juice and quickly heat in a skillet with the olive oil to stabilize the color. Spread thinly over a silicone baking mat. Freeze until firm and cut into 20 rectangles (1 ¼ × 6 inches/4 × 15 cm). Place in the freezer. Place any leftover puree in a piping bag and reserve.

For the grapefruit marmalade: Rinse the grapefruit and slice very finely with the skins. Soften gently with the vanilla bean and sugar and reduce slowly. Allow to cool, then chop very finely to make a marmalade.

For the coconut mousse: Make an Italian meringue by preparing a syrup with the sugar and water and heat to 250°F (121°C). In a stand mixer, whisk the egg whites until they hold soft peaks and drizzle the syrup into the bowl. Whisk until the meringue is firm and shiny and has cooled to lukewarm. Whip the cream until it is foamy. Add the vegan gelatin powder to a small quantity of coconut puree and heat for 20 seconds at 195°F (90°C). Stir in the remaining puree. Liquefy the Italian meringue with the coconut puree mixture, then incorporate the whipped cream. Pour into the molds, filling them to three quarters. Place in the freezer until frozen, turn out of the molds, and then assemble them two by two to form two differently sized "cushions." Allow to thaw and hollow out the center with a ½-in. (1-cm) cutter. Roll them in the ground coconut.

For the grapefruit: Use a ¾-inch (1.5-cm) diameter cutter to cut out the candied grapefruit peel. Peel the fresh grapefruit, removing all the pith, and cut out the segments between the membranes. Reserve 20 of the whole segments and cut 20 other segments into halves. Place on a nonstick baking sheet and sprinkle with the sugar.

Place in a 350°F (180°C/Gas Mark 4) oven for 2 minutes, then leave to cool.

For the orange zest: Peel the oranges and cut the skins into fine julienne sticks. Blanch them three times. Bring the sugar and water to a boil and cook the julienned zest in it over low heat until translucent.

For the coconut shavings: Open the coconut. Cut some of the flesh into small dice and, using a vegetable peeler, make shavings with the rest of the flesh.

For the coconut sorbet: Heat the coconut milk with the trimoline. Combine the sugar, neutrose, and dextrose. When the coconut milk reaches 104°F (40°C), pour in the sugar mixture and bring to a boil. Stir in the pureed coconut. Let rest for the flavors to develop, then process in an ice-cream maker.

For the grapefruit caviar: Scoop out the grapefruit flesh and place in the freezer.

To serve: On each plate, place a rectangle of the frozen avocado puree. Next to that, place three spoonfuls of grapefruit marmalade, flattened out into fine disks, and on each one place a cushion of coconut mousse. Fill the hollowed-out center of the mousse with the avocado puree reserved in the piping bag. On each coconut cushion, place a disk of candied grapefruit skin. Place two half-segments of roasted grapefruit on the avocado rectangle. Place two segments of fresh grapefruit over them. Arrange the orange zest and coconut cubes and shavings on the plate and, to finish, add a scoop of coconut sorbet over the larger cushion and some grapefruit caviar on the avocado puree.

Ingredients

Pie crust

2 cups (9 oz./250 g) unbleached flour

½ teaspoon fine salt

1 stick plus 1 tablespoon (5 oz./130 g) butter, chilled and diced

1 egg yolk

1 teaspoon white wine vinegar

1-2 tablespoons ice water

Filling

1 ¼ lb. (600 g) onions

1 lb. (500 g) cooking apples

3 tablespoons (1 ½ oz./40 g) butter

1 bay leaf

3 sprigs dried thyme

2 tablespoons maple syrup

1 tablespoon cider vinegar

1 tablespoon whiskey or bourbon

1 teaspoon mild smoked paprika

¼ teaspoon smoked chili pepper, such as chipotle

¼ teaspoon grated nutmeg

Onion, Apple, and Whiskey Pie ★

Serves 4 to 6
Preparation time: 30 minutes
Cooking time: 1 hour 15 minutes

For the pie crust

Combine the flour with the salt. Make a well in the center and add the butter. Working with your fingertips, rub the butter into the flour. Alternatively, use a food processor fitted with a blade knife. Do not attempt to incorporate all the butter; traces should be visible. Add the egg yolk, vinegar, and cold water and combine rapidly until the ingredients form a ball. Cover in plastic wrap and chill until needed.

For the filling

Peel the onions and chop them finely. Peel the apples, remove the core and seeds, and dice them. Melt the butter in a skillet and briefly sauté the apples until golden. Set them aside.

Place the onions in the skillet, season with salt, and add the bay leaf and thyme. Cover with the lid and cook gently over low heat for 30 minutes, stirring regularly, until the onions have softened. Stir in the maple syrup, vinegar, whiskey, apples, and spices. Mix through and cook for 15 minutes, until all the liquid has evaporated and the onions are well softened. Adjust the seasoning.

To finish

Preheat the oven to 350°F (180°C/Gas Mark 4). Spread the softened onion and apple mixture evenly in a rectangular ovenproof dish. Roll the dough out between two sheets of parchment or waxed paper to a thickness of ¼ inch (8 mm). Set the dough over the filling and make a cross-shaped incision in the center. Roll up a piece of cardboard (preferably) or aluminum foil and place it in the cross so that it does not close up during baking. Place in the oven and bake for 30 minutes, until the pastry is golden and crisp. Serve the pie hot.

● Good to know

This type of recipe, where apple and onion are combined in a savory dish, can be traced back to the sixteenth century. It was frequently served during Lent in English-speaking countries.

❘ Techniques

Dicing Onions, p. 39
Making Shortcrust Pastry Dough, p. 65
Rolling Out Pastry Dough, p. 66

Tomato and Berry Salad with Balsamic Vinegar ★

Serves 4
Preparation time: 15 minutes

Rinse the cherry tomatoes, strawberries, raspberries, and red currants. Cut the tomatoes into halves or quarters, depending on their size. Hull the strawberries and cut them into halves or quarters, depending on their size. Pick the red currants off their stems. Rinse and dry the sorrel and basil leaves. Roll them up and shred them.

At the bottom of a salad bowl, combine a good pinch of fleur de sel, some freshly ground pepper, the olive oil, and balsamic vinegar. When blended, place all the fruit, almonds, sorrel, and basil leaves in the bowl. Mix carefully until the salad is coated evenly in the dressing and serve immediately.

● Chef's notes

If you don't have fresh almonds, soak your almonds in hot water for 1 hour: this will add a degree of moisture to them.
Experiment with the berries used depending on what is in season and your preference: cherries, blackberries, and gooseberries all work well.
This summer salad is great served as an appetizer or a dessert. It's sure to be a hit with lovers of sweet and sour flavors.
It makes an excellent accompaniment to goat cheese.

Ingredients
8 oz. (250 g) cherry tomatoes
4 oz. (125 g) strawberries
4 oz. (125 g) raspberries
2 ½ oz. (75 g) red currants
10 sorrel leaves, or 1 handful baby spinach leaves tossed in 2 teaspoons lemon juice
10 basil leaves
3 tablespoons olive oil
2 tablespoons balsamic vinegar (preferably 8-year-old vinegar from Modena)
1 handful fresh almonds
Fleur de sel and freshly ground pepper

Ingredients

1 ripe pineapple
1 tablespoon blackstrap molasses (black treacle)
1 unwaxed lime

White chocolate sauce

1 ¼ cups (300 g) Greek sheep yogurt,
  or strained cow milk or goat milk yogurt
3 ½ oz. (100 g) white baking chocolate

Pineapple with Molasses, Lime, and White Chocolate Sauce ★

Serves 4
Preparation time: 15 minutes
Cooking time: 5 minutes
Chilling time: 2 hours

For the white chocolate sauce
Take the yogurt out of the refrigerator for 15 minutes, to allow it to come to room temperature. Roughly chop the white chocolate. Melt it over a hot water bath until smooth, then leave to cool to lukewarm for 10 minutes, stirring regularly. Whisk the yogurt and white chocolate together, pour it into four bowls or one large dessert dish, and place in the refrigerator.

For the pineapple
Peel the pineapple, taking care to remove all the eyes. Cut it into slices and place them in a serving dish. Lightly oil a tablespoon and scoop up 1 tablespoon of blackstrap molasses. Drizzle it in a zig-zag pattern over the pineapple slices. Finely grate the lime zest and sprinkle it evenly over the slices. Serve with the chilled white chocolate sauce.

● Chef's notes
Molasses is extremely sticky, so it is recommended that you oil all equipment that will come into contact with it. You can also use a squeeze bottle—or even a baby bottle—to drizzle just the right quantity.

● Good to know
The two components of this dessert were inspired by Spanish chef Ferran Adrià's dishes, served to his staff.

Techniques
Preparing Pineapples, p. 137

Ingredients

1 ²/₃ cups (400 ml) sweet white wine

¼ cup (60 ml) agave or rice syrup

1 bay leaf

1 ½-inch (4-cm) licorice stick,
  slit in two lengthwise

1 cinnamon stick

1 thin slice peeled fresh ginger

4 cooking pears

Equipment

Cast-iron pot or Dutch oven, large
  enough to hold the pears snugly

Pears Poached in White Wine ★

Serves 4

Preparation time: 15 minutes
Cooking time: 30 minutes
Cooling time: 3 hours
Chilling time: 3 hours

Preheat the oven to 300°F (150°C/Gas Mark 2).

In the cast-iron pot, bring the wine and agave syrup to a boil with the bay leaf, two pieces of licorice stick, cinnamon, and ginger.

Peel the pears and place them in the boiling syrup. Cover with the lid and bring back to a boil.

As soon as the liquid boils, remove from the heat and place the pot in the oven for 30 minutes. When you remove the pot from the oven, do not open it. The temperature inside will drop slowly and the pears will finish cooking gently.

Place in the refrigerator for 3 hours. Serve with plain strained or Greek yogurt.

● Chef's notes
Feel free to vary the spices. Cardamom and ginger, for example, with a few saffron threads added after the syrup has boiled, is a superb combination.

⦙ Techniques
⦙ Peeling Fresh Ginger, p. 29

Ingredients

Meringue
4 egg whites from jumbo eggs (UK extra large)
1 pinch salt
½ cup (3 ½ oz./100 g) granulated sugar
½ cup (2 ½ oz./70 g) confectioners' sugar
2 teaspoons cornstarch (see Chef's notes)
2 teaspoons white vinegar or lemon juice

Topping
1 ¼ cups (300 ml) passion fruit pulp
⅔ cup (4 oz./125 g) sugar
3 eggs, lightly beaten
1 tablespoon cornstarch
1 passion fruit
1 pomegranate

Equipment
Electric beater

Passion Fruit and Pomegranate Pavlova ★★

Serves 6
Preparation time: 30 minutes
Cooking time: 1 hour 15 minutes

For the meringue
Preheat the oven to 250°F (120°C/Gas Mark ½). Line a baking sheet with parchment paper.

In a large mixing bowl, whisk the egg whites with the salt. When they begin to hold peaks, pour in the sugar, whisking constantly, until dense and shiny. With a flexible spatula, fold in the confectioners' sugar.

In a small mixing bowl, combine the cornstarch with the vinegar, then fold into the whisked meringue mixture.

Pour the meringue over the prepared baking sheet and spread into the shape of your choice: disk, rectangle, etc. Slightly hollow out the center so that the sides are high enough to hold the filling. Bake for 1 hour 30 minutes and allow to cool in the oven. Keep in a dry place until you are ready to decorate it.

For the topping
In a heavy-bottom saucepan, combine the passion fruit pulp, sugar, lightly beaten eggs, and cornstarch; mix together. Place over low heat and stir constantly until the mixture thickens. Remove from the heat and cover with plastic wrap, pressing it down directly onto the surface to prevent a skin forming. Leave to cool to room temperature.

Cut the pomegranate open and remove the seeds. Cut the passion fruit in half and scoop out the seeds with a teaspoon.

Spread the cooled cream over the meringue. Spread the passion fruit seeds over the top and scatter with pomegranate seeds. Serve immediately.

● Chef's notes
You can prepare all of the components of this dessert a day ahead and assemble the pavlova at the last minute, to ensure that the meringue retains its crisp texture.
Using starch together with an acidic ingredient (vinegar or lemon juice) ensures that the texture inside the pavlova is deliciously chewy. If you prefer your pavlova to be drier and even crisper, omit the cornstarch.

Techniques
Preparing Pomegranates, p. 134

Dried Apricot Flan ★

Serves 4 to 6
Preparation time: 30 minutes
Soaking time: 1 hour
Cooking time: 45 minutes

Bring ¾ cup (200 ml) water to a boil. Pour it over the dried apricots and leave to soak for 1 hour, until plump.

Preheat the oven to 350°F (180°C/Gas Mark 4). Butter the cake pan well (make sure that the butter that will be incorporated into the cake is returned to the refrigerator) and dust it lightly with flour.

Drain the apricots well and arrange them over the base of the pan. In a mixing bowl, combine the flour, sugar, and salt. Make a well in the center and break in the eggs one by one, incorporating each one before breaking the next. Stir briefly, then gradually pour in the milk and rum, stirring constantly, until the batter is fairly fluid. Pour it carefully over the apricots. Cut the cold butter into knobs and scatter over the top of the batter.

Bake for 30 minutes, until well risen and golden. Serve warm or cool. If you wish, you may sprinkle it with a little extra sugar.

● Chef's notes
Organic dried fruits do not retain their original color because, of course, they contain no preservatives. Organic dried apricots will be a dull brownish color but don't be put off: the taste is excellent!

● Good to know
This flognarde, as it is known in the French regions of Corrèze and Auvergne, where it is a specialty, is a cross between a clafoutis and a flan. Made with dried plums or fresh fruit such as apples and apricots, it has a melt-in-the-mouth texture, particularly when eaten warm.

❙ Techniques
Soaking Dried Fruits, p. 143

Ingredients
7 oz. (200 g) dried apricots, preferably organic
1 cup (250 ml) whole milk
3 tablespoons (1 ½ oz./40 g) butter, well chilled, plus a little extra for the pan
1 cup (4 oz./125 g) buckwheat flour, plus 1 tablespoon for the pan
3 ½ tablespoons (1 ½ oz./40 g) sugar, plus extra for serving
1 pinch salt
4 eggs
1 tablespoon rum

Equipment
9-inch (22-cm) cake pan

Ingredients

Coconut whipped cream

1 ⅔ cups (400 ml) full-fat coconut milk
½ vanilla bean, slit lengthwise and seeds scraped

"Torn pancake"

10 oz. (300 g) seasonal mixed red berries
  of your choice, fresh or frozen
3 jumbo eggs (UK extra large)
1 cup plus scant ½ cup (6 oz./170 g)
  all-purpose flour
2 ½ tablespoons (1 oz./30 g) sugar,
  plus an equal amount for sprinkling
1 teaspoon baking soda
1 cup (250 ml) whole milk (cow or soy)
1 pinch salt
3 tablespoons (1 ½ oz./40 g) butter

Equipment

Electric beater

Techniques

Making Soy Milk, p. 86
Making Coconut Whipped Cream, p. 127

Red Berry "Torn Pancake" with Coconut Whipped Cream ★ ★

Serves 4
Preparation time: 20 minutes
Cooking time: 10 minutes
Chilling time: 3 hours

For the coconut whipped cream

Chill the coconut milk for at least 3 hours. When you open the can, use a spoon to scoop out the upper layer of thick cream. In a small mixing bowl, mix the coconut cream with the seeds from the vanilla bean and place in the refrigerator so that it is well chilled when you need to whip it.

For the "torn pancake"

If you are using frozen fruit, allow them to thaw and drain any liquid. If you are using fresh fruit, rinse, dry, and pick them off their stems, if necessary.

Separate the eggs. In a mixing bowl, combine the flour with the sugar and baking soda. Whisk in the milk and egg yolks.

Whisk the egg whites with a pinch of salt until they hold soft peaks. Carefully fold them into the batter, taking care not to deflate the mixture. Then, gently fold in the berries.

In a large skillet over medium heat, melt the butter. Carefully pour in the batter and cook for 7 to 8 minutes, until the bottom of the pancake is set. Using a wooden spatula, roughly cut the pancake into strips and turn the pieces to color on the other side for 2 to 3 minutes, until golden.

To finish

With the electric beater, whisk the coconut cream until it holds soft peaks. Sprinkle the torn pancake with the sugar and serve immediately with the whipped coconut cream.

● **Chef's notes**

The cream at the top of a can of full-fat coconut milk makes delicious, lactose-free whipped cream. Use the thick creamy part only, and reserve the more liquid coconut milk that is left to make a smoothie or a marinade.

● **Good to know**

The name of this Austrian specialty—Kaiserschmarrn—can be translated as "the Emperor's mishmash." There are several versions, but the story goes that Emperor Franz Josef I and his wife Elisabeth stopped at an inn and asked to eat there. The host tried to make a delicious pancake but due to his nervousness he scrambled it; another version says the innkeeper's wife was unable to flip or turn the pancake out of the pan and had to shred it. To disguise the mess, it was covered with fruit jam and the Emperor found it delicious!
This dessert was originally garnished with raisins and plum or apple compote, but now it is made with all sorts of fruit.

Coconut and Verbena Tapioca with Raspberry Coulis ★

Serves 4
Preparation time: 15 minutes
Cooking time: 10 minutes
Chilling time: 4 hours

For the coulis
Rinse and dry the raspberries. Set aside 12 of the most attractive raspberries. Place the remaining ones in a small saucepan over medium heat with the agave syrup, and cook for 5 minutes.

For the tapioca
Over medium heat, bring the coconut milk, milk of your choice, and syrup to a boil with the verbena. Pour in the tapioca pearls, reduce the heat to low, and cook, stirring regularly, until the tapioca is transparent and the mixture has thickened. This should take 5 to 10 minutes, depending on the brand of tapioca. Discard the verbena leaves.

To finish
Divide the raspberry coulis between four bowls, glasses, or ramekins. Pour the tapioca mixture over it and leave to cool. Cover with plastic wrap flush with the surface, to prevent a skin forming, and place in the refrigerator for at least 4 hours.

Decorate with the reserved raspberries just before serving.

● Chef's notes
Instead of stewed raspberries, mangoes and pitted cherries prepared in the same way are also excellent with this dessert.
A fruit salad can be used as an alternative topping.
All varieties of tropical fruit pair particularly well with tapioca.
This dessert will keep for up to 2 days in the refrigerator.

Ingredients
Coulis
8 oz. (250 g) fresh raspberries
2 tablespoons agave syrup

Tapioca
1 ²/₃ cups (400 ml) coconut milk
¾ cup minus 1 tablespoon (180 ml) milk
(cow, soy, or rice)
2 tablespoons (30 ml) agave or rice malt syrup
2 sprigs fresh verbena, or 2 tablespoons
dried verbena leaves
¹/₃ cup (2 oz./50 g) tapioca pearls

Ingredients
14 oz. (400 g) rhubarb
3 ½ oz. (100 g) red currants
¾-inch (2-cm) piece ginger
Generous ⅔ cup (4 ½ oz./130 g)
    granulated sugar
4 egg yolks
3 tablespoons (50 ml) vodka
1 ¼ cups (300 ml) whipping cream,
    30-35 percent butterfat

Equipment
Electric beater
6 ramekins

Rhubarb, Red Currant, and Ginger Parfait ★

Serves 6
Preparation time: 30 minutes
Resting time: 1 hour
Cooking time: 15 minutes
Freezing time: 6 to 12 hours

Clean the rhubarb, pull off the outer fibers, and cut it into pieces. Rinse and dry the red currants and pick them off the stems. Peel and grate the ginger.

Combine the prepared rhubarb with half of the sugar and the grated ginger. Leave to macerate for 1 hour at room temperature, so that the juice rendered by the rhubarb forms a syrup with the sugar.

Transfer the rhubarb-sugar mixture to a saucepan and bring to a boil over medium heat. Simmer for 15 minutes, until completely softened. Remove from the heat, stir in three quarters of the red currants, and leave to cool.

In a heat-resistant bowl, whisk the egg yolks with the remaining sugar and the vodka until the sugar has dissolved. Place the bowl over a saucepan of hot water and whisk continuously for 3 to 4 minutes, until the mixture is foamy and has tripled in volume. The whisk must leave clear traces in the foam. Fold in the stewed rhubarb.

With the electric beater, whisk the whipping cream until it has doubled in volume and is no longer shiny. Carefully fold it into the egg yolk-rhubarb mixture.

Divide the preparation between the six ramekins and place in the freezer for at least 6 hours.

To unmold, briefly dip the bases of the ramekins into hot water and turn the mini parfaits onto plates. Decorate with the remaining red currants and serve immediately.

● Chef's notes
Other berries, such as raspberries or black currants, are also excellent in this dessert, as they counterbalance the acidity of the rhubarb.
The alcohol used in this recipe enables the parfait to remain soft and prevents icy flakes from forming. The taste of the vodka is barely discernible, especially as most of the alcohol content evaporates when it is heated. You can use any other alcoholic beverage of your choice, even white wine. Should you prefer an alcohol-free version, simply use fruit juice.
Iced parfaits may be frozen for up to 6 weeks.

❙ Techniques
Peeling Fresh Ginger, p. 29
Preparing Rhubarb, p. 138

Index

Gluten-Free Recipes    Vegan Recipes

Bibliography

America's Test Kitchen. *The Complete Vegetarian Cookbook*. Boston: America's Test Kitchen, 2015.

Bittman, Mark. *How to Cook Everything Vegetarian*. Hoboken, NJ: Wiley Publishing, Inc., 2007.

Britton, Sarah. *My New Roots*. New York: Clarkson Potter Publishers, 2015.

Carr, Kris. *Crazy Sexy Kitchen: 150 Plant-Empowered Recipes to Ignite a Mouthwatering Revolution*. Carlsbad, CA: Hay House, 2012.

Chaplin, Amy. *At Home in the Whole Food Kitchen*. Boston: Roost Books, 2014.

Cohen, Amanda, and Ryan Dunlavey. *Dirt Candy, a Cookbook: Flavor-Forward Food from the Upstart New York City Vegetarian Restaurant*. New York: Clarkson Potter Publishers, 2012.

Corrett, Natasha. *Honestly Healthy in a Hurry*. London: Hodder & Stoughton, 2016.

Corrett, Natasha, and Vicki Edgson. *Eating the Alkaline Way: Recipes for a Well-Balanced Honestly Healthy Lifestyle*. New York: Sterling, 2013.

Corrett, Natasha, and Vicki Edgson. *Honestly Healthy for Life: Eating the Alkaline Way Every Day*. New York: Sterling, 2014.

Cotter, Dennis. *Café Paradiso Seasons: Vegetarian Cooking Season-By-Season*. New York: Skyhorse Publishing, 2014.

Cotter, Dennis. *For the Love of Food: Vegetarian Recipes from the Heart*. London: Collins, 2011.

Ducasse, Alain. *Nature: Simple, Healthy, and Good*. New York: Rizzoli, 2012.*

Duff, Gail. *Gail Duff's Vegetarian Cookbook*. London: Pan Books, 1979.

Fearnley-Whittingstall, Hugh. *River Cottage Veg: 200 Inspired Vegetable Recipes*. Berkeley: Ten Speed Press, 2013.

Fearnley-Whittingstall, Hugh. *River Cottage Veg Every Day!* London: Bloomsbury Publishing, 2011.

Frenkiel, David, and Luise Vindahl. *The Green Kitchen*. London: Hardie Grant Books, 2014.

Frenkiel, David, and Luise Vindahl. *Green Kitchen Travels*. London: Hardie Grant Books, 2014.

Frenkiel, David, and Luise Vindahl. *Vegetarian Everyday*. New York: Rizzoli, 2013.

Jones, Anna. *A Modern Way to Eat*. London: Fourth Estate, 2014.

Katzen, Mollie. *The Moosewood Cookbook: 40th Anniversary Edition*. Berkeley: Ten Speed Press, 2014.

Katzen, Mollie. *The New Moosewood Cookbook*. Berkeley: Ten Speed Press, 2000.

Kayser, Éric. *Éric Kayser's New French Recipes*. Paris: Flammarion, 2009.*

Madison, Deborah. *The New Vegetarian Cooking for Everyone*. Berkeley: Ten Speed Press, 2014.

Madison, Deborah. *Vegetable Literacy*. Berkeley: Ten Speed Press, 2013.

Madison, Deborah. *Vegetarian Suppers from Deborah Madison's Kitchen*. New York: Broadway Books, 2005.

Ottolenghi, Yotam. *Plenty*. London: Ebury Press, 2010/San Francisco: Chronicle Books, 2011.

Ottolenghi, Yotam. *Plenty More*. London: Ebury Press, 2014/Berkeley: Ten Speed Press, 2014.

Swanson, Heidi. *Super Natural Every Day*. Berkeley: Ten Speed Press, 2011.

Woodward, Ella. *Deliciously Ella*. London: Yellow Kite, 2015.

Woodward, Ella. *Deliciously Ella Every Day*. London: Yellow Kite, 2016.

World cuisine

Ando, Elizabeth. *Kansha: Celebrating Japan's Vegan and Vegetarian Traditions*. Berkeley: Ten Speed Press, 2010.

Butcher, Sally. *Salmagundi*. London: Pavilion, 2014. *

Ducasse, Alain. *The Provence of Alain Ducasse: Recipes, Addresses and Places*. Paris: Assouline, 2011.

Grogan, Bryanna Clark. *World Vegan Feast: 200 Fabulous Recipes from Over 50 Countries*. Woodstock, VA: Vegan Heritage Press, 2011.

Hage, Salma. *The Middle Eastern Vegetarian Cookbook*. London: Phaidon, 2016.

Hingle, Richa. *Vegan Richa's Indian Kitchen*. Woodstock, VA: Vegan Heritage Press, 2015.

Jaffrey, Madhur. *Vegetarian India: A Journey Through the Best of Indian Home Cooking*. New York: Knopf, 2015.

Kazuko, Emi, and Yasuko Fukuoka. *Japanese Cooking: The Traditions, Techniques, Ingredients and Recipes*. New York: Hermes House, 2002.

King, Si, and Dave Myers. *The Hairy Bikers' Great Curries*. London: Weidenfeld & Nicholson, 2013.*

Mittal, Vidhu. *Pure & Simple: Homemade Indian Vegetarian Cuisine*. Northampton: Interlink Publishing Group, 2009.

Mittal, Vidhu. *Pure & Special: Gourmet Indian Vegetarian Cuisine*. Northampton: Interlink Publishing Group, 2014.

Roden, Claudia. *The Book of Jewish Food: An Odyssey from Samarkand to New York*. New York: Knopf, 1996.*

Roden, Claudia. *The New Book of Middle Eastern Food*. New York: Knopf, 2000.*

Selva Rajah, Carol, and Priya Wickramasinghe. *Food Of India: A Journey For Food Lovers*. Sydney: Murdoch Books, 2005.

Shulman, Martha Rose. *Mediterranean Harvest: Vegetarian Recipes from the World's Healthiest Cuisine*. New York: Rodale, 2010.

Singleton Hachisu, Nancy. *Japanese Farm Food*. Kansas City: Andrews McMeel Publishing, 2012.*

Vegan cuisine

Bailey, Charlotte, and David Bailey. *The Fresh Vegan Kitchen*. London: Pavilion, 2015.

Carlin, Ainé. *Keep It Vegan*. London: Kyle Books, 2014.

Carlin, Ainé. *The New Vegan*. London: Kyle Books, 2015.

Coscarelli, Chloe. *Chloe's Kitchen*. New York: Atria Books, 2013.

Coscarelli, Chloe. *Chloe's Vegan Desserts*. New York: Atria Books, 2013.

Lafôret, Marie. *The Best Homemade Vegan Cheese and Ice Cream Recipes*. Toronto: Robert Rose, 2016.

Lafôret, Marie. *Vegan Bible*. London: Grub Street Publishing, 2015.

Liddon, Angela. *The Oh She Glows Cookbook*. New York: Avery, 2014.

Mattern, Mary. *Nom Yourself: Simple Vegan Cooking*. New York: Avery, 2015.

Moskowitz, Isa Chandra. *Isa Does It*. New York: Little, Brown And Company, 2013.

Nixon, Lindsay. *The Happy Herbivore Cookbook*. Dallas: BenBella Books, Inc., 2011.

Patalsky, Kathy. *Healthy Happy Vegan Kitchen*. New York: Houghton Mifflin Harcourt, 2015.

Shultz, Dana. *Minimalist Baker's Everyday Cooking*. New York: Avery, 2016.

Steen, Celine, and Joni Marie Newman. *The Complete Guide to Vegan Food Substitutions*. Beverly, MA: Fair Winds Press, 2011.

Turner, Kristy. *But I Could Never Go Vegan!* New York: The Experiment, 2014.

History, philosophy, and health

Page, Karen. *The Vegetarian Flavor Bible*. New York: Little, Brown and Company, 2014.

Plutarch. *Moralia; Twenty Essays: Translated by Philemon Holland*. London: Forgotten Books, 2015.

Safran Foer, Jonathan. *Eating Animals*. New York: Little, Brown and Company, 2009.

Stuart, Tristram. *The Bloodless Revolution: A Cultural History of Vegetarianism from 1600 to Modern Times*. New York: W.W. Norton & Company, Inc., 2007.

Taylor, Thomas, and Esme Wynne-Tyson. *Porphyry on Abstinence from Animal Food*. Whitefish, MT: Kessinger Publishing, 2006.

Products

Boyce, Kim. *Good to the Grain: Baking with Whole-Grain Flours*. New York: Stewart, Tabori & Chang, 2010.

Cupillard, Valérie. *Sprouts and Sprouting: The Complete Guide with Seventy Healthy and Creative Recipes*. London: Grub Street, 2007.

Dragonwagon, Crescent. *Bean by Bean: A Cookbook*. New York: Workman Publishing Company, 2012.*

Hester, Kathy. *The Great Vegan Bean Book*. Beverly, MA: Fair Winds Press, 2013.

Madison, Deborah. *This Can't Be Tofu!* New York: Broadway Books, 2000.

Marcon, Régis. *Champignons*. Paris: La Martinière, 2013 (book in French).*

Mikanowski, Lyndsay, and Patrick Mikanowski. *Vegetables by 40 Great French Chefs*. Paris: Flammarion, 2006.*

Seaver, Barton. *Superfood Seagreens : A Guide to Cooking with Power-Packed Seaweed*. New York: Sterling, 2016.

Vergé, Roger. *Roger Vergé's Cooking with Fruit*. New York: Harry N. Abrams, 1998.*

Vergé, Roger. *Roger Vergé's Vegetables in the French Style*. New York: Artisan, 1994.*

Wells, Patricia. *Vegetable Harvest: Vegetables at the Center of the Plate*. New York: William Morrow Cookbooks, 2007.*

*Not exclusively vegetarian books, but include numerous vegetarian recipes

Acknowledgments

The author wishes to thank the following people:

- Ryma Bouzid for her trust and faith in me.
- Clélia Ozier-Lafontaine for her careful coordination of the project and her infectious enthusiasm.
- Catherine Roig, to whom I owe so much that not even an entire book would suffice to thank her.
- Laurence Auger from Éditions La Plage, for opening my eyes to the world of vegetarian cuisine.
- Beena Paradin for listening, offering advice, and for her garam masala.
- Claire Chapoutot, Joëlle Dubois, Déborah Dupont, Emilie Fléchaire, Marie Grave, Linda Louis, Camille Oger, Anne-Laure Pham, Céline Pham, Elisabeth Scotto, and Estelle Tracy, for lending me their expertise and their support as chefs of the heart and the world.
- Patrick Cadour for his good humor and seaweed.
- The chefs who have done me the great honor of contributing to this book.
- Philippe, Virgile, and Rodrigue, for their love, patience, and endless support, as without them none of this would have meaning.
- For the food photography and styling in this book, I would like to thank Nathalie Carnet, a photographer whose mantra is "simple and refined," Alexandre Cernec and Anaïs Gensellen, her eager assistant stylists, and Catherine Mounier and Maison Jars (www.jars-ceramistes.com) for their inspiring tableware.